HUMAN LIFE-
A PHILOSOPHICAL AUDIT

HUMAN LIFE-
A PHILOSOPHICAL AUDIT

(a special audit report)

by, Ahmed Sayeed

PARTRIDGE
A Penguin Random House Company

To order additional copies of this book, contact
Partridge India
000 800 10062 62
www.partridgepublishing.com/india
orders.india@partridgepublishing.com

CHAPTER	CONTENTS	PAGE

Acknowledgement

I am grateful to be a student of Philosophy which is a mother of all branches of knowledge including science, and which has fragmented the facts of our life. This philosophy encouraged me to write this book and placed before all human beings.

I also acknowledge all the NOBLE and NOBEL laureates, Philosophers & Scientists who bloomed the knowledge of Universe into wisdom for humanity

—Ahmed Sayeed

PREFACE

My aim throughout this book has been to give fellow human an easily intelligible exposition of the HUMAN LIFE and I have taken special pains to present impartiality, the different aspects of human life which is an 'event' by itself.

Human Knowledge has become unimaginably vast; every field of knowledge has become unimaginably vast, the telescope revealed stars and systems beyond the mind of man to number and to name, geology spoke in terms of millions of years, where men before had thought in terms of thousands, physics, found a universe in the atom and biology in the cell, Physiology discovered inexhaustible misery in every organ; and psychology in every dream; Anthropology reconstructed the unsuspected antiquity of man; archeology, unearthed buried cities, and forgotten states, history proved all history false; theology crumbled, and political theory cracked, inventions, complicated life and war & and economic creeds overturned governments and inflamed the world. Human knowledge had become too great for the human mind.

Day has generated to know more and more about less and less' facts replaced fictions and knowledge split into thousand of isolated fragments. Men has learned more about the world and he found himself ever less capable of expressing to his educated fellow men what he learned in the past. The days when common man found himself forced to choose unintelligible permission and theological priest hood mumbling incredible hopes have melted away in the history.

II

Our 'minds' 'souls' 'spirit' 'consciousness' are all physical in nature. Thousand years of research have shown that our brains comprise and produce our true selves. Souls and spirits do not exist. Our bodies run themselves. We know from cases of brain damage and the effects of psycho active drugs, that experiences are caused by physical chemistry acting of our physical neurons in our brains. Our innermost self is our biochemical self.

In this context of obtaining knowledge of both physics and psychology or say 'body' and 'brain' morality is the objective law of reason: just as objective physical laws necessitate physical actions (for example apples fall down because of gravity), objective rational laws necessitate rational actions. Thus as we are rational beings we should believe that perfectly rational being must also be perfectly moral. Besides human also act upon instinct some time, and so human must conform their subjective will with objective rational laws, which can be said as conformity obligation. Rational morality is universe and they cannot change depending on circumstances. Fact always remain fact where as fiction changes always. Therefore Rational Ethics is law of Human and this categorical Imperative is HUMANITY which is dressed with Love and Affection till you diminish into dust.

TABULA RASA

Prologue

BABY OF HUMAN is born without built in MENTAL CONTENT and the knowledge comes from experience and perception. The brain of the kid would be in the phase of A TABULA RASA. Generally proponents of Tabula Rasa thesis favor the 'the nurture' side of the 'nature verses nature' debate; when it comes to aspects one's personality, social and emotional behavior and intelligence. The Term in Latin equates to the English 'blank slate' or 'scraped tablet' and this theory was proposed by the Great English Philosopher John Locke. Ibn sina, a Persian Philosopher argued that the human intellect by birth is rather like a tabula rasa, a pure potentiality that is actualized through education and comes to know and KNOWLEDGE is attained through empirical familiarity with objects in this world from which one abstracts 'concept'. Present day Psychologists and Neurologists also support the idea. There is no substance called INNATE IDEA or SPIRITUAL CONCEPT. To sum up the HUMAN BABY is neither, a Muslim, a Christian, a Hindu nor a Buddhist. It is his parental, societal and cultural realms that envelops him in to the so called the religion he belong after baptizing him into that frame. Thus his brain is constructed socially as he grows up to the level as an INDIVIDUAL.

The primary objective of writing this book is to elucidate that individual is brought up under an umbrella of cultural and social dictums that promotes him to builds up his character. It is however, the RIGHT EDUCATION AND RIGHT SOCIAL CIRCUMFERENCE ELITES HIM TO ATTAIN RIGHT KNOWLEDGE AND FINALLY HE PROMOTES HIMSLEF INTO A RIGHT CITIZEN. But before encountering with right education the preliminary aspects of customs rituals and religious concepts would already have laid foundation to great extent for getting himself shaped into an INDIVIDUAL. It is the parental initiation in building him up in to right character which is most important and hence this is my appeal to all the civilized parents to drive him to become sustainable individual without any biased and prejudiced malignant ideas which may dictate his personality. Everybody must be watching that the present system of human life is engulfed with biased ideologies, prejudiced and envious thinking with fellow humans thus causing perennial conflicts and global chaos.

It must be duty of social actors to Train him to become good human, good citizen till he completes his tenure of life in the world. Artificial utopias and manipulating motivations are like viruses causing unrest in human thoughts and behavior. Facts are so stubborn things and whatever may be our wishes, or inclination or the dictation of passions they cannot alter the state of facts and evidence. Patience and preservance have a magical effect before which difficulties disappear and obstacles vanish. If he has talent in particular field of knowledge better encourage him as an amplifier to his ambitions. KNOWLEDGE IS POWER and that power will certainly lead him to emancipate his GOAL. Whatever is gained and achieved is meant or relates to the present state of affairs on the earth and there neither a permanent nor heavenly life after death. HEAVEN AND HELL ARE FELT THROUGH PLEASURE AND PAIN, HERE ON EARTH ITSELF and not anywhere else. PERMANANT LIFE IN HEAVEN AFTER DEATH is

ONLY A FAIRY TALE in my opinion. If you still have any doubt you please go through this book at least once which I feel is an abridged booklet of life in general and helps in enlightening you AND YOUR CHILD.

CHAPTER I
MEANING OF LIFE

The meaning of life is a philosophical one concerning the significance of life or say existence in general. It can also be expressed in different forms such as WHY ARE WE HERE? WHAT IS LIFE ALL ABOUT? WHERE FROM WE ARE? And WHAT WOULD BE PURPOSE OF LIFE?

It has been the subject of much Philosophical, Theological and Scientific speculation throughout the history of mankind.

The meaning of life entrenched in the Philosophical and Religious conception of existence, social ties, consciousness and happiness and borders of many other issues such as symbolic, meaning, ontology, value, purpose, ethics, good and evil, free will and the existence of God conception of God, the Soul and after life.

Is life really a question—WHICH NOBODY KNOWS, some say Life is secret that God alone knows (if at all He exists) while living a LIFE we are asking a question OURSELF—Does it not sound like a strange?

Do all living things move? Do they all eat and breathe? Even Biologists have tough time in describing WHAT LIFE IS? But many years of studying living things biologists have determined that all living things do share something in common:

- **Living things need to take energy;**
- **Living things get rid of waste;**
- **Living things grow and develop;**

- ☐ **Living things respond to environment;**
- ☐ **Living things reproduce and pass their traits on to their Off-SPRING.**
- ☐ **Living things evolve (change slowly) respond to the environment;**
- ☐ **Living things grow old;**
- ☐ **Living things have death finally.**

Therefore in order for something to be considered "to have life'" as well as to know, it must possess these characteristics.

Life looks increasingly like chemical experiment that took over the laboratory. All living things turn to dust and ashes when they die or put in another way to constituent of atoms, and molecules of hydrogen, oxygen, carbon phosphorous and so on.

But in another sense living things do not die they begin again from a tiny cell and scavenge dust, the air and water to find elements necessary to fashion and ASPIDISTRA an ELEPHANT, OR ADOLF HITLER, USING A RAW MATERIAL TO HAND AND ENERGYFROM THERMO NUCLEAR REACTOR 93 million miles away(SUN). The freshly minted self—replicating organism then grows up, grows old and melts away, but not before imparting a fragment of itself to generate yet another copy, but not an identical copy. This process is visible and transparent everywhere on the Planet, but it is ultimately mysterious. It has been going on for at least 3.5 billion years, may never satisfactorily explain how it ever got started.

The mystery may endure because once up and running the life machine kicked up enough dust, to cover its original track. It altered the air, muddled the water and recycled the rocks around it. For at least 30 centuries, thinkers ascribed the beginning of life to an extra terrestrial agency. They talked of the hand of GOD the divine afflatus, the vital spark or of seeds of travelling through the COSMOS.

BY 1850, however Chemists, Physicists Geologists and Biologists including Anthropologists and Historians—many of them religious and Philosophical—had begun to take the problem seriously and concluded that COMPLEX OF LIFE HAD IN SOME SENSE "EVOLVED" FROM SIMPLER BEGINNING EXPLOITING THE MATERIALS AROUND ITS OWN SURVIVAL.

Scientists like DARWIN in 1859 proposed that LIFE may have brewed in a soup of organic chemicals in some "WARM LITTLE POND" on the surface of the Primordial Earth.

We have also come to know as of date that life exists on earth only and not elsewhere. This is a puzzle because at one level the UNIVERSE looks as though it was set up to generate life.

In the first place the constants of Physics are so finely tuned that they even INFINITESIMALLY different; there would be no stars or planets, no carbon, no oxygen, no aspidistras, elephants, Adams or Adolf Hitler.

In the second place between the stars where no life could ever exist, is rich in life' prime ingredients—"the organic chemicals. Astronomers have identified more than 100 of these including a cyanide formaldehyde, alcohol, ammonia and acetylene. Comets are rich in hydrocarbons. A meteorite that fell to Earth in Austria in 1969 has so far yielded more than 70 amino acids. These are all building blocks of protein. In 1953, two Chicago chemists filled a flask with ammonia, methane, water and hydrogen—the Earths primitive atmosphere must have contained all these—and ran an electric current through it. After just a week they had 13 of the 22 amino acids that are the constituents of protein, the stuff of all living material. If that happened in a week in one laboratory, they reasoned, it could certainly have happened through billion of years of lightning strikes.

But it is a big jump from life's building blocks to self replicating planet—altering life. YET LIFE EXISTS. It shares a common bio—chemistry and species are grouped in such way as to suggest common ancestry. But how it began and precisely WHEN and WHERE, remains to be traced since billions of years have been melted in the history of universe, or say in our Planet EARTH.

Life looks after itself but human look after the classification of life and that is what humans argue. The process of classification of species began long ago before any one realized that life's microbes and their parasitic viruses dominate all LIFE ON THE PLANET. Complex life was late arrival. But this was long before DNA. This microbial influence is so profound that another biologist CARL WOESE proposed three kingdoms (I) ARCHEA (ii) BACTERIA (III) EUCARYOTA. All of these are family trees with many branches, but the last group the microbes with nuclei end with three twigs from which evolved all the planets, plants, fungi and animals. Biologists with the latest discoveries now argue that the case is for either five kingdoms (MONERA, PROTISTA, PLANTAE, FUNGI, and ANIMALA) OR six kingdoms (PLANTS, ANIMALS, PROTISTS, FUNGI, ARCHE BACTERIA, AND EUBACTERIA)

Accordingly some argue that, to this scenario our universe itself embedded in larger evolutionary process that shaped LIFE including HUMAN LIFE organism that complete this transition to intentional evolution will drive the further development of life and intelligence in the UNIVERSE. Humanity is fast APPROACHING THE THRESHOLD OF THIS CRITICAL EVOLUTIONARY TRANSITION.

The analysis elucidates that LIFE exists and HUMAN BEING is also a part of biological kingdoms. The greatness of this HUMAN SPECIES is INTELLIGENCE, which stands super conductivity of life motor. Human intelligence drive progress is more rapid than animal. Animals can adapt to problems and make inventions but no faster than natural selection. But we human have the ability to internalize the world and conduct "what if's" in heads, we can solve many problems thousand times faster THAN NATURAL SELECTION—just because of his intelligence. Simulationsly at much higher speeds, we are entering a regime as radically different from our own HUMAN PAST as humans are far above from the lower animals. Development that before thought might only happen in a million years will likely happen in next century.

Stephen Hawkins a great Astrophysicist has rightly said that the "HUMAN RACE IS CHEMICAL SCUM ON MODERATE SIZED PLANET". In other words he meant that life is key part of evolution of the Universe based on which Mind will turn out to be a fundamental significance in the grand story of COSMOS.

Around two centuries ago Scientists believed that life is indeed fundamental phenomenon because they thought that some sort of life force was responsible for the remarkable properties that living organism display. This life stuff was treated as a basic property of biology. Life is distinctive not as a result of the material from which it is made, but because of things it does.

The life and mind are intrinsically fundamental to the working of natural not relevant aberrations implies that they are written into the LAWS OF UNIVERSE and there they are expected even inevitable product of working out these laws. This point of view is sometime called "THE STRONG ANTHROPIC PRINCIPLE" and has received support from prominent Scientists.

MAN'S ROLE IN UNDERSTANDING UNIVERSE

IT is often assumed that the Science—based world view implies that life on this planet is meaningless accident in a universe that is indifferent to our existence. Human struggles to find purpose within this purely naturalistic understanding of reality and so they supplement it with BELIEFS in SUPERNATURAL process and entities.

However recent advances in our understanding of evolution are revealing a bigger picture than can by itself give meaning to life. This new world view locates humanity within much larger evolutionary process that appears to offer us meaningful ROLE to play.

The new understanding of evolution is founded on the recognition that evolution is headed somewhere—it has trajectory. In particular evolution on earth repeatedly gathered small—scale entities into co—operative organization on a progressively larger and larger scale, self replicating molecular process were organized into first simple cells. Communities of these simple PROKARYOTIC cells formed multi—cellular organisms and organisms were organized into COOPERATIVE SOCIETIES.

A SIMILAR SEQUENCE APPEARS TO HAVE UNFOLDED IN HUMAN EVOLUTION FROM FAMILY TO GROUPS, TO BANDS, TO TRIBES, TO AGRICULTURURAL COMMUNITIES AND CITY STATES, TO NATIONS AND SO ON.

The trajectory has applied regardless of whether evolution proceeds be gene based NATURAL SELECTION or CULTURAL PROCESS, it is driven by the potential at all levels of organization for cooperative teams united by common goal to be more successful than ISOLATED INDIVIDUALS.

This cooperative transition on EARTH would be the emergence of sustainable and GLOBAL SOCIETY would curb internal conflict and destructive competition including WAR and POLLUTION. Past transition demonstrates how this might be organized.

UNIVERSAL TRAJECTORY—Extrapolating the Trajectory further would see the continued expansion of the scale of cooperating organization out into the Solar system and beyond. Whenever possible this expansion would likely to occur through cooperative linkage they are hereby high and while the details of evolution on other PLANETS are likely to differ, the general form of the evolutionary trajectory would be UNIVERSAL TRAJECTORY.

IF the trajectory continued in this way the scale of cooperative organization would expand in this way. The scale of cooperative organization would expand throughout the Universe, comprised of living process and intelligence from multiple origins. As it increased in INTELLIGENCE and scale, its command over matter, energy, and other resources would also expand as would its power to achieve objectives it choose.

According to this scenario, our universe itself is embedded in larger evolutionary process that shape universe. And life, that is HUMANITY as a function and purpose within these larger processes in to the same sense that our Eyes have a purpose within the evolutionary process that shaped humanity.

Organism that completes this transition to intentional evolution will drive the further development of life and intelligence in the universe. Humanity need fast approached to the threshold of this critical evolutionary transition.

As per the statistics available as of 2011 human population has crossed 700 billions of which 84% is in roaming in the fairy dreams of DOGMATISM that goal of life is to go to HEAVEN after death and in consequence they have developed a negative and fearful way of life neglecting their duty as a human beings and reluctantly ignoring their attitude over SCIENTIFIC feat achieved by 16% of humans since two centuries. It is well known fact that there is no supernatural element as such hence they are suppose to join this cooperative movement and for this they need to go through the efforts exercised since 3000 years how human being became the product of nature and get himself enlightened on going through the ensuing chapters on HUMAN LIFE, A PHILOSOPHICAL AUDIT.

Before entering into the ongoing articles, let me compass few more words which would help as a stepping stone for the achievement of the goal entrusted by our mother EARTH.

OWN YOUR MIND DO NOT LET IT IMPRISON YOU—AWARENESS REVEALS YOUR SECRET FRUSTUATIONS YOUR HIDDEN APPREHENSIONS TOWARDS YOUR UNWARRENTED BELIEFS AND EMOTIONS AND YOUR REPRESSIONS.

Awareness is true power. Use it in proper way it will give everything you need in this bliss of life. WHY IS AWARENESS SO POWERFUL? Because your mind has surrounded you like a maze. You have got lost inside and will stay lost for the rest of life. Your mind has fantastic power over you and you are helpless in the face of its might. In fact, you never had any power over your mind at all simply because you have no clue except blind belief.

When the mind tells you to feel angry you feel angry, your blood pressure will rise and you will yell like a madman. When in the event while regretting is you to feel greedy you salivate and pant for desires you do not actually need. When the mind tells you that your pride is hurt, you will go into dizzy and the most stupid things a human is capable of, then regret it for years. Even while regretting it you remain a victim of your MOODS. What is this? Your moods are all emotional implants, hormonal stents shoved inside your cranium as and when the mind feels like it. if you have even IOTA of independence, you should be able to pluck out a bad "mood" like a loose thread from a garment and throw it away. Can you do it? No way. The mind is your master and you are always a mere slave. As you are a PRISONER of your mind, and since you have been like this from your birth, you do not even know that you can escape. AWARENESS is the only key you will ever get out of the prison. Doors of knowledge are around you to walk free.

The mind is great and fantastic tool and a great help to cope with the outside the world. YOU HAVE TO OWN YOUR MIND, IT SHOULD NOT OWN YOU. FOR GETTING AWARE OF YOURSELF YOU BETTER KNOW THE KNOWLEDGE SINCE KNOWLEDGE IS SUPERCONDUCTOR FOR COOPERATION WITH THE UNIVERSE YOU BORN. AND FOR THIS I THINK THE ENSUING CHAPTERS CONSISTING THE KNOWLEDGE OF ALL BRANCHES OF LIFE YOU HAVE BEEN ENCOUNTERED WITH. IT IS SO BECAUSE UNIVERSE IS BORN FROM ATOM AND YOU ARE AN ATOM AND THEREFORE YOU ARE THE UNIVERSE.

"IF WE GO BACK TO THE BEGINNING WE SHALL FIND THAT IGNORANCE AND FEAR CREATED THE 'GODS' THAT FANCY, ENTHUSIASM OR DECIET ADORNED OR DISFIGURED THEM, THAT WEAKNESS WORSHIP THEM THAT CREDULITY PRESERVES THEM AND THAT CUSTOM RESPECTS AND TYRANNY SUPPORTS THEM IN ORDER TO MAKE THE BLINDNESS OF MEN SERVES ITS OWN INTEREST"

VOLTAIRE

CHAPTER II
HUMAN ROLE
IN UNDERSTANDING LIFE

2.1 THEOLOGICAL PERSPECTIVE

THEOLOGY OR SAY RELIGION is a collection of cultural systems and belief systems and world views that relates humanity to spirituality to moral values. Many religions have narratives, symbols, traditions and sacred histories that are intended to give meaning to LIFE or explain the origin of LIFE or the UNIVERSE itself, out of which they derive morality, ethics, laws or style of living and ideas and about the COSMOS and human nature.

The word RELIGION is derived from the Latin RELIGIO the ultimate origins which are obscure. RELIGION was originally used to mean only "reverence for God or the Gods, careful pondering of the divine piety"

Many languages have words that can be translated as "RELIGION" but they may use them in a different way and some have no word for religion at all. For example, the Sanskrit word DHARMA sometimes translated as "Religion also mean "LAW". Medieval Japan at first had a similar Union between 'imperial law' and "Universal or BUDDHA LAW".

One important way in which religious beliefs accomplish this by providing a set of ideas about how and why the World is put together that allows people to accommodate anxieties and deal with misfortunes. Some academies studying the subject have divided Religions into three broad categories like

TRANSCULTURAL INTERNATIONAL FAITHS AND INDEGENOUS RELIGION.

Having defined religion, we now move to the most common schemes employed for differentiating between different types of religions. Those religions that preaches POLYTHEISM, MONOTHEISM, FOLKTHEISM, THESOPHISM, SCIENTIOTHEISM etc. Out of 700 billion of total population of the world (as of June 2012) 84% of people are adherent of some religion or other. Only 16% people are either none-religious or atheist. To go, however, in detail about religions like JUDAISM, CHRISTIANITY, ISLAM BUDDHISM, HINDUISM AND JAINISM may be studied what when where and how these religions became popular or populous.

2.2 JUDAISM

It is an oldest Abrahamic religion originating in the people of ancient ISRAIL AND JUDEA. Judaism is based primarily on the TORAH; a text which the Jews believe was handed down to the people of Israel through the Prophet MOSES. This along with rest of HEBREW BIBLE and TALMUD are the central texts of JUDAISM. The Jewish people after the destruction of the Temple in Jerusalem by Roman Empire in 70 BCE spread over many parts of the world. Today there are about 13 million Jews about 40 % living in Israel and 60% in United States of America.

HISTORY: Hebrew Bible (Old Testament) preserves the stories of Judaism. The religion is centered on the covenant revealed to MOSES at MOUNT SINAI and preserved in TORAH, the first five books of Hebrew Bible. It tells the history of the people of Israel from their first ancestor ABRAHAM and SARAH (perhaps 1800BCE) and attempted to rebuild the Kingdom of JUDAH (in South ISRAEL) after the Babylon exile ended in 539 BCE.

They believe the conviction that there is one eternal, omniscient, incorporeal God who created the Universe, that he alone deserve worship and that he revealed the UNCHANGING TORAH to MOSES as a guide to life. Jews generally speak of God in male terms.

The Torah received its name because it contains instructions how to live. The most famous instructions are the TEN COMMANDMENTS which God gave to Moses in Mount Sinai. In all the RAQBBIS identify 613 MITZVOT or commandments in the TORAH. It is written by hand on scrolls of parchment and are kept in the front of the SYNAGOGUE IN A CHEST known as an ark.

The Genesis creation narrative is primary myth of Judaism, Christianity and Islam. It is presented in the first two chapters of GENESIS, the first book of Bible. In Chapter I GOD(Hebrew ELOHIM) creates the world in six days as detailed below then rests on blesses and sanctifies the SEVENTH DAY. God creates by spoken command LET THERE BE . . . . the characteristic Hebrew verb used to describe Gods creative act in this Chapter BARA which throughout the Genesis is used only with God as its subject, ONLY GOD.(GENESIS1. 1:2:3)

FIRST DAY: Light is commanded to appear. The light is divided from the darkness and they named Day and Night.

SECOND DAY: GOD makes firmament to divide the waters above from the waters below. The firmament is named SKIES.

THIRD DAY: GOD commands the water below to be gathered together in place and dry land appear EARTH and

SEA are named. God commands the earth bring forth grass, plants and fruit bearing trees.

FOURTH DAY: God puts light on the firmament to separate light from darkness to mark days, seasons and years and two GREAT lights SUN and MOON are made to appear.

FIFTH DAY: God commands Sea to term with living creatures and birds to fly across the heaven.

SIXTH DAY: God commands the land to bring forth living creatures. He ordered to make wild beasts, live stock and reptiles and finally creates HUMANITY in his image and likeness. They are commanded to be fruitful and multiply and fill the earth and subdue it. To this point he has seen his work on each day and described it as "GOOD" and totality of creation is described by as "VERY GOOD"

SEVENTH DAY: Thus the heavens and Earth were finished and all the host of them GOD having completed the work of heavens and earth rests and blesses and sanctifies the Seventh day.

(GENESIS2:1:3) Yahweh (God) plants a garden in Eden and sets man in it and causes pleasant trees necessary for food and also "The Tree of Knowledge of good and evil" and unnamed river is described which goes out from Eden to water the garden after which it parts into four streams. YEHWEH sets the man in the garden to work it and keep it and tells him he may eat the fruit of all trees except the tree of knowledge of good and evil for on that day thou shall surely die.

YEHWEH see it is not good for the man to be alone and resolves to make a HELPER for him. He makes domestic animals and birds for which man gave their names, but none of them is fitting helper and takes a RIB when he fell asleep and forms woman. The woman proves to be the fit mate for the man and statement instituting marriage follows and ordered them to be one flesh.

TEN COMMANDMENTS: The ten commandments refers the words (EXODUS 20) that God wrote on the two stone tablets that Moses brought down from Mount Sinai and smashed upon seeing the idolatry of the Golden Calf (EXODUS 32:19). In the Hebrew bible these words are called ASERET HADVAREEM (THE TEN Things and in rabbanised texts they are called ASERET HA DIBROT (the ten sayings or Utterances). Jews tradition holds that the Ten Commandments are the ideological for 613 commandments (MITZVOT) in the Bible. When the Israelites accepted Ten Commandments from God they committed themselves to the following moral code of behavior:

- □ I am the lord your God who brought out slavery in Egypt.
- □ You shall have no other gods but me.
- □ You shall not misuse the name of the Lord, your God.
- □ You shall remember and keep SABBATH DAY a holy.
- □ Honor your father and mother.
- □ You shall not murder.
- □ You shall not commit adultery.
- □ You shall not steal.
- □ You shall not bear false witness against thy neighbor.
- □ You shall not covet.

The rabbis teach that the first five sayings on the left side of the tablet and the second five saying on right side of the tablet. The first five concerns mans relationship with God and second five concern with fellow people. In Judaism disrespect to the parents is considered as an insult to God and thus life of man would be meaningless.

The central Jewish religious observance is keeping the SABBATH, the time from sun down FRIDAY to sun down SATURDAY since God took rest on seventh day and hence they observe fast on the whole day and the Sabbath meal on Friday evening, the mother of an observant family will light Sabbath candles and welcome queen Sabbath. During Rituals performed soon after the birth a Jew enter into covenant with God and receive their names. The ritual for boys is CIRCUMCISION known as BRIT MILAH. Sometimes they perform on eighth day of birth. Rituals for girls vary from boys as the traditional ritual is for fathers to introduce the baby girl to the community at the Synagogue service. Female circumcision is not allowed in Judaism. Judaism as rule does not allow cremation, embalming is forbidden and ideally the corpse should be buried within 24 hours.

2.3 CHRISTIANITY.

The religion centered on the belief in Jesus as son of God. The most important teaching of Christianity is that JESUS WAS FULLY GOD AND FULLY HUMAN AND THAT GOD WAS A TRINITY—Father (creator) Son and Holy Spirit and the Christian part of the Bible is NEW TESTAMENT. It is believed that Jesus is a son of Virgin Mary from God took birth to save the humanity. Jesus is the son of God thus unites two natures, Devine and Human in person that Jesus was conceived apart from human Sexual activity as he is a son of Virgin that forgiveness of sins is available through Jesus, death and RESURRECTION AND THE END OF TIME THE DEAD WILL BE RAISED AND JUDGED.

Most Christians follow a cycle of annual festivals linked to the life of JESUS; CHRISTMAS celebrated his birth, EPIPHNY celebrates his manifestation as GOD; LENT which begins on ASH WEDNESDAY is time for preparation and repentance;

PALM SUNDAY recalls JESUS ENTRY INTO Jerusalem JUST BEFORE HIS death; MONDAY; THURSDAY his last meal with his followers and GOOD FRIDAY his Crucification ; EASTER celebrates Jesus resurrection from the death.

BIBLE FOR THE CHRISTIANS: Christians call Hebrew scriptures as old Testament and recognize them as part of their Bible and to this they add another 27 books and call it NEW TESTAMENT WHICH TOOK PLACE DURING SECOND TO FOURTH CENTURY (ADE).

CREATION OF WORLD: As detailed I Judaism creation of world in Christianity was taken place in six days but with small change. As told in second chapter of GENESIS THE LORD GOD FORMED ADAM FROM EARTH'S DIRT, BREATHED LIFE INTO HIM AND PLACED HIM IN THE GARDEN OF EDEN. After futile attempt to companion for him among the animals God put him deep sleep and took one of his ribs and fashioned a woman from it whom Adam eventually named eve. In Genesis 3 God expelled Adam and eve from the Garden because they disobeyed God's command NOT TO EAT FROM TREE OF KNOWLEDGE. Christians used the image of Adam in defining Special role of JESUS. For example PAUL saw Jesus as second Adam undoing consequences of First Adam (1 Corinthians 15, 22.45) and for Muslims Adam is the first line of Prophets that culminates into PROPHET MUHAMMAD.

Christianity claims miracle powers for Jesus. The New Testament presents him as healing, casting out demons and performing like curing leprosy patient, giving life to a dead body of child etc.

FASTING: Catholic orthodox and some protestant Christians have traditionally fasted during 40 days period before EASTER known as LENT.

TEACHINGS: According to one account Jesus identified two predominant commandments: LOVE GOD and LOVE YOUR FELLOW HUMAN BEINGS. In the famous sermon on the Mount (Mathew 5—7) Jesus shows how far these commandments extend. For example he teaches that if one strikes a person on one cheek that person should turn the other cheek and allow it to be struck too and if some takes a person's coat that person should give away his or her coat too.

Jesus also characterizes his followers in metaphors" I am the bread of life—I am the light of world—I am vine you are branches and the best is I AM THE GOOD SHEPARD AND THE GOOD SHEPARD LAYS DOWN HIS LIFE FOR SHEEP (John 10-11)

2.4 ISLAM.

ISLAM is the second largest religion followed by world population. Islam in Arabic means" submission ". Specifically submission to the will of God, a religion that took final form in Arabia after revelation to the Prophet Muhammad(570—632 AD) People who practice the religion are called Muslims(earlier period MOSLEM).

After the death of Prophet the revelations he had received were collected and compiled into a Book called THE QURAN. After the next 300 years Scholars collected stories of Prophet's deeds and sayings and named as HADITH.

Muslims also speak Allah in masculine. As per QURAN 'HE IS ALLAH, THE CREATOR, THE GOVERNER OF

SECURITY, THE WATCH OVER OF HIS CREATURES; THE ALMIGHTY, THE COMPELLER, THE SUPREME INVENTOR OF ALL THINGS AND THE BESTOWER OF FORMS. It is ALSO ALLAH SAYS" INDEED YOUR LORD CREATED THE HEAVENS AND THE EARTH IN SIX DAYS AND ROSE OVER THE THRONE(ISTAWA) HE BRINGS NIGHT AS A COVER OVER THE DAYSEEKING IT RAPIDLY AND HE CREATED THE SUN, MOON, AND STARS (Surat Al-Araf 7:54) Allah reveled his final Scripture the QURAN to the last of his Messenger Muhammad. The TORAH THE INJEL (GOSPEL) and Allah's word be followed for your guidance (Surat Al-Araf 7-158)

The QURON constitutes the most comprehensive legislation of Islam on practical as a source of SHARIAH(The Divine Laws)It is comprehensive because it includes the laws as well as underlying purposes and moral principles to which every Muslim must subscribe.

There are FIVE FUNDAMENTAL PRINCIPLES OR COMMANDMENTS FOR MUSLIM (1) SHAHDAH— BELIEVING ALLAH PROPHESSED BY MUHAMMAD (2) SALATH—prayer to be offered to the God five times a day (3) ROZAH—Fasting for 30 days in the month of RAMADAN the month during which QURAN was reveled to the Prophet. (4) ZAKAT—Alms giving annually at the prescribed rate to the poor and (5) HAJJAH—performing Pilgrimage to Mecca by every Muslim provided he is capable of doing so.

HADITH an Arabic word for story or news in reliable reports about the Prophet. HADITH are for the most part records of what Prophet Muhammad SAID, DID and ALLOWED They define what Muslims call SUNNAH—Tradition. In 10th century CE Scholars made six authoritative collections and

SHIITE'S PARTITIONED and FOLLOW THEIR OWN HADITH. They are the supporters of ALI, SON-IN-LAW of Prophet Muhammad.

2.5 ASIAN RELIGIONS—CONFUSCIANISM:

THIS RELIGION originated with CONFUCIUS AT THE 6th CENTURY BCE and since then it became an official ideology of Chinese State.

CONFUCIUS (Latin for KUNG-FU-T ZU) Master Kung 551—479 BCE was profoundly influential Teacher who emphasized that BECAUSE HUMAN BEINGS ARE SOCIAL CREATURES A GOOD SOCIETY IS IMPORTANT TO GOOD HUMAN LIFE. He also realized that good Society in turn depends on good and highly motivated people. First Goal must be to cultivate HUMANNESS within one self.

He is said to have edited five classic books of Chinese thought and disciples gathered his own teaching into collection known as the ANALECTS. Later he taught proper behavior in terms of FIVE RELATIONSHIPS: RULER—SUBJECT, FATHER-SON, ELDER BROTHER-YOUNGER BROTHER, HUSBAND-WIFE, and FRIEND-FRIEND. He recalls that HUMANNESS is present in all human beings; it simply need right nurturing in order to blossom and flourish.

When CONFUCIANISM was temporarily eclipsed on account MENICIUS DOMINITATION in 220 (BCE) its place was taken by BUDDHISM AND TAOISM. BUT AROUND 1000 ADE the fortunes of Confucianism began to rise again. Later Confucianism equipped with rituals like sacrificing under neo CONFUCIAN thinkers like CHUHSI.

Pigs, sheep and Ox were given as sacrifice under the presence of either Emperor or high Official and offer prayers after burning Incense and loud music

2.6 TAOISM

Taoism is a Chinese religion pronounced with an initial of "d" and therefore spelled Daoism. It teaches that by living in harmony with the TAO (the way of nature), it is possible to prolong life and even become immortal.

There are two types of Taoism one Philosophical and other religious. Religious Taoism refers to movements and practices like ALCHEMY (Transforming metals into medicines that were thoughts grant immortality. The founder Taoism is known as LAO—TZU "Old Master". He dictated classic book on Taoism that has 5000 Chinese characters who had come into existence that advocated yielding to the way of nature in all things. It called Prime characteristic human life. Another book was named CHUANG—TZU after a person who supposedly wrote it. On account of these books rituals and institutions developed. They looked a golden age to come in future and this age was known as GREAT PEACE Another, Taoist movement that began in 184 BCE is known as THE WAY OF HEAVENLY MASTERS. LAO-TZU was considered as GOD who can heal sick. They perfected many techniques that were said lead long life and if done just right immortality achieved. They quote an analogy if water is flowing in a stream means it simply yields to the forces exerted on it and that force is gravity and if it moves out of the way when it hits a stone and still it moves since water force is more powerful than boulder. Thus human actions is action that forced not deliberately unless human exercise the force of intention. They believed that there are five mountains in China the most sacred of which is TAISHAN in eastern province of SHAN TUNG where there are life giving properties such as gold.

Taoism analyzes human being in detail the most important life forces concentrate in three centers—THE HEAD, THE HEART, AND THE NAVEL. These three centers the head the heart and the navels are where the three holy ones the most important immortals dwell. They are also home to three beings known as WORMS that devour VITAL ENERGY and bring about death. There are two main practices: EXERCISE TO PROLONG ONE'S LIFE AND LARGE, ELOBERATE RITUALS FOR THE WELL BEING OF COMMUNITY WHICH IS CALLED EXTERNAL ELEXIR INVOLVING EATING AND DRINKING (EVEN GOLD) then one get long life. Around 1000CE the external elixir was replaced by an INTERNAL ELIXIR means gymnastic exercise which give peace, health and protection to the community as a whole. They have both monks and Nuns. Taoism was attracted by Europeans in 20th century for its exercise through martial arts called TAICHI.

2.7 SHINTOISM

Shintoism, a Japanese religion of indigenous of the country. The word Shinto means "the way of the Gods" Shinto is worship of KAMI an ancient Japanese God. Kami in other words means Sun Goddess. The Kami of most Shrines are peaceful deities protectors of families and local communities, honored in festivals during agricultural year.

Symbol of SHINTO AS RECOGNIZABLE AS Christian Cross or Jewish Star of David. Passing under the TORIL the visitor will approach the Shrine itself, a small wooden building. Japanese give sacrifice in token of getting the blessing of Goddess. Spiritually it emphasizes the importance of Purity for the Kami and their Shrines are thought to be very pure places and one can purify one's own mind and heart. As a polytheistic religion one affirming many gods and goddesses Shinto suggests that divine can be found in many different local forms and by this means is close to the lives of communities.

2.8 ZOROASTRIANISM

Zoroastrianism begun in Iran by the Prophet ZARATHSTRA. Its followers worship only God, AHURA MAZDA. It teaches that the world is site of a struggle between good and evil. It also maintains that there will be a final judgment after death

No one knows when Zarathustra lived. Some date him close to 1000BCE, others in 600BCE. In any case he lived in eastern Iran and reformed the traditional religion. He advocated the worship of AHURAMAZDA (Lord of Wisdom) as the one true God. He also conceived of the traditional DEEVAS a word related to the English word DIETY. He eliminated sacrifices that DEEVAS originally received.

Zoroastrianism religion flourished under Persian emperors known as ACHEMENIDS and it became official religion and the priests were known as MAGI. After the conquest of ALEXANDER the Great (356-323 BCE) Zoroastrianism adopted very low profile. Further Muslim armies invaded and conquered Persia and with the result majority of Persians converted into Islam. Only 25000 Zoroastrians known as GABARS remain in Iran today. By 1000CE Zoroastrians from Persia began settling in western Indian region and are being called as PARSEES. The central figure of the religion is AHURA MAZDA or ORMAZD and he is eternal and uncreated and said to have seven heavenly attendants led by SPENTA MAINYU also known as Holy Spirit opposed to AHURA MAZDA is ANGRA MAINYU an EVIL SPIRIT and also known as AHRIMAN. Human being are now called upon to choose truth over the lie, goodness over evil. There will be final battle at the end of time in which AHURA MAZDA will defeat ANGRA MAINYU once for all. They also teach that human beings are judged after death and they must walk across the Bridge of recompense which traverse an abyss.

2.9 HINDUISM

Religion as practiced in Indus Valley Civilization also called the HARAPPAN civilization. Around 3500(BCE) a city based way of life began to emerge in the plains of Indus Valley. Asset of religions that arose and are especially practiced in India is something of an Umbrella term and acknowledged the authority of the sacred text known as VEDAS.

A number of organizations advocates the Hindutva ideal and according to common scheme Hindus follow one of the three margas or paths, the paths of right, moral action and devotion to the Gods. Hinduism does not have any founder or one scripture or even way of life. It speaks on one side Monotheism and on other side Polytheism. Gods are being worshipped by different people but essence of belief of different sects is same. Only authorized scriptures areVEDAS which means revelation. They are four in number—RIGVEDA, YAJURVEDA, SAMAVEDA AND ATHARVANAVEDA. They are reported to be called as APOURUSHEYA (not written by humans). They are written and preached by God. The first three Vedas are considered as Bird with one wing and the fourth one with two wings.

Sage Vyasa is reported to have compiled these four Vedas. Later UPANISHADS which are said to be the concluding part of four Vedas and it denotes a student sitting close to the teacher. They are also called JNANA KANDA of Vedas which deals with JNANA AND VIJNANA. The central theme is the Self (ATMAN) joining with Universal Self (PARAMATMA). There are as many Upanishads as 108 in number of which 11 have special importance.

The problems of Upanishads mentioned includes:

- □ What is reality from which all things originate?
- □ What is that by knowing of which everything is known?
- □ What is that by which unknown becomes known?
- □ By which one can attain immortality?
- □ What is BRAHMAN?
- □ What is Atman?

And response these questions is that:

- □ The ultimate reality is Brahman(God)
- □ The ultimate reality is self(Atman)
- □ The Ultimate reality is SAT(Sense)

Upanishads shift the center of interest from Vedic gods to the Self of man. The real is pure consciousness—ATMAN. The Vedic belief in sacrifice was moved and shaken by Upanishads. Since according to MANDUKYA UPANISHAD these sacrifices cannot help in achieving the highest goal and the highest goal can only be through the knowledge of Self and God (ATMA AND PARAMATMA) which is ultimate source of joy. Self realization is greatest joy. Realization of identity between the self and Brahman is liberation from Bondage JEEVAN MUKTI.

Finally one more holy book was called revealed to the
NAR (Man) by NARAYANA (God) named after as
BHAGAVATGITA. When Upanishad called cream of
VEDAS the BHAGAVTGITA IS suppose to be the essence of
Upanishads. BHAGAVATGITA exhorts one to equip oneself
for the battle of life, Karma (doing one's duty) that is enacting
our role righteously and bravely in the cosmic play of action
without fear be it a friend or foe, relative or outsider. It says
strength nurtures life, weakness wear it away and then only
he would shine and enjoins with THE ONE (Paramatman).
It analogically describes this act conveying that man's life is
in ambush, dirt but he should come out as pure light as lotus
arises out of mud. It also states that renunciation does not
mean cessation of action, but rather it connotes renunciation
of desire for fruits while performing out actions. And man
gets MOKSHA through three ways (1)JNANA MARGA (way
of enlightenment) (2) KARMA MARGA (way of action) and
BHAKTI MARGA(way of devotion)

Finally comes PURANAS which are also called
(ITHIHASAS) or epics. According to these epics VISHNU
(THE PROTECTOR) BRAHMA(THE CREATOR) AND
SHIVA(THE DESTROYER) Each set of people choose
particular God for their worship depending upon their mind
set. It is stated that God incarnates himself among human
beings whenever it deems necessary, to destroy Evil and restore
Dharma. Hindu heritage proclaims NARAYANA THE GOD
OF PROTECTOR whenever occasion arises to wipe out evil
he incarnated into himself for nine times which include:

- ☐ MATSYAVATARA (fish incarnation)
- ☐ KURMAVATHARA(Tortoise incarnation)
- ☐ VARAHAVATHARA(Pig incarnation)
- ☐ NARASIMHAVATHARA(Man-Lion incarnation)
- ☐ VAMANAVATHARA(Dwarf incarnation)
- ☐ PARASURAMAAVATHARA(Dutiful sage incarnation)

☐ RAMAAVATHARA(Ideal King and demon killing incarnation)

☐ BALARAMAAVATHARA(Demon destroyer and ideal brother incarnation)

☐ KRISHNAVATHARA(Complete MAN incarnation)

and it is supposed that another incarnation called KALKIAVATHARA is yet to take incarnation and some scholars do not accept *BALARAMAAVATHARA as Brahmas incarnation. Hindu Religion being a VEDANTIC expounds universal truths and leaves the individual to follow to attain emancipation because it is only the ULTIMATE TRUTH, otherwise they will reap the result of their action and suffer by taking births after births in the cycle of creation.

Hindu sages and philosophers say that Hinduism was much maligned by cast system like Brahmins, Kshatriyas, Vaisyas and Sudras which is purely functional arrangement in Society for orderly conduct of affairs in society and not sanctioned by this Vedic religion. The only way to attain emancipation is JNANAMARGA in other words good deeds and dutiful deeds without expecting fruit as reward.

2.10 BUDDHISM.

Buddhism, a religion that traces its history back to BUDDHA, Siddhartha Gautama(560-480 BCE) it is practiced widely throughout South East and East Asia. It has also strong traditional ties with Tibet. Siddhartha Gautama is said to have discerned the path that leads to release from suffering and rebirth(samsara) at the age of 35. Although sometimes hears that the Buddhists are atheist this is not quite correct Buddhism does not deny truth of other religions instead it tries to supplement another truth with a truth of its own. But in Buddhism it is ultimately more important to follow the Buddhist path than worship Gods. According to tradition the Buddha, discovered four truths during the night of enlightenment which termed as Noble truths.

Buddhist path to redress the root problem that all sentient or conscious being face SUFFERING for which Buddha like doctor sets to cure the disease that plaques all sentient being by prophesying the truths of suffering. First noble truth tells what are the symptoms of disease, Second being identifying what causes them, third sets what can be done about the disease and finally fourth Noble Truth to provide a detailed prescription. Buddha says symptoms of disease is suffering, cause is craving, and then rout out craving and fourth for providing detailed prescription is to adopt eight fold path which include:

- ☐ SAMYADRISTI (Right view)
- ☐ SAMYAKSANKAKALPA (Right to resolve)
- ☐ SAMYAGVAK (Right speech)
- ☐ SAMYAK KARMANTA (Right conduct)
- ☐ SAMYOGVYAMTA (Right effort)
- ☐ SAMYAKSMRTI (Right Mindfulness)
- ☐ SAMYAGJIVA (Right livelihood)
- ☐ SAMYAKSAMAQDHI (Right concentration)

All these eight fold path shall lead human being to NIRVANA(emancipation) or relief from the bondage of suffering. Further Lord Buddha is very obvious about four explicitly stated views:

- ☐ The theory of dependent origination OR conditional existence of these things
- ☐ The theory of karma or action
- ☐ The theory of Change
- ☐ The theory of non existence of soul.

Buddha attributes the Principal causation for the existence of individual which is due to KARMA and the present existence of an individual is due to causation of PAST AND FUTURE. He also states that everything arises from condition and therefore impermanent. Everything which has the beginning also has an end that is momentary or KSANIKAVADA.

Basically there are as many as 32 Schools of later Buddhism. However of these Schools FOUR schools are distinguished and they are 1)Nihilist(sunyavadi) 2)Subjective idealist(Vijnanavadi) 3)Critical realists(Bahyanumeyavadi)and 4)Direct realist(Bhahyapratyakavada) or MADHYAMICA, YOGACHARA, SOUTRANTIKA AND VAIBHASIKA respectively.

2.11 JAINISM

Jainism is religion in India and they get their name because they follow the teaching and example of the JINA or Victor and that Victor is MAHAVIRA(599 BCE), Jains claim that their religion is millions of years old and for them MAHAVIRA is24th THIRTHNKARA.(FORD MAKERS)These are people who have made fords across the stream of life(SAMSARA). HE WENT ABOUT STARK NAKED. HE DID NOT EVEN POSSESS A BOWL FOR COLLECTING FOOD BUT PREFERED TO EAT FROM HOLLOW OF HIS PALMS.

The main goal is to make good conduct which lead to salvation say MOKSHA and according Jaina there are two kinds of bondage, bondage due to thought and due to matter. Or sway BHAVA BANDHA AND DRAVYA BANDHA. JAINA proposes THRIRATNAS or three gems and they are RIGHT FAITH, RIGHT KNOLEDGE, and RIGHT CONDUCT. AND FOR WHICH FOLLOWER HAS TO

TAKE FIVE VOWS and which are AHIMSA SATHYAM ASTEYAM BRHMACHARYA AND APARIGRAHA or Non-violence, truth, non-stealing, bachelorhood and non attachment to wealth. JAINS do not believe in the existence of GOD because his existence is unwarranted and unreasonable. In the first century CE the community split in two groups, one group proposed to give up non-clothing another remained orthodox and these groups are named SWETHAMBARAS AND DIGAMBARAS. DIGAMBARAS(naked) tend to live in south Indian State of Karnataka and SWETHAMBARAS.(white-clad) lived in west Indian State of Gujarat.

2.12 SIKHISM

A RELIGION FROM North west India that traces itself back to 10 GURUS, beginning with GURUNANAK (1469—1539). Today the Sikhs venerate above all a book writing known as the ADIGRANTHA OR GURUGRANTH SAHIB. Sikhs worship together in a building called GURUDWARA.

Sikhs believe that by following Gods path inscribed in the holy book, people become pure and over succession of rebirths eventually unite with the ETERNAL. In GURUDWARA the GURUGRANTH rests upon the plat form where it is decorated with flowers and fanned and the followers worship and listen to and participate in singing from GURUGRANTH. They also present gifts and receive sweet in turn.

2.13 GANDHISM

AHIMSA meaning Non-violence became the new modern religion which was advocated by MOHANDAS KARAM CHAND GANDHI. It is the basic law in view of God is of our beingness. That is the religion of religions for which no God is required to reveal to human being through any Prophet or Messiah. Ahimsa is in deep accord with Truth of man's nature itself and corresponds to innate desire for peace, order freedom and personal dignity. It is religion by itself that exists in every human being ever since he attained wisdom in evolutionary process from Ameba to Adam. Gandhi is careful to state that he does not want to practice it perfectly. However all men should be willing to engage in the risk and wager of Ahimsa because violent policies have not only proved bankrupt but threaten man with extinction.

There is half way between truth and non-violence on the one hand and untruth and violence on the other. We may never be strong enough (to be entirely strong enough) to be entirely non-violent in thought, word and deed. But one should keep non-violence as our goal and steady progress towards it. The attainment of freedom whether for a man, nation or the world, must be in exact proportion to the attainment of non-violence by each. It is a commandment in itself one need not go to any temple or mosque or synagogue or not even for meditation. Non-violence is not garment to be put on and off at will. It s seat is in the heart and it must be an inseparable part of every being. There is no such as defeat in non-violence. Given proper training and proper generalship non-violence can be practiced by masses of mankind. Man as an animal is violent but in spirit is non-violent. In the empire of non-violence every true thought counts, every true voice has its full value. Prayer from heart can achieve what nothing else can do in the world.

The first principle of non-violent action is that of non-cooperation with everything that is humiliating. True non-violence, Gandhi means "For an individual who is non-violent the Golden rule is that he will have nothing. "If I decided to settle and walk among criminal tribes, I should go to them without any belonging and depend on them for my food and shelter. The moment they feel that' I am in their midst in order to serve them, they will be my friends." In that attitude it is Non-violence. Prayer is not an old man or old woman's idle amusement. Properly understood and applied the truth, is itself the most potent instrument of action. Finally Gandhi says hatred, untruth generates violence where as truth and love flower non-violence. The future will depend on what we do in the present.

2.14 ATHEISM

Denial of existence of any God or Supernatural being is ATHEISM In ancient India, China and Greece few Philosophers said that gods were only figments of human imagination and everything that happens in the universe could be given natural explanation. Religionists have also accused one another among themselves. Orthodox Christians negates Protestants, Muslim Sunnis negates Shiites and they fight and kill among themselves then their God never comes to rescue. Similarly so many wars have been waged between one religion to another—between Christians and Muslims, Muslims and Jews and Christians and vice versa ; Muslims and Hindus and vice versa but history has never recorded any interference of their gods to establish peace among their followers. Atheism, probably grown in Modern world with a rise of Science and through its powerful ideologies like communism and socialism.

In terms of Great Psychologist Edmund Freud that "Religion and belief in God is nothing but a mental illness"

"Philosophy is mental activity"—Levison.

"It is rigorous disciplined guarded analysis of some of most difficult problems which men have ever faced."

"Education without philology is blind and philosophy without education is invalid"

"Philosophy gives a synoptic view of universe"—Henderson

"Philosophy is mother of all branches of knowledge including sciences. It is comprehensive picture of the universe. It is daily activity. It gives direction to life, offers & design for living"—Author

Chapter III
PHILOSOPHICAL PERSPECTIVE

In order to talk about the nature of the Universe and discuss the questions such as whether it has beginning or an end, we have to be clear what the Matter is. It must accurately describe large class of observation on the basis of model that contain only a few arbitrary elements and it must make definite predictions about the result of future observations. Elements like EARTH, AIR, FIRE, WATER AND SPACE are all forms of matter and their combination results to great chemical outcome is LIFE. Our Goal is however, to provide a single theory that describe WHOLE LIFE.

The approach must follow to separate the problem into two parts—First there must be laws that tell us how and when the UNIVERSE that is Matter in total started from and Secondly what was the state of Universe before it change from time to time. It is not like "LET THERE BE—as studied in Religious perspective. It was only a fiction rather than factual. Fact should be perceived, felt, smelt touched and heard and perceived as our five senses do conceive. Philosophy, however, attempted to analyze and describe the factual position of Universe matter and there with life too.

3.1 ETIMOLOGY

Philosophy is a Greek term that denote LOVE OF KNOWLEDGE or say LOVE OF WISDOM. The introduction of the term Philosopher and Philosophy has been ascribed to the Greek thinker PYTHAGORAS.

"PHILOSOPHER was understood as a word which contrasted with SOPHIA (from SOPHI) travelling SOPHISTS or WISEMEN, were important in classical Greece, often earning money as teachers, where as Philosophers are LOVERS OF KNOWLEDGE are not professionals. The main areas of study today include METAPHYSICS, EPISTOMOLOGY, LOGIC, ETHICS, AESTHETICS, ONTOLOGY, SOCIAL AND POLOTICAL PHILOSOPHY. To be Philosopher is not merely to have subtle thought nor even to found school but to know what is reality, what is universe, what is knowledge and explain it with an independent magnanimity and trust. The person who knows and tells it frankly is real philosopher. In every man there is something where one may learn and is that we become his pupil. List of Philosopher and their proposition from earliest period of time to date include:.

3.2 THALES (624-546 B CE):

Thales belonged to Miletus in Asia Minor and was among the Seven sages of Greece. He tried to explain the natural Phenomena without taking the help of Mythology. He brought revolution not only in Philosophy but also in Science. Thales became the first person to describe general principles and put forward HYPOTHESIS and for the same he was called father of reasoning. In order to solve the mathematical problems he took the help of Geometry like calculating Pyramid's height and distance between SHORE and SHIP. Thales is recognized with the usage of deductive reasoning, application. He can be said as first person to study about ELECRICITY. He was more and above True Mathematician. He forecasted solar eclipse and thus he became the first Astrologist too in the history of mankind.

3.3 DEMOCRITUS (460-360 BCE):

At first, Philosophy was Physical it looked upon the material world and was the final and irreducible constituent of things. The natural termination of this line of thought was materialism of Democritus. He said in reality there is nothing but ATOM AND SPACE and which became main stream of Greek speculation. There is no real philosophy until the mind turn s around examine itself.

3.4 SOCRATES (469-399BCE):

He started with the slogan KNOW THY SELF and started questioning the certainties. He started deflating dogmas and puncturing presumptions, with a sharp point of questions and for this his enquiring became a concept of SOCRATIC IRONY and SOCRATIC METHOD or ELENCHUS. He did not write Philosophical texts about the knowledge of life nor he established any School of thought but his Philosophy is entirely based on writing by his students and contemporaries and foremost among is PLATO. His method was DIALECTIC and which later became Socratic Method. To solve the problem he used to break down into series of questions, the answer to which gradually distil the answer a person would seek. The influence of this approach is most strongly felt today in the use of SCIENTIFIC METHOD in which hypothesis is the first stage. This method is one of Socrates most enduring and the factor in earning his mantle as the Political Philosophy, ethics or moral philosophy and as figure head of all the central themes in western philosophy. Many of the beliefs traditionally attributed to the historical Socrates have been characterized as PARADOXICAL because they seem to conflict with common sense which include:

- ☐ No one desires evil
- ☐ No one errs or does wrong willing fully or knowingly

☐ Virtue-all-virtue is Knowledge
☐ Virtue is sufficient for happiness.

Socrates' best saying is I ONLY KNOW THAT I KNOW NOTHING AND KNOW THY SELF. His stature in western Philosophy returned full force with RENISSANCE AND AGE OF REASONING. And to this day THE 'SOCRATIC METHOD' is still used in class room and Law schools discourse to express underlying issues in both subject and speaker.

3.5 PLATO: (424—347BCE)

He was classical Greek Philosopher, mathematician and prominently known as Student of Socrates. He founded THE ACADEMY IN ATHENS, THE FIRST INSTITUTION OF HIGHER LEARNING IN THE WESTERN WORLD. His famous book is REPUBLIC. The precise relationship between Plato and Socrates remains an area of contention among scholars. Platonism is a term coined by scholars to refer to the intellectual consequences of denying, as Socrates often does, the reality of the material world. He states that reality of material world is unavoidable to those who use senses but at the same time he says material world as it seems to us not the real world but only an image or copy of the real world.

EPISTOMOLOGY: Many have interpreted as stating that knowledge is justified true belief, an influential view that future development in modern analytic epistemology. Plato argues himself in the TIMAEUS that knowledge is always proportionate to the realm from which it is gained. That is if no one derives one' account of something by way of the non-sensible forms, because these forms are unchanging, so too is the account derived from them. It is only in this sense that Plato uses the term Knowledge. In geometrical example to expound Plato's view that knowledge is acquired by recollection. Plato asserts that Society have a triplicate class of structure—PRODUCTIVE, PROTECTIVE AND GOVERNING. He also viewed that unless and until Philosopher rule as Kings who lead men genuinely and adequately philosophize that is until political power and philosophy entirely coincide, cities will have no rest from evils—nor think will the human race(Republic 473-d) Plato describes these philosopher kings as those who love the sight of truth(Republic 475)and support the idea with an analogy of a captain and his ship or doctor and his medicine with patience. A large part of Republic then addresses how the educational system should be set up to produce these Philosopher Kings. Plato's Dialectic is process of eliciting the truth by means of questions aimed at opening out what is already known or at exposing the contradictions and muddies of opponents position.

3.6 ARISTOTLE (384-322 BCE)

Aristotle was a Greek Philosopher a student of Plato and Teacher of ALEXANDER THE GREAT. His writing cover many subjects including PHYSICS, METAPHYSICS, POETRY, THEATRE, MUSIC, LOGIC, RHETORIC, LINGUISTICS, POLITICS, ETHICS, BIOLOGY AND ZOOLOGY. The term logic he reserved to mean '"dialectics". The logical works of Aristotle were compiled into six books in about the early 1 century AD

- ☐ Categories
- ☐ On interpretation.
- ☐ Prior Analytics,
- ☐ Posterior Analytics,
- ☐ Topics.
- ☐ On sophistical refutations

Aristotle's Scientific Method: Aristotle's Philosophy aims at the universal. He however found the Universal in particular things which he called essence of things. For Aristotle, FORM still refers to the conditional basis of Phenomena but it is particular substance. Thus Aristotle's method is both INDUCTIVE AS WELL AS DEDUCTIVE. Aristotle go too far in deriving laws of universe from simple observation and stretched reason: for example he says that;

- ☐ Earth which is cold and dry corresponds to the modern idea of SOLID.
- ☐ Water which is cold and wet corresponds to the modern idea of LIQUID.
- ☐ Air which is hot and wet corresponds to the present idea of GAS.
- ☐ FIRE which is hot and dry corresponds to the present idea of HEAT.
- ☐ Ether which is divine substance related to the present idea of SPACE.
- ☐ Aristotle defined motion as the actually of a potentiality as such it is ENERGY as termed by Einstein as Causality.

Four causes, he suggested that reason for anything coming about can be attributed to Material cause; formal cause; efficient cause and final cause. He used the device to make observation of the sun and noted that no matter what shape the sun would be still be correctly displayed as round object. He used optical concepts as are being used in Modern cameras for observing sun. He also observed and states that when distance between the aperture and surface with the image increased the IMAGE IS MAGNIFIED. In his book "ON THE HEAVENS" Aristotle put forward two good arguments for believing that the Earth is a round sphere rather than flat plate and secondly he realized that ECLIPSE OF THE MOON CAUSED BY Earth coming between the Sun and Moon

In his book "Ladder of life "(SCALA NATURAE) ARISTOTLE classified animals and living organisms placing them according to the complexity of structure and function so that higher organisms greater vitality and ability to move. In terms of Aristotle Man is also an animal or say rational animal because of the complexity of organisms and nervous system. And finally he conceptualized CHANCE might be thought to coincidence and not luck. What is cannot capable of action cannot do anything by chance and luck only mere term. To be in short in terms Renan "SOCRATES GAVE PHILOSOPHY TO MANKIND ARISTOTLE GAVE SCIENCE. And so he can be better termed as **FATHER OF SCIENCE**.

3.7 EPICURUS (341-270BCE)

Epicurus was ancient and last Greek Philosopher and a prominent in Hellenistic period . . . He was the founder of EPICUREANEANISM. The basic purpose was to acquire a happy and tranquil life which was characterized by ATARAXIA which has complete freedom from worry and opinion or absence of pain. According to him PLEASURE AND PAIN measures of good and evil and the death is the end of body and the soul hence there is nothing to fear. He thought that GODS could not punish or reward humans and man should not worry about life. He also thought that universe is infinite and eternal atoms are responsible for the events that took place in the world.

Like Democritus, Epicurus believed that the world is made up of indivisible little bits of matter flying through space. According to him everything occurring or happening in the world is due to colliding, rebuilding and entangling of atoms which have no aim or purpose behind their action. He further confirmed that his concept of free will, he was the first man to negate the God fearing and God worship, traditionally prevalent at that time. In his opinion God does not furnish evil and reward for the bad and good deeds of human being, instead he claims that all good and bad that happen to the people are based on pleasure and pain. Anything that gives pain is bad and anything that gives pleasure is good. He also states not to fear for the death as death is nothing to do to us and after that no pleasure and pain are felt and hence the role of God does not necessitate here.

3.8 EASTERN PHILOSOPHY

3.8.1 HETERDOX SYSTEMS

Indian Philosophy (in SANSCRIT called DARSHNAS) refers to several traditions of philosophical thought originated in the Indian sub-Subcontinent, including Hindu Philosophy, Buddhist philosophy and Jain Philosophy. It is considered by Indian thinkers to be practical and its goal should always be to IMPROVE HUMAN LIFE. The main heterodox (NASTIKA) schools do not accept the authority of Vedas and Supernatural elements like God.

3.8.1.1 CARUVAKA:

Also known as LOKAYATA CARUVAKA is a materialistic Skeptical and aesthetic School of thought. It was CARVAKA, the author of BARHASPATYA SUTRAS in the final century BCE, although the original texts have been lost and our understanding of them is based largely on Criticism of ideas by other Schools. As early the 5 century SADDHANTI and BUDDHA GHOSA connected the LOKAYATAS with VITANDAS(or SOPHISTS) and the term CARVAKA was recorded in 700BC by the PURANANDARA and in 800 BCE by KAMASILA and HARIBHADRA. It was founded in MOURYAN period.

CARVAKA deemed VEDAS to be tainted by three faults of untruth, Self-contradictory and TANTOLOGY. CARVAKA, felt that consciousness was an emancipation from body and it ended with destruction of the body. He denied that inference as means of knowledge and held sensory indulgence as the final objective of life. He held the view that Invariable concomitance (VYAPAT) a theory of Indian logic refers to the middle term and major term freed from all conditions could not be ascertained. The Basic tenets of CARVAKA Philosophy are (i) Metaphysics—Matter is reality (ii) Epistemology—perception is the only authority(PRAMANA) and (iii)Ethics—Heaven is myth hence pleasure is the ideal life(HEDONISM)God Soul, Heaven, life before and after death are not perceivable hence are not real. He says the World is made up of four elements (i) air (vayu) (ii) Fire (agni) (iii) Water (apa) and (iv) Earth (Ksiti) and all living things are made up of these four elements. The world is created by natures own inherent in them wherein they form combine together to form this world. He believed in pain and pleasure and said as much pleasure as possible in our life should be experienced. Sacrifice of pleasure for the sake of unknown achievements is meaningless.

3.8.1.2 JAINA PHILOSOPHY:

According to BHAGAVATA(5.3.6) story revealed is that RIBASA a great saint-king who sacrificed everything including his clothes and got liberated is the first teachers i.e. THIRTHNKARAS AND the last teacher is VARDAMANA MAHAVIRA. These 24 teachers are the founders of this Jain Philosophy. Mahavira lived during 600BCE and contemporary of GOUTHAMA BUDDHA. The first 22 teachers lived during the Prehistoric period.

The word etymologically means a conqueror which can be applied to all teachers, as they all have conquered all passions and could attain liberation from bondage. They are said to have become omniscient, omnipotent, true, perfect and blissful. They believe that every spirit (JIVA) is in the bondage. According JAIN philosophy the basic concepts of reality are (i) conception of substance(ii) classification of substance (iii) Soul Or JIVA (iv) Innate substances like Matter, space, time and duty. And they viewed that each substances has qualities(GUNAS) and Modes(PARAYA). A substance is real and possesses three factors which are (i) performance (ii) origination and (iii) Decay. JAINA philosophy held that Soul is eternal but it undergoes change in its state and it is different from body. It has the capacity to illumine itself and other objects. Pleasure and pain are perceived by it. The denial of something for example "There is no God" some place includes its presence or Knowledge about its existence. Another example "I do not exist" is as absurd as to say that my mother is barren etc.

According JAINA there are three kinds of knowledge(i) Perception (ii) Inference (iii) Testimony(iv) immediate and mediate knowledge. Another most important dimension of this philosophy is CONDUCT i.e. Good conduct which leads salvation. Good conducts are (i) right faith (ii) Right knowledge (iii) Right conduct or say behavior. They also laid five steps which everyone has to follow (i) AHIMSA—Abstinence from injury (ii) SATYAM— Truth and abstinence from falsehood (iii) ASTEYAM— Non-stealing (iv) BRAHMACHARYA—Bachelor/spinster and (APARIGRAHA—Nonattachment to Wealth.

3.8.1.3 BUDDHIST PHILOSOPHY:

Great heroic legend of Asia and also called Light of Asia and founder of BUDDHISM, was born in Royal family of Nepal-KAPILAPILAVASTU, during 600BCE. His teachings recorded are called TRIPITICAS, which are considered as his philosophy. They are

- (i) VINAYAPITIKA—Conduct for the Congregation
- (ii) SUTTA PITICA—sermons and dialogues and
- (iii) ABHIDHAMMA PITIKA which denotes dialogues and philosophical theories. There are two schools of Buddhism—MAHAYANA and HINAYANA. His teaching include four noble truths
    a. Life is full of suffering
    b. Causes of suffering cessation of suffering and
    c. Path of liberation which has eight fold path. Basically his teaching show anti-speculative attitude, and has ethical dictation rather than metaphysical.

He believed in three phases of life-Past, present and future. By practicing the Eight fold path one will get liberation and the eight fold paths are (i) Right views (ii) Right resolve (iii) Right speech (iv) Right conduct (v) Right livelihood (vi)Right effort (vii) Right mindfulness and (viii) Right concentration. Buddhism believed in the law of causation since NOTHING HAPPENCE BY CHANCE. Buddhist philosophy mainly has four Schools namely—NIHILISM, SUBJECTIVE IDEALISM, CRITICALREALISM and DIRECT REALISM.

3.8.2 ORTHODOX SYSTEMS OF EASTERN PHILOSOPHY;

3.8.2.1 NYAYA PHILOSOPHY:

The founder of this School of thought was AKSAPADA GOUTAMA. NYAYA SUTRAS (logical formulae) was emphasized by this School on the conditions of correct thinking and means of acquiring a true knowledge of reality. It is basically a system of logic and Epistemology but also considered as philosophy of life.

NYAYA SUTRAS are divided into five ADHYAYAS(books) and each consists of two sections or AHNICAS and this can be understood under four dimensions which are;; (i) Theory of knowledge (ii) Theory of Physical world (iii) Theory of individual self and liberation and (iv) The theory of God. These are called PRAMANAS. An objects of true Knowledge are Self, Body, Senses, Sensible qualities, cognition, Mind activity, mental defects, Rebirth, Pleasure and pain, sufferings and finally Liberation. According to this philosophy existence of objects and things of the world are independent of the knowledge or mind where as the images, ideas, feeling pleasure and pain are dependent and an independent mind which experiences them. Logical grounds and critical reflections are the source of true knowledge and true knowledge in reality emancipate LIBERATION.

The Theory of reality or the source of knowledge are (i) perception—PRATYAKHSHA (ii) Inference—ANUMANA (iii) Comparison—UPAMANA and (IV) Testimony—SABDA. This philosophy says that PRAMANAS like Space, time and AKASA are all products of forms of the atoms. The Self is distinct from Mind(MANAS), body and also consciousness. To attain liberation self need to know itself the knowledge of liberation through the knowledge of truth, scriptural authority, self reasoning and conformity with the principles of YOGA(Nidhi asana).

In NYAYA Philosophy there is no explicit mention of God, but they feel God is necessary for liberation of self. They also feel God is the eternal, infinite self who is the basis for the creation, sustenance and destruction. The existence of God can be proved through CAUSATION (ADRSTA),authority of Scriptures(SRUTI) and testimony(PRAMANA).

3.8.2.2 VAISESIKA PHILOSOPHY:

This philosophy was founded by Sage KANADA also known as ULKA. It also aims for the liberation of individual life, feel that ignorance is the root cause of all pain and suffering. Unlike NYAYA this School accepts only two sources of knowledge and they are (i) Perception and (ii) Inference.

According this school all four substances i.e., EARTH (PRTHVI), WATER(JALA), LIGHT(TEJAS and AIR(VAYU) are made up of atoms called PARAMANUS. The fifth substance SKY or SPACE i.e. AKASA including TIME cannot be perceived. Soul is eternal, all pervading which is related to consciousness. And Finally MANAS is the internal sense (an ATENDRIA)to perceive internal soul and its qualities like pleasure and pain which helps to fix our mind on the object of perception (MANO YOGA).

Further it held that quality cannot exists on its own but it exists in substance which is motionless and it has 24 qualities (VISESHA). Action is the dynamic QUALITY OF SUBSTANCE. It is a movement. It is not also universal but it is unique. It also says formation of the World, its origin and destruction can be reduced again in to four kinds of atoms—Earth, Water, Fire and Air. This is in other words the world is made of atoms (PARAMANUS),

3.8.2.3 SAMKHYA PHILOSOPHY:

SAMKHYA system which initially known as SAMKHYA SUTRA. SAMKHYA means Number. It is dualistic realism that is there exists two realities PRAKRTI and PURUSHA i.e. Nature and God. It has the dimensions which are in four in kind—Causation, Nature and qualities, Super Self and evolution of the world. It argues that if cause exists, effect must also exist. Explicit and implicit aspects of cause and of the the same substance can be interpreted as transformation (PARIMANA) which is real. As the effect must potentially be contained in the cause that indicates effect exists in the cause in an un manifested form of its production or manifestation.

According to this philosophy Nature or (PRAKRITI) is the ultimate cause of world of objects and all objects of the world including our body and mind, senses, intellect, are products of combination of certain elements. PRAKRITI has three qualities (GUNAS) which are called Pleasure Pain and indifference SATTVA, RAJAS and TAMAS respectively). These qualities does get changed and they cannot remain without changing and these changes are homogenous and heterogeneous

The second ultimate reality is self. All the objects of the world are the means to ends of other beings and they are said to be conscious unless it exists in itself. All the material objects including mind intellect etc. should be controlled by an intelligent Principle to achieve their end and that principle is SELF (PURUSHA. This Philosophy believes in plurality of selves i.e. each body will have self and thus there are many selves in the world.

According this philosophy the Evolution arises from various elements: Self, Nature, mind, light and ego . . . It also accepts three kinds of elements for acquiring knowledge and they are Perception, Inference and testimony. It further states man's life on earth is a mixture of pain and pleasure. No living being can escape and cannot avoid decay and death. It is, however, possible for every self to liberate itself which can be obtained from emancipation of self with Super Self (GOD). The liberation can be obtained when one requires to realize one's self, to develop a real personality, train all organs appropriately and to provide knowledge and function of all the organs process and their role in self determination and acquiring good and valid knowledge.

3.8.2.4 YOGA SYSTEM OF PHILOSOPHY:

YOGA school of thought which is closely allied to SAMKHYA system, Sage PATANJALI promulgated 55 SUTRAS of YOGA. It has both theoretical as well as practical. They are basically divided into four PADAS—(i) SAMADHI PADA (ii) SADHANA PADA (iii)VIBHUTI PADA and (iv) KAIVALYA PADA. YOGA is practical side of philosophy of life where self purification and purification of body, mind and intellect. It has been compared to VEENA which gives heavenly music only when stings are tuned adequately and played harmoniously. Unless man wipe out five distresses (KALESHAS) like error, egoism, attachment, selfishness, attachment, hatred (AVIDYA, ASMITHA, DWESHA, RAGA, ABINEVASA) Self cannot attain liberation and for this, one requires to practice YOGA or action like abstinence, non-violence, Truthfulness of thought and speech stead fastness in truth which enables actions fruit full, control of carnal desires and passions non acceptance of gifts, and surrender on self to God by way of meditation and finally emancipation(SAMADHI) or (YOGA).

3.8.2.5 MIMAMSA PHILOSOPHY.

The ritualistic side of VEDIC culture called as MIMAMSA School of Philosophy. The Main objective is to support ritualism which is of two types:—(i) to make VEDIC rituals more clearly understood without difficulty and (ii) providing philosophical justification for rituals. They believe that Soul exists and survives even after death and enjoys the fruit s of rituals in heaven and there is power which is preserved by the rituals performed. According to it the world is real, the action done in this world are no more than dreams.

It believes in diverse objects of world and which are real and the souls are permanent and there is law of KARMA (DUTY). They believe in atomic theory of VAISESHIKA but for creation these atoms God is necessary. It is pluralistic realism. According this philosophy there are two types of Knowledge—Perception and non—perception. One who realizes this truth will control his desires and passions, otherwise if man has desire in worldly pleasures he will take birth repeatedly.

3.8.2.6 VEDANTHA PHILOSOPHY (2000-1500BCE)

VEDANTHA means the end of VEDAS, in other words it may be considered as UPANISHADS. The literature of this period can be categorized into three types—(I) VEDIC HYMNS (2) BRAHMANAS (3) UPANISHADS. Based on this three main schools of VEDANTHA were founded which include

    (i)   ADVAITHA
    (ii) DVAITHA and
    (iii) VISISHDVAITHA.

(i)   ADVAITHA:

Monism:—Sankaracharya wrote about MONISM (NON-DUALISM) to prove reality is one. According to him, MAYA as the magical power of creation is indistinguishable from God. God creates Physical world which also called WORLD-SHOW. Individuals out of their ignorance feel that this world is real. This is nothing but ignorance since some times the MAYA or illusion could produce positively some illusionary images (like rope for snake). It is also called RAJJU SARPA BHRANTI. He views change as only apparent, not real, since God being the creator does not undergo change.

According to him concept of self, its bondage, and liberation is also illusionary because it is created between (i)objects and subjects(ii) object and self and (iii) Self and God. As the soul is ignorant of this it gets attached to the body(both gross and subtle) and this is called bondage. This ego as self is only unreal. Only when it realizes self it will be relieved from its bondage. According him the PRAMANAS like perception, inference, testimony, comparison postulation and non-cognition are accepted. God is absolute transcendental non lucrative. To describe God with some qualities is limiting his qualities, so he is indeterminate NIRGUNA or attributeless or indefinable

(ii) DVAITA:—MADHVACHARYA(1254-1333AD)

He considered individual soul and God (BRAHMAN) as reality which are different to each other. This established the tradition of Dualism (DVAITHA). According to him God is supreme and everything is controlled by him and the individual soul is Part of Supreme soul i.e. God or PARAMATMAN.

(iii) VISITADVAITHA—Qualified monism.

Ramanujacharya is a founder of the school of thought and according to him God as existing knowledge and bliss is eternal, infinite, omnipotent and supreme. He viewed that Nature (PRAKRITI) is unconscious matter (ACHIT) which is part of God. During Dissolution (PRALAYA) nature remains as subtle (SUKSHMA) and non-differential. As per deeds of souls God creates diverse objects—Fire, water and air and they are the parts of God only. However though man is product of God, he is finite where as GOD is infinite and also qualified Infinite. (VISISHTA SAKHYAM) Man has soul and body but his soul is eternal and infinitely small. He identified Soul as "I" or AHAM. Bondage and attachment are due to KARMA (action). It is possible to attain liberation of his soul through work, knowledge and devotion(JNANA KARMA and BHAKTI).

3.8.2.7 UPANISHADS:

According to different interpretations there are thousands of interpretations of seers and sages but only 108 were preserved out of which only 12 are major that are popular and prevalent.

UPANISHADs are considered as breath of eternal self that is one God. Self is one, moving which is faster than thought and senses also cannot supersede it. There is no life without self. Soul remains with its KARMA or deeds and soul is reminder of his past deeds.

According to UPANISHAD everything is done by reality of God who is behind every action and activity. Those who realize BRAHMAN (God) while living become immortal. Secret of immortality is to be found in purification of the heart in Meditation and immortality is union with God. Meditation include continuance, truthfulness not deceitful wicked and false.

There are five elements (PANCHABHUTAS) which include Fire, Water, Air, Earth and ether which constitutes body. According this there are two kinds of knowledge—higher and lower, self-thy self are compared with birds on a tree one on lower branch and the other on higher branch. To reach higher, the lower soul should be praying and praising the greatness of BRAHMA (GOD) who is supreme and everything.

3.9 CHINESE PHILOSOPHY

CONFUCIUS (551-479): Confucius belong to China, and according to whom Compassion(REN) or loving others, cultivating or practicing such concern for others involved depreciating self. His philosophy emphasize on personal and governmental correctness of social relationship, Justice and sincerity. His principles had basis in common Chinese tradition and belief. He championed strong family, loyalty ancestor worship, respect of elders by their children, husband by their wives. He also recommended family as a basis for ideal Government. He propounded a well known principle "Do not do others what you do not want to do yourself and this is called Golden Rule.

3.10 MODERN EUROPEAN WETSERN AND AMERICAN PHILOSOPHY

After the death of Aristotle, advent of religious trend dominated the entire human civilization. Religion became the thought, practice and way life to human beings in total. Human mind was put in the cage of belief—religious.

Religion wars became the art of culture in those days. Nearly thousand years of human intelligence was kept in darkness and only religious dogmas prevailed.

However after thousands of years of tillage the soil bloomed again, goods were multiplied surplus that compelled trade and trade in its cross roads built again great cities wherein men might cooperate to nourish culture and rebuild civilization. The Crusades (wars between religions) opened routs to the East and let in stream of luxurious and heresies that doomed dogmas. Papers now became cheaply available Egypt replacing costly parchment that had made learning Monarchs to priests, printing which had long awaited inexpensive medium, broke out like a liberated explosive and spread it was destructive and clarifying influence ever where. Brave mariners armed now with compass, ventured out into the wilderness of the sea and conquered mans ignorance of the sky. Effort lodged baser metal into gold alchemy was transferred into chemistry out of astronomy men developed of the fables of speaking animals came as the science of zoology.

Awakening began with Roger beacon(1294AD) Leonardo(1452-1519) and it reaches its fullness in the astronomy of COPERNICUS(1473) who exploded the thought that the Earth is not the center of Solar system, but Sun is the center of Solar system, around whom Earth including the other planets rotate. GALILIO (1584CE) whose telescope, according to which there are number of galaxies in which Solar system is tiny part of the Universe. The research of GILBERT (1544-1603) in Magnetism and Electricity of Vesalius (1514-1564) in anatomy and HARBEG (1578-1657) on circulation of blood. As knowledge grew, fear (genesis of theosophy) decreased; men thought of worshipping unknown and overcoming of it. There was no bound now to what might do. It was achievement, hope, vigor; a new beginning and enterprise in every field. An age of renaissance started with Philosopher Bruno and Francis Bacon, the most powerful mind of modern times who rang the bell that called wits together and announced the Europe had come of age.

3.11 BRUNO (1548-1600)

Bruno was a Romantic Italian who had wealth of ideas. He sponsored that "First master of unity; all this reality are one. He also stated Mind and matter are one every particle of reality is one substance, one in cause, one in origin; God and this reality are one. Further he stated that every particle of reality is composed inseparably to PHYSICAL and PSYCHICAL. The object of Philosophy is therefore is to perceive UNITY in DIVERSITY, Mind in matter and Matter in mind, to find the synthesis in which opposite and contra directions meet and merge to rise to that highest knowledge of Universal unity which is intellectual equivalent of love God. This Physical and Psychic combination of Philosophy roused angry to the Biblical Society and the result was that BRUNO was buried alive.

3.12 FRANSIS BACON (1615):

Bacon started his Philosophy with his first dialogue "WITHOUT PHILOSOPHY I CARE NOT LIVE" In his book NOVUM ORANUM he argued that man never put move life into logic making an epic adventure and conquest. He proceeds to give an admirable description of Scientific method called EMPERICISM.

He quotes "costly men condemn studies simple men admires them and wise men use them" Bacon in his terms "simple experience" which if taken as it comes, is called accident that is EMPERICAL. If sought for experiment, the true method of experience first lights candle shows the way (arrange and delimit experiment) "commencing as it does experience duly ordered and delighted not bungling, nor erratic and from it educing axioms and from established axioms and again new experiment starts by this INDUCTIVE results"

3.13 RENE DESCARTE (1595-1650)

Rene Descartes as a famous French Mathematician, Scientist and Philosopher. He was arguably first Major Philosopher in the modern era to make serious effort to defeat skepticism as well as his views about relationship between Mind and body have been very influential over the last three centuries. His famous quote I THINK THEREFORE I AM (COGITO ERGOSUM) from discourse on Method, influenced many scientists of last three decades. He was also called as the father of SUBJECTIVE IDEALISM, unlike Bacons objective idealism. The central notion of Descartes was "Primary consciousness has apparently obvious proposition that mind know itself immediately and directly that it knows the EXTERNAL WORLD only through that world impress upon the mind in sensation and perception; that philosophy must in consequence (though it should not doubt everything else) begin with individual mind and self and make its first argument in three words I THINK THERFORE I AM.

3.14 BENEDICT SPIONOZA (1630-1677)

European rather than a Nationalist. He changed his name from BARUCH to BENEDICT lest he will be killed by Jews since he was staunch atheist. He wrote on the Improvement of intellect (DE INTELLECTUS EMENDATIONE) and Ethics for which he was sent to Jail and died there.

He was called "the impious atheist that ever lived upon the face of earth". He said that masses think God, if so, he is there inactive so long as nature works in her accustomed order and vice versa, the power of nature and natural causes are idle so long as God is living thus they imagine two powers are distinct from one another that is Powers of God and Powers of nature. He declares that the God and the process of nature are one. He questions that "how do I know that nature that my knowledge that my senses can be trusted in material which bring my reason can be trusted with conclusion which it derives from material sensation" So he says that NATURE itself God and there is no separate God for doing so. He says substance as literally that stands beneath and that inner being or essence is substance. That is NATURE NATURATA. Nature be gotten the material and contents of nature, its wood, winds, water, hills, and fields and myriads are external forms of substance. He further says "neither material nor the matter mental; neither is the brain process and there is no two entities, there is but one process" It is seen no inwardly as mind, not outwardly as matter but in reality an inextricable mixture and unity of both.

3.15 JOHN LOCKE (1632-1704)

John Locke was an English philosopher and physician regarded as one of the most influential ENLIGHTENMENT thinkers. His work had great impact upon the empiricists, following the tradition of Francis Bacon. He is equally important to social contact theory. His works on Epistemology and Political philosophy influenced VOLTAIRE and ROUSSEAU and many Scottish Enlightenments including American revolutionaries.

Locke's theory of mind is often cited as the origin of modern conceptions of Identity and the Self, figuring prominently in the work of later Philosophers such as Hume and Kant. Locke was to define self through continuity of Consciousness. He postulated that Mind was a slate or TABULA RASA. Contrary to pre-existing CARTISAN philosophy, he maintained that we are without any INNATE IDEAS and the knowledge is instead determined only by experience derived from sense of perception. His political theory was founded on SOCIAL COTACT theory. He believed that "human nature is characterized by reason and tolerance". He held that "human nature allowed men to be selfish". In a natural state all people were equal and independent and everyone had natural right to his LIFE, HEALTH, LIBERTY, or POSSESSIONS". Locke advocated Governmental SEPERATION of POWERS and believed that revolution is not only right but obligation in some circumstances.

3.16 DAVID HUME.

David Hume was Scottish Philosopher, Historian, Economist and Essayist, known especially for his philosophical EMPERCISM.

Beginning with his book "A Treatise on Human Nature" (1739) Hume strove a total naturalistic SCIENCE OF MAN that examined the Psychological basis of human nature. He concluded that DESIRE rather than REASON govern human behavior, saying REASON OUGHT ONLY TO BE THE SLAVE OF PASSION. Being an eminent personality in the Skeptical Philosophical tradition and determined empiricist, he contented the existence of INNATE IDEAS. He further argued that human only has the knowledge of things he experiences in his life, dividing PERCEPTION among strong lively, direct sensations and fainter ideas. Without direct impression of metaphysical SELF he concluded that humans have no actual conception of the Self, only a BUNDLE OF SENSATIONS associated with the self.

Hume advocated COMPATIBULIST theory of FREE WILL that proved extremely useful and influential on subsequent moral philosophy. Understanding a problem of induction is the central to grasping is the Philosophical system of Hume.

Hume notices that we tend to believe that things behave in regular manner i.e. the pattern in the behavior of the objects will persist into the future and THROUGH OUT UN-OBSERVED PRESENT. This persistence of regularities is called UNIFORMITARIANISM or the Principle of the Uniformity of Nature.

3.17 VOLTAIRE

Francis Marie AROUTE, better known as Voltaire, a French ENLIGHTENMENT writer, historian and Philosopher famous for his WIT and for his advocacy of CIVIL LIBERTIES including freedom of religion, freedom of expression, free trade and separation of Church and State. His trade was "to say what I think" as what he said was always said incomparably well. In his opinion "all the people are equal except those who are idle", one must give one's self all the occupation one can make life supportable in this world . . . . Further advance in age, the more I find work necessary. It becomes in the long run the greatest of pleasure and takes the pleasure of illusion of life". In terms of Victor Hugo "ITALY HAD RENAISSANCE, GEMANY HAD REFORMATION BUT FRANCE HAD VOLTAIRE AND HE WAS FOR HIS COUNTRY BOTH RENAISSANCE AND REFORMATION" and half of the REVOLUTION Voltaire has characterized entire eighteenth century as viewed by Victor Hugo.

Voltaire terms History "must lie in applying Philosophy and endeavoring to trace beneath the flux of political events of history". He also states that "History should be written in such a way that we should transform the past to suit our wishes for future but not as a pack of tricks which play upon the dead"

He was so frank in saying that "If we go back to the beginning we shall find that ignorance and fear created the Gods, that fancy and enthusiasm or say, deceit adorned them, that weakness worship them, that credulity preserves them and that custom respects and tyranny supports them in order to make the blindness of men serves its own interest"

He bluntly and openly proclaims "THE EARTH WILL BE INTO ITS OWN ONLY WHEN HEAVEN IS DESTROYED". Materialism may be an over-simplification of the world—all the matter is probably instinct with life and it is impossible to reduce the unity of consciousness to matter and motion: must spread knowledge and encourage industry, industry will make for peace and knowledge will make a new and natural morality.

Voltaire's determines that "If philosophy end in the total doubt, it is greatest adventure of man and noblest. Let us learn to content with modest advances in knowledge rather than for ever weaving new systems out of our effortful imagination. Let us leave the matter to Scientists and to Socialists. Socialist concern must be to lead a life peacefully, ethically, contently after attaining basic biological and social needs.

He further states that WHEN WE KNOW NOTHING OF FIRST PRINCIPLE, IT IS TRULY EXTRAVAGANT TO DEFINE GOD, ANGELS, HEAVENS AND MINDS TO KNOW PRECISELY WHY GOD FORMED WORLD,

WHEN WE DO NOT KNOW WHY WE MOVE OUR ARMS AT WILL" In his concluding part, He advocates that "Society is a growth in time, not syllogism in logic and when the past is out through the door, it comes in at the window. The problem is to show precisely by what changes we can diminish misery and injustice in the world in which we actually live". Voltaire rejected the Adam and Eve story and was polygamist who speculated that each race had separate origins. He divided humanity into varieties of races. He wondered, if blacks fully shared in the common humanity or intelligence of WHITE due to participation in slave trade.

3.18 IMMANUEL KANT (1724-1804)

Immanuel Kant hails from Prussia and he wrote famous books: "Critique Pure reason "Critique of Practical Reason" "Critique of Judgment" and "Ground works of Metaphysics and Morals". According to Kant 'Metaphysics' as dark ocean without shores or light house. Hence he gave reasoned argument against skepticism and idealism of thinkers like DECARTE, BERKELY and HUME. He is known for his transcendental idealist Philosophy, which stated that time and space are not materially real but merely ideal APRIORI CONDITION OF OUR INTERNAL INTUTION. He discovered that TIME is not a thing itself determined from experience, objects, motion and change but it is an avoidable frame work of the human mind that preconditions possible experience.

Kant maintained that one ought to think autonomously, free of the dictates of external authority. Kant asserted that because of limitation in the absence of irrefutable evidence, no one could really know whether there is God and an after life or not. The sense of enlightenment approach and the critical method required that "If one cannot prove that IT IS he may not try to prove that IT IS NOT" And if he succeeds in doing neither (as often occurs)he may still ask whether it is in his interest to accept one or the other of the alternatives hypothetically from the theoretically and practical point of view.

The presupposition of God, Soul, and freedom was then practical concern of morality by itself, constitutes a system, but happiness does not have value unless it is distributed an exact proportion of morality. This however, is possible in an intelligible world under a wise author and ruler. Reason compels us to admit such a ruler together with life in such a world in which we must live as future life, or else all moral laws are considered as idle dreams

Kant claimed to have created COPERNICAN REVOLUTION in Philosophy. This involved two interconnected foundations of his critical Philosophy.

- The EPISTOMOLOGY of transcendental idealism (ii) the moral philosophy of anatomy of practical reason.
- He made significant astronomical discovery when he discovered the retardation of the ROTATION OF EARTH. He described that TIME is not a thing itself determined from experience, objects, motion and change; but it is an unavoidable FRAME WORK of the human mind that preconditions possible experience.
- In his work "General History of Nature and Theory of Heavens" (1755) Kant proposed the NEBULAR HYPOTHESIS which states that solar system formed from large cloud of Gas" A NEBULA". He also said that Milky wave was a large Disc of stars formed from larger spinning of cloud of Gas. His prediction opened new horizons in the field of astronomy, the solar system of Galactic and extra Galactic realms.

3.19 ARTHUR SCHOPENHAUER (1788-1860)

ARTHER SCHOPENHAUER was German Philosopher known for his pessimism and philosophical clarity. As he claimed that the world is fundamentally what humans recognize in themselves as their WILL. His analysis will led him to conclusion that emotional, Physical and Sexual desire can never be satisfied. The corollary of this is an ultimately painful human conditions, he considered that a life style of negating desires, similar to ASCETC TEACHING OF VEDANTHA, BUDDHISTS and CHRISTIANITY, was the way to attain liberation.

The metaphysical examination of desire, he viewed that an human motivation and will and also his aphoristic writing technique showed great influence on ALBERT EINSTEIN, SIGMUND FRUAD, TOLSTOY etc.

For Schopenhauer, human desire was futile, illogical, directionless and by extension, so was all human action in the world. He proposed a moral theory according which there are three primary moral incentives COMPASSION, MALICE and EGOISM. He felt that ultimate aim of love affair is nothing less than the composition of the next generation. His pessimistic view on marriage reflects in his following quote:

Marrying means to halve one's rights and double one's responsibilities" and "Marrying means to grasp blindfolded into a sack hoping to find out an EEL out of an assembly of snakes"

3.20 G.W.F. HEGEL.

Hegel was a German philosopher and creator of German Idealism. His HISTORICIST and IDEALIST account of reality has revolutionized European Philosophy, and an important precursor to CONTINENTAL PHILOSOPHY and MARXISM.

Hegel developed a comprehensive philosophical frame work or system of ABSOLUTE IDEALISM to account in an integrated and developmental way for the relation of MIND and NATURE., SUBJECT and OBJECT OF KNOWLEDGE and PSYCHOLOGY, the state, history art religion and philosophy. In particular he developed the concept that mind and Spirit manifested itself in a set of contradictions include those between nature and freedom and between immanence and transcendence.

Hegel made distinction between civil society and state in his "Elements of Philosophy of Right" In his work, civil society was stage in the dialectical relationship that occurs between, Hegel perceived, opposites, the micro— community of the State and the micro-community of the family. Broadly speaking, the term was split, to political LEFT and RIGHT. On left it became Communism-civil Society on ECONOMIC base and to the RIGHT, it became a description for all Non-State aspects of Society including culture, Society and Politics. His famous triad IS OFTEN DESCRIB ED THE THOUGHT includes:

- □ THE THESIS IS AN INTELLECTUAL PROPOSITION.
- □ THE ANTI-THESIS IS SIMPLY NEGATION OF THE THESIS AND
- □ THE SYNTHESIS SOLVES THE CONFLICT BETWEEN THE THESIS AND ANTI-THESIS BY RECONCILING THEIR COMMON TRUTHS AND FORMING A NEW PROPOSITION CALLED THESIS AGAIN.

3.21 BERTRAND RUSSEL (1872-1970)

Russell was a prominent anti-war activist, he championed anti—Imperialism. Russell is generally credited with being one of the founders of ANALYTIC PHILOSOPHY and in particular METAPHYSICS, logic mathematics, philosophy of languages and EPISTOMOLOGY.

3.22 SANTAYANA (AMERICAN PHILOSOPHER)

George Santayana was a philosopher, essayist, poet and Novelist, born in MODRID in 1863. His great saying" Those who cannot remember the past are condemned to repeat and dead have seen the end of war". His main philosophical work consists of "THE SENSE OF BEAUTY" He was a pragmatist and well versed in Evolutionary theory. He was committed metaphysical naturalism. He believed that human cognition, cultural practices and social institutions have evolved so as to harmonize with conditions present in environment. Their value may be adjudged by the extent to which they facilitate human happiness. The alternative title to the "LIFE OF REASON" AS "THE PHASES OF HUMAN PROGRESS" is indicative of this metaphysics. He is agnostic, he held, fairly benign view of religion in contrast to RUSSEL who held that religion was harmful.

Chapter IV
SCIENTIFIC PERSPECTIVE-HUMAN ACHIEVEMENT

Scientific method is a body of techniques investigating PHENOMENA acquiring new knowledge or correcting and integrating previous knowledge. To be termed scientific, a method of enquiry must be based on empirical and measurable evidence subject to specific principles of reasoning. Oxford Dictionary says that Scientific method is 'method or procedure that has characterized natural science since the 17 century consisting in systematic observation, measurement and experiment and, testing and modification of HYPOTHESIS.

The chief characteristic which distinguish a Scientific method of enquiry from other methods of acquiring knowledge is that Scientists seek to let reality speaks itself, supporting a theory' s prediction are confirmed and challenging a theory when its predictions prove false. Scientific steps must be repeatable to guard against mistakes or confusion in any particular experimenter. Theories that encompass wider domains of enquiry may bind many independently derived by hypothesis together with coherent, supportive structure. Theories, in turn may help from new hypothesis or place of groups of hypothesis into context. Scientific inquiry is generally intended to be AS OBJECTI VE as possible in order to reduce biased interpretations of results. Another basic expectation is data that is achieved and share all data and methodology so they are available for careful scrutiny by other scientists. Giving them opportunity to verify results by attempting reproduce them. This practice, called full disclosure and reliability of the data. We have gone through both theological and philosophical perspective view of life which were not subjected for the experimentation of the fact that how the LIFE has come into existence. Each theological perspective and Philosophical perspective, to some extent are proved biased interpretations without supportive structure of methodology as practiced in Scientific approach. It is therefore let us study the scientific perspective also, how methodologically and verifiably explain the origin and growth of life from ameba to Adam and for this purpose the study of the Universe and its beginning and formation of earth as an entity in the Solar system and how formation of LIFE resulted through various fields of SCIENCE, is required to be studied in the ongoing chapters with an authenticated and reliable source of KNOWLEDGE.

4.1 ASTRONOMY OR COSMOLOGY

Gazing up to the night sky you wonder about the stars twinkling above us: How far away these tiny glimmers of light? What lies beyond the stars? And where does our tiny planet fit in? Let us join on an exploration to answer these mysteries. This will help us to find out how was the UNIVERSE is, how and when it all began, what astronomical events could trigger dooms day on Earth, statistics on planets and much more . . . . THE UNIVERSE: The Universe can be defined "all matter, energy including the earth, solar system the galaxies and contents of Intergalactic space regarded as whole" Cosmology is Scientific study of the large scale of properties of the universe as a whole. It endeavors to use the Scientific method to understand the origin, evolution and ultimate fate of the entire Universe. Like any field of cosmology involves the formation of theories or hypothesis about the Universe which make specific predictions of the phenomena that can be tested with observation. Depending on the observations, the theories will need to be abandoned, revised or extended to accommodate the data. The prevailing theory about the origin and evolution of universe is the so called BIG-BANG THEORY.

The Big Bang theory is broadly accepted for the evolution of our Universe. It postulates that 14 billion years of the portion we can see today was only a few millimeters across. It has since expanded from this hot dense state in to vast and much cooler COSMOS we habituated of. We can see remnant of this hot matter as the very cold cosmic microwave background radiation which still pervades the universe and is visible to Microwave detectors as a uniform glow across the entire sky.

The first key idea refer to 1916 when EINSTEIN developed his grand Theory of relativity which proposed as a new theory of gravity, which generalizes ISAAC NEWTON's original theory of gravity during 1680. Newton's gravity is only valid for bodies of rest or moving slowly compared to the speed of light.

After the introduction of General relativity a number Scientists including EINSTEIN tried to apply the new gravitational dynamics to the Universe as whole. To be clear, that if you viewed the contents of universe with sufficiently poor vision, it would appear roughly the same everywhere and in every direction. That is matter in the Universe is homogeneous and isotopic when averaged over very large scales and this is called COSMOLOGICAL PRINCIPLE. This assumption is being tested continuously as we actually observe the distribution of Galaxies on over larger scales. In addition THE COSMIC MICROWAVE BACKGROUND RADIATION the remnant heat from the BIG—BANG, has temperature which is highly uniform over the sky. There is uniform distribution of measured Galaxies is over 70 degrees swath of the sky. This fact strongly supports the notion that gas which emitted this radiation long ago was very uniformly distributed.

These two ideas form the entire theoretical basis for Big Bang cosmology and lead to specific predictions for observable properties of the Universe. There are number of free parameters in this family of Big-Bang models that must be mixed by observations of our Universe. The most important are geometry of the Universe—Open, flat or closed. The event of expansion rate (The Hubble Constant); the overall course of expansion, past and future, which is determined by the fractional density of different types of matter in the Universe. Thus the present age of the universe follows from the expansion history at the present expansion rate. As such the Geometry and evolution of the Universe are determined by the fractional contribution of various types of matter, both energy density and pressure contribute to the strength of gravity in general gravity, cosmologists classify types of matter by its "equation of state" the relationship between its pressure and energy density which include,

- ☐ Radiation—composed of mass less particles that move at speed light.
- ☐ Baryonic meter—ordinary matter having pressure.
- ☐ Dark matter—refers to exotic non baryonic matter that enter between matter to matter.
- ☐ Dark energy—this is truly form matter or the property of vacuum itself.

4.2 TEST OF BIG-BANG COSMOLOGY

The big-Bang model is supported by number of important observations,

a) EDWIN HUBBLE's 1929 observation that Galaxies were generally receding from us provided first clue that Big-Bang theory must be right;

b) The abundance of light elements H He L1: The Big Bang theory predicts that these light should have been fused from protons and neutrons in the few minutes after Big-Bang.

c) The cosmic microwave Back ground(CMB): the early universe should have been very hot. The cosmic microwave background radiation is the remnant heat left over from Big-Bang.

These three measurable signatures strongly support the notion that the Universe evolved from a dense futureless hot gas, just as BIG-BANG predicts. The existence of the CMB was predicted by RALPH ALPHER, ROBERT HERMAN and GEORGE GAMOW in 1948. It was inadvertently observed in 1965 by PENZIAS and ROBERT WILSON for which they shared the 1978 NOBEL PRIZE in Physics.

4.3 OUR UNIVERSE

We have theoretically proved that Big-Bang model on general terms the Universe appears nearly uniform and it is currently expanding and there is strong evidence that it was hotter and denser in the past. Now certain doubts in the format questionnaire include,

□ What types of matter and energy fill the Universe? How much of each?

□ How rapidly is the universe expanding today?

□ How did the Universe today?

□ What is the overall shape of the Universe? Open, flat, or otherwise?

□ How is the expansion changing with time?

□ What is the ultimate fate of the Universe?

For all these questions latest findings as published in Gulf News Dt. July 5, 2012through REUTERS and AFP reveals the theory HIGGS BOSOM as detailed below,

All the while we were referring about the Universe, Galaxies, Sun Stars, Big-bang Theory, atoms, Neutrons, Protons, Gravitational powers, Relativity, radiation, Dark energy, Dark matter, and how is Universe expanded, the age of cosmos, Hubble constant, clusters, Microwave, and the Structure of universe, but all these what is the phenomena that constitutes matter, having molecules, electrons, neurons how, when and Where it was formed that in one word "God Particle" that formed the Universe? Since centuries together Scientists, Philosophers, were breaking their heads to know the constituent of the Universe.

- □ In 5 century BCE Greek Philosopher DEMOCRITUS suggests the universe consists of empty space and invisible particles called atoms.

- □ In 1802 JOHN DALTON, a quake—educated English Physicist and chemist, lay ground work of Modern theory of the elements and atom.

- □ In1932 Neutron similar to the Proton but with no electrical charge was discovered by JAMES CHADWICK of Britain.

- □ In 1934, Italy's ENRICO FERMI postulates the existence of the NUTRINO((Italian for the little neutral one)

- □ In 1964 British Physicist PETER HIGGS postulates existence of particle known as HIGGS BOSON that provides mass to otherwise particles.

□ In 1974 Development of Standard Model a theory that every thing in universe comprises 12 building Blocks made of LEPTONS and QUARKS.

□ In 2008 European organization for Nuclear Research (CERN) starts LARGE HADRON COLLIDER (LHC) the biggest particle Lab established.

□ On July 4, 2012 CERN announces it has discovered a new particle consistent with HIGGS, which termed MYSTERIOUS SUB-ATOMIC PARTICLE.

What is HIGGS Boson: The HIGGS is the last missing piece of the standard model, the theory that describes the basic building Blocks of the Universe. The other 11 particles predicted by model have been found or finding some more exotic would force a rethink on how the Universe put together. (as imaged in overleaf).

Scientists believe that first billionth second after the Big Bang, the universe was gigantic soup of particles racing around at the speed of light without any mass to speak of. It was through their interaction with the HIGGS field that they gained MASS and eventually formed the UNIVERSE.

The HIGGS field is theoretical and invisible energy field that pervades the whole COSMOS. Some particles, like PHOTONS that make up light are not affected by it and therefore have no mass. Others are not so lucky and find it drags on them as porridge drags on spoon.

Picture George Clooney (the particle) walking down a street with gaggle of Photographers (the HIGGS field) clustered around him. An average guy on the same street (PHOTON) gets no attention from the Paparazzi and gets on with his day.

The HIGGS particle is the signature of the field—an eyelash of one of the Photographers.

The particle is theoretic first posited in 1964 by six Physicists including Briton Peter Higgs. The search began in earnest in 1980s, first FERMILAB now mothballed TEVATRON particle collider near Chicago and later in a similar machine at CERN, but intensively since 2010 with start-up of European Center's large HADRON COLLIDER as diagramed below. (REUTERS—GULF NEWS 5July 2012).

After a quest spanning nearly half century Physicists on July 4, 2012 found a new sub-atomic particle consistent with the elusive HIGGS BOSON which is believed to confer mass. European organization for Nuclear Research(CERN) presented astonishing new data in their search for the mysterious data. Many hailed it as a MOMENT IN THE HISTORY OF MAN KIND. The find is CONSISTENT with the long sought HIGGS BOSON—CERN declared in statement CERN Director General ROLF HEUR overwhelmingly shouted and said that further work was needed to identify what exactly had been found. He also said "We have discovered a bosom and now we determine what kind of BOSOM IT IS.

Mooted by HIGGS and several others the BOSON is believed to exist in TREACLY, invisible ABQUITOUS field created by BING BANG 13.7, million years ago. When the particles encounter the HIGGS, they slow down and acquires mass according to theory. Others such as particles of light, encounter no obstacle. CERN uses giant—underground laboratory where protons are smashed together at nearly the speed of light yielding sub-atomic debris that is then scrutinized for sings of the fleeting Higgs.

The task is arduous because they are trillions of signals, occurring among particles at different ranges of mass. The HIGGS has been dubbed the God particle because it is powerful and ubiquitous yet so hard to find.

Two CERN Laboratories working independently of each other to avoid bias, found in the new particle in the mass region of around 125-126 GIGAELECTRON VOLTS(G e V) according data they presented on 4th July 2012. Both said that the results were "Five Sigma" meaning there was just 0.00006 percent that what the two laboratories found is mathematically QUIRK. The results are preliminary but five sigma signal at around 125 G e V we are seeing is dramatic stated CERN.

This is indeed a new particle, we know it must be BOSON and it is the heaviest boson ever found. The implications are very significant and it is precisely for this reason that we must be extremely diligent in all our studies and cross checks"

4.4 WHAT IS THE UNIVERSE MADE OF

The air we breathe and the distant stars are all made up of protons, neutrons and electrons. Neutrons are bound together into nuclei and atoms are nuclei surrounded by full complement of electrons. According to WILKINSON MICRO WAVE ANTISTROPY PROBE(WMAP) the Universe is made up of 4.996percent atoms 72pecent dark energy and 23 percent Dark matter (position include HIGGS BOSON FINDING which has 0,00006% as of July 2012 as detailed above). By measuring the motion of stars and gas astronomers can weight GALAXIES. In our solar system we can measure velocity of the earth around the sun to measure Suns mass. The Earth moves around the sun at 30 KM per second(roughly 60,000 miles per hour)

If the Sun more massive then Earth would need to move around the Sun at 60KM per second in order for its stay on its orbit. The sun moves around the Milky way at 225 KM per second. We can use this velocity to measure the mass of our Galaxy.

4.5 HOW FAR IS THE UNIVERSE EXPANDING

EDWIN Hubble discovered his measurements of Cepheid based galaxy distance determination with measurements of relative velocities of these galaxies. He showed that more distant galaxies were moving away from us more rapidly— V=H o d—where V is the speed at which galaxy moves from us and "d" is its distance and "H o" is now called Hubble constant. The common unit used to measure the speed of Galaxy is called Mega per second(MPC) which is equal to 3.26 million light year or 30,800,000,000,000,000,000 KM. The structure of all stars including Sun and CEPHEID variable stars is determined by the capacity of matter in the star. The more massive Stars are more luminous and have more extended and density in their envelops is lower, than variability period which is proportional to the inverse square root of the density if the layer is longer.

If the matter is very nearly transparent, then Photons move easily through the star and erase any temperature gradient. Cepheid Stars oscillate between two states, when the star is in compact state, the Helium in a layer of its atmosphere is singly ionized. Photons scatter off of the bound electron in the singly ionized helium atoms, the, layer is vary opaque and large temperature and pressure gradients build up across the layer. These large pressure causes the layer (and the whole star) to expand. When the stand is in its expanded state the, Helium in the layer is doubly ionized, so that the layer is more transparent to radiation and there is much weaker pressure gradient across the layer. Without the pressure gradient to support the star against gravity, the layer(and the whole star contracts and the star returns to the compressed state.

4.7 HOW OLD IS THE UNIVERSE

Until recently astronomers estimated that the BIG BANG occurred between 12 and 14 billion years ago and to put this perspective our solar system is thought to be 4.5 billion years old and human have existed as genus for only a few million years.

4.8 WILL THE UNIVERSE EXPAND FOR EVER:

The expansion of Universe is determined by a struggle between the EXPANSION and PULL OF GRAVITY. If the density of Universe is less than the CRITICAL DENSITY which is proportionate to the square of HUBBLE CONSTANT (H o) the Universe will expand forever and if the density of the Universe greater than the CRITICAL DENSITY then gravity will eventually win and the Universe will collapse back on itself the so called BIG CRUNCH. However the result of WMAP mission and observations of distant SUPER NOVA have suggested that the expansion of the Universe is accelerating which implies the existence form of matter with strong negative pressure such as COSMOLOGICAL CONSTANT.

4.9 HOW DID THE UNIVERSE START AND EVOLVE

The WMAP determined that 4.99994 % (latest report as of July 2012—HIGGS BASON) of the mass and energy of the Universe contained in atoms (protons and neutrons) which are made of up of mass and energy. The only chemical element created at the beginning of our universe were HYDROZEN, HELIUM and LITHIUM, the three lightest atoms in periodic table. These elements were formed throughout the universe where elements higher than LITHIUM would never form and life never develop. But that is not happened in our Universe. We are carbon-based life forms. We are made of and drink water (H_2o). We breath oxygen. Carbon and oxygen were not created in the BIG BANG but much later in stars. All the CARBON and OXYGEN in all living things are made in the nuclear fusion reactors that we call Stars. The early stars are massive and short lived. They consume their HYDROGEN, HELIUM and LITHIUM and produce heavier elements. When these stars die with a bang they spread the elements of life carbon and oxygen throughout the Universe. New stars condense and new Planets form from these heavier elements, The stage set for life to begin. Understanding when and how these events occur offer another window on the evolution of life in the universe.

WMAP DETERMINED THE FIRST STARS IN THE UNIVERSE AROSE ONLY 400 MILLION AFTER BIG BANG.

4.10 MILKY WAY-GALAXY

Milky way is gravitationally bound collection of roughly a hundred billion stars. Our Sun is one of these stars and is located roughly 24000 light years(or 8000PARSECS) from center of Milky way.

4.11 MODERN RESEARCH

In 1944 HENDRAK VAN DE HULST predicted Microwave radiation at Wavelength of 21 CM resulting from interstellar atomic hydrogen gas, this radiation was observed in 1951. In 1990 HUBBLE SPACE TELESCOPE yielded improved observations. The HUBBLE DEEP FIELD extremely long exposure of a relativity empty part of the sky, provided evidence that there are about 125 billion (1.25 x10 to the power of 11) galaxies in the universe. However improved technology allow detection through radio telescopes, infra-red cameras and X-ray telescopes have revealed number of new more galaxies.

4.12 TYPES OF GALAXIES

Galaxies come in three main types—ELLIPTICALS, SPIRALS and IRREGULARS.

i)   ELLIPTICAL Galaxies show little structure and they typically have little inter stellar matter. The stars in it contain low abundance of heavy elements because Star formation ceases after initial burst and they have much smaller globular cluster.

ii) SPIRAL galaxies consist of rotating disc of Stars and interstellar medium along with central followed by letter (a, b, or c)that indicates degree of tightness of the spiral arms and the size of the central bulge. Our own Galaxy is large disc-shaped bared Spiral Galaxy about 30 KILOPERSEC and it contained two hundred billion(2x10 to the power of 11)stars has a total mass of about six hundred billion times the mass of the SUN.

iii) IRREGULAR GALAXIES:: Peculiar Galaxies are Galactic formations that develop unusual properties due to tidal interactions with other galaxies. They have ring like structures, which are also called DWARFS and MILKY WAVE Galaxy is member of an associated named local group, relatively smaller group of Galaxies that has diameter of approximately one MEGAPERSEC.

The current era of star formation is expected to continue for up to hundred billion years and then the STELLAR AGE will wind down after ten trillion to one hundred trillion years (10 to the power of 13-10 to the power of 14 years)At the end of STELLAR age galaxies will be composed of compact objects; BROWN DWARFS, WHITE DWARFS, BLACK DWARFS and NEUTRON STARS and BLACK HOLE. Eventually as result of gravitational relaxation, all STARS will either fall into central Super massive BLACK HOLE or be flung into inter galactic space as result of collisions.

ULTRA VIOLET and X-RAY TELESCOPES could observe highly energetic Galactic phenomena, on account of which an Ultra-violet flare was observed when Star in distant galaxy was torn apart from the tidal forces of BLACK HOLE. The distribution of hot Gas in Galactic clusters could be mapped by X-Rays. The existence of SUPER MASSIVE BLACK HOLES AT THE CORE OF GALAXIES was confirmed through X-Ray astronomy. In recent time that is during July 2012, through NASA-CHANDRA X-RAY laboratory(a joint venture of United States and India) astronomers detected that fill field view of spiral galaxy shows the low medium and high energy X-rays observed by Chandra in red, green and blue respectively. The new X-ray data from the remnant of SN 1957D provide an important information of this explosion that astronomers think happened when a massive star ran out of fuel and collapsed. The distribution of X-rays with energy suggests that SN 1957D contain neutron star formed when the core of pre-supernova star collapses (ANI dt.31July2012 D.C India), as shown below.

4.13 OUR GALAXY-PLANETARY SYSTEM—OUR SUN AND EARTH.

As elucidated in earlier chapter Our Milky way-Galaxy is a large scale disc shaped galaxy about 30 KILO PER SECS in diameter and a KILOPER SEC in thickness. It contain about two hundred billion (2X10 to the power of 11) Stars and has a total mass of about six hundred billion (6X10 to the power of 11)time the mass of the SUN.

The standard model of the formation of the Solar System (including Earth) is the SOLAR NEBULA HYPOTESIS. In this model the solar system formed from large rotating cloud of inter stellar dust and gas called the solar nebula. It was composed of hydrogen and the helium created shortly after the BIG BANG 13.7 G a (billion years ago) and heavier elements ejected by Supernova. About 4.5.G a nebula began a contraction that may have been triggered by the shock wave nearby Supernova.

The center of nebula not having much angular momentum, collapsed rapidly the compression heating it until nuclear fusion of hydrogen into helium began. After more contraction a TTAURI star ignited and evolved into the Sun. Meanwhile in the out part of the nebula gravity caused matter to condense around density perturbations and dust particles, and the rest of the proto planetary disc began separation into rings. In a process known as runaway accretion successively larger fragments of dust and debris clumped together to form PLANETS.

Earth formed in this manner about 4.5.billion years ago (with an uncertainty of 1%)and was largely completed with in 10-20 million years. The solar wind of the newly formed TTAURI star cleared out most of the material in the disc that had not already endorsed into larger bodies.

4.13.1 SOLAR SYSTEM:

The Solar system is located 26,100 light years from the center of the Milky way and was formed about 4540 million years ago as referred above.

4.13.2 MERCURY

Mercury's surface is dominated by large basins representing different epochs in the formation of the crust. The high density of the planet is due to its iron-rich core which is 3600KM(2200miles) in diameter and accounts for 65%of mercury mass. The atmospheric pressure is only one trillionth(10-12) that of Earth and without the protection of an atmosphere. The variation in surface temperature, from up to 420degreesC(t90 degrees F) in the day down to-180 degrees C(-290 degrees F)at night.

4.13.3 VENUS

Though similar size to Earth, Venus is an extremely hostile planet with an atmosphere rich in carbon dioxide. It has surface pressure of 94 times that of Earth at an overall temperature of 464 degree C (867 degree F). A thick planet-wide cloud cover 50-75 KM above the surface, contains high concentration of droplets of sulfuric acid which may be due to to emissions from active Volcanoes. Venus is essentially flat(with 80% being within 1 KM of the planets average radius. It is relatively young only 500 million years old. Although the rotation period is longer than its year, A VENUSIAN Day (Sun rise to Sun rise) is equivalent to 116 Days

4.13.4 MARS

Like Venus, the atmosphere in Mars is mainly Carbon dioxide, but only at a surface pressure about 116th that of Earth at an average temperature of—53 degrees C(—63 degrees F) which 68 degrees C(122 degrees F) lower than earth. The surface is highly complex consisting of flat plains, craters, dormant volcanoes and pole caps. There are also number of large channels such as VALLLES MARINERS which is at least 4000KM long up to 600KM wide and 7KMdeep. It now appears that life could only have developed to a microbiological level. Though there is evidence that many channels must have been fashioned by large quantities of water in the past, there is no evidence of water in the out most surface layers or in atmosphere although water ice is still present under the frozen carbon outside polar caps.

It is also learnt that there is GALE CRATER is one of the lowest places on Mars, as reported by NASA Rover. Gale crater is one of the lowest places on Mars "It is like a little bowl capturing any water that may have been present there" said the Project Scientist, JOHN GROTZINGER, California Institute of Technology.

4.13.5 JUPITER

A model Jupiter suggests that it may have a central rock iron core about 15000KM in diameter, weight about 15 earth masses and is surrounded by a shell of metallic hydrogen extending to a radius of 55000KM from its center. "The great Red Spot" which was first seen in 1964, is long lived swirling storm which rises up to 8KM above the surrounding cloud deck. The Planet has a very strong magnetic field, about five to ten time stronger than that of Earth. The results in the formation of extremely lethal radiation belts about 10,000miles more powerful than those of Earth. The ring system of Jupiter was discovered in 1979 and has three components.

4.13.6 URANUS

Uranus can just seen with naked eye, this much smaller gas planet is believed to have a rock iron core surrounded by "sea" of water, methane and ammonia. The outer atmosphere is composed mainly of hydrogen, but with about 26% helium and a small amount of methane which is responsible for the greenish color of the atmosphere. The large tilt of Uranus axis(98 degrees) means that day and night on some parts of the planet may last up to 21 years, but sunlit "South pole and dark North pole differ very little in temperature.

4.13.7 NEPTUNE

The planet Neptune is invisible to naked eye. It is an extremely dynamic world with many dissemble cloud features and extremely high with speeds. The planet radiates 161% more heat back into space than it receives from the Sun. The bluish color of the planet is due to the presence of methane in the atmosphere.

The Voyage 2 encounter proved that there were three distinct rings and defuse ring material between 38,000 to 59,000 KM from Neptune's center. In 1989, the Voyager imaging team discovered six new satellites in addition to the two already known. The largest satellites, TRITON, has large orbital indication (157 degrees) and retrograde orbit(opposite direction0f Neptune's rotation.

4.13.8 SATURN

Saturn internal structure is generally considered to the similar to that of JUPITER, but with much smaller metallic hydrogen layer extending to only 26,000 KM from the center of the Planet. The true nature of Saturn's rings initially vaguely observed by Galileo in 1610, was deduced by CHRISTAN HUYGENS(Netherlands) in 1659 composed mainly of water ice, the main ring system is 273,550 KM diameter but only about 10 M (33Ft.) thick.

Although officially Saturn has eighteen Satellites, many more candidates have been observed from re-examination of Photographs from the VOYAGER 2 encounter and from HUBBLE Space Telescope observation. The largest of the moon TITAN, is the only Satellite in the Solar system with an extensive atmosphere.

4.13.9 EARTH

The Earth is biggest and densest of the inner planets with an atmosphere consisting mainly of 78% nitrogen and 21% oxygen at an average temperature of 15 degree C(59 degree F) towards the surface is covered by oceans and mean (average). Sea level can be used as reference from which the maximum deviation are a depth of 11,022 Meters(36,16 Ft) for the MARIANA TRENCH in the Pacific Ocean and maximum height of 8863 meters(29,078Ft) for mount Everest in the Himalaya, a difference of 19.9KM—only 0.3% of Earth's radius

4.13.10 MOON

With an educational dia-meter of 3476KM, Polar diameter of 3471.9 KM and mass of 7,348 X1019 tones or.0.123 Earth mass, the Moon is the fifth largest and fifth most massive satellite in our Solar system. Extensive space probe Photography, has now recorded the whole Lunar surface showing the presence of crates, mountain ranges and broad planes of frozen lava known as SEAS or MARIA. Because the moon has no atmosphere, there is wide variation in surface temperature from 117 degrees C(243 degrees F) at the EQUATER at mid-day to—163degrees C(-261 degrees F) after night fall.

The current theory of Moons formation is the "Giant Impact" theory, suggesting that the violent early history of the Solar System, the newly formed Earth was struck by at least one and possibly several very large PLANETESIMALS.

4.13.11 SUN

At the center of Solar system is the Sun, a mass composed of 73% hydrogen, 25% helium 2% other elements.

The internal structure of the Sun consists of Helium. The atmosphere of the consists of CHROMOSPHERE which extends to about 10,000KM above the PHOTOSPHERE. It has sufficiently high temperature. The CHROMOSPHERE only becomes visible during total Eclipses, when the PHOTOSPHERE is blocked out. The outer atmosphere or CORONA is an extremely thin Gas at a high temperature which appears as white HOLLOW. It allows the continuous dispersal into space of the Sun's matter in the continuous dispersal into space of Sun's matter in the form of PLASMA of charged particles. This Solar Wind pervades the whole

Solar system. Solar flares are huge jets of gas flung many thousands of Kilo meters from the CHROMOSPHERE. COSMOLOGIST ALEX VOLZEV and his team of PEN University announced that SUN on account of his growing age will become old Star of 500 billion years and emerges in to such a big size that it will swallow the Earth. These Scientist have already discovered a new Planet in Solar family and acknowledged by cosmologist as great discovery. They have also discovered that a Planet was swallowed by another Giant Star than the Sun. That Giant star had larger quantity of LETHIUM cell to an extent of BD+48740(RED Giant STAR) on whose a small planet was evolving around which was suddenly disappeared. This was discovered the change while observing HABBI—EBERLY TELESCOPE. On its disappearance chemical combination was found noticed. This must have been occurred due to magnetically affected Boom rang which would have attracted to that Giant size Star, In the same way our Sun may also become Red Giant and finally swallow out planet. (WASHINGTON DT. 21.8.2012. published in DC on 22,8,2012 PTI)

4.14 A SOLAR SYSTEM LIKE OUR OWN

Researchers from MASSACHUSETTS Institute of Technology, University of California at Santa Cruz and other Institutions have detected first Ex-planetary system which lined up in an aligned orbits similar to those in our Solar system, which is 10,000 light years away with regularly aligned orbits similar to those in our Solar system.

At the center of this far away system is KEPLER-30 a star as bright and massive as our Sun. After anal sing data from NASA's KELPER Space Telescope, they discovered that the Star much alike the Sun rotates around vertical axis and it three planets have orbits that are all in the same plane" In our Solar system the trajectory of the planets is parallel to the rotation of the Sun, which shows they probably formed from spinning disc" says ROBERT SANCHIS-OJEDA, a Physics graduate at MIT who led the research effort. "In this system we show the same thing happens he said in a statement.(PTI Deccan Chronicle Hyderabad, India, Dt. July 27,2012.)

4.15 PLANET WITH FOUR SUNS FOUND: (GULF NEWS NDT 17.0CT.2012)

Astronomers have found a planet whose skies are illuminated by different SUNS—the first known of its type. The Planet, located just under 5,000 light-years away, has named PHI after PLANET HUNTER SITE (A report on the ARXIV Server has been submitted to the ASTROPHYSICAL JOURNAL—Dr. Chris Lintott University of Oxford (IMAGE APPENDED)—KEPLER was launched by U.S. on March 2009 to search for Earth like Stars orbiting other stars. (Agency gulf News).

CHAPTER V
GEOGRAPHY

5.1 HISTORY OF EARTH

The History of Earth elucidate the most important events and fundamental stages in the development of the Planet Earth from its formation to the present day. Nearly all branches of \physical and natural Sciences have contributed to the understanding of main events of the Earth's past. The age Earth is approximately one third of the UNIVERSE.

Earth formed around 4.54. billion years ago by accretion from the Solar Nebula. Volcanic out gassing likely created the Primordial atmosphere, but it contained almost no Oxygen and would have been toxic to humans and most modern life. Much of Earth was molten because extreme Volcanism and frequent collisions with other bodies. One very large collision is thought to have been responsible for titling the Earth at an angle and forming the moon.

5.2 HOW LIFE FORMED

5.2.1 General

Over a time, such cosmic bombardments ceased allowing the planet to cool and form a Solid crust. Water that was brought by comets and asteroids condensed in to clouds and oceans took shape. Earth was finally hospitable to life, and the earliest forms that arose enriched the atmosphere with oxygen. About 3.5.billion years ago first one celled life forms were formed, as per American Miller who formed in 1951, an organic matter out of mixture of ammonia(NH_3) Methane(CH_4) Hydrogen (H_2) and water (H_2O) by exposing this mixture to an electric current. During the experiments different organic mixture formed among them amino acids and nucleonic acid which are essential for the building of proteins and chromosomes

Through lightning organic connections were formed and fell into the prehistoric Seas. Evaporation of these inside seas, concentration might have occurred giving rise to organic "Primal soup". In this primal soup first bigger molecules were formed and the first forms of life formed. This origin of life out of lifeless matter of called BIOGENESIS.

Life on earth remained small and microscopic for at least one billion years. About 580 million years ago complex multi cellular life arose and during the CAMBRIAN period experienced a rapid diversification in to major PHYLA. Around six million years ago, the primate lineage that would lead to Chimpanzees(the close relative of humans) diverged from lineage that could lead to modern humans.

Biological and geological change has been constantly occurring on our planet since the time of formation. Organisms continuously evolve, taking on new forms or going extinct in response to an ever changing planet. The process of PLATE TECHTONICS has played role in the shaping of earth's oceans and Continents as well as the life they harbor. The biosphere, in turn has had a significant effect on the atmosphere and other biotic conditions on the planet, such as formation of OZONE layer, the proliferation of oxygen and the creation of soil. Though humans are unable to perceive it due to their relatively brief life spans, this change is ongoing and will continue for next few billion years.

5.2.2 FORMATION OF MOON

The Earth's relatively large natural satellite, the Moon, is larger relative to its planet than any other satellite in the Solar family. During the APOLLO program rocks from the Moon's surface were brought to Earth. Radio metric dating of those rocks has shown that Moon to be 4.53+or—.1 billion years old, at least 30 millions after the Solar system was formed. New evidence suggest that the moon even later, 4.48+ or—o.2.Ga or 70-110 million years after the start of Solar system.

First the moon has low density 3.3 times that of water, compared to 5.5 for the Earth and a metallic core. Second, there is virtually no water or other Volatiles on the moon. Third, the Earth and Moon have the same oxygen isotopic signature(relative abundance the oxygen isotopes) The GIANT IMPACT HYPOTHESIS proposes that moon originated after a body size of Mars struck the proto-Earth a glancing blow.

The collision between the impact some time named THEIA and Earth released about 100 million times more energy than the impact that caused the extinction of the DINOSARUS. This was enough to vaporize some Earths outer layer and melt both bodies. The Giant Impact hypothesis predicts that moon was depleted of metallic material explaining its abnormal composition. The eject in orbit around the Earth could have condensed into single body with couple of weeks. Under the influence of its own gravity the ejected material became a more spherical body: MOON.

5,2,3 OCEANS AND ATMOSPHERE

Earth is often described as having had three atmospheres: The first atmosphere, captured from the Solar Nebula, was composed of light(ATMOPHILE) elements, mostly hydrogen and helium. A combination of the Solar wind and Earth's head would have driven off this atmosphere as a result of the atmosphere is now depleted in these elements compared to Cosmic abundances. After the impact the MPLTEN earth released VOLATILE GASES; and later more gases were released by volcanoes, completing second atmosphere rich in green house gases but poor in oxygen. Finally third atmosphere, rich in oxygen emerged when bacteria began to produce oxygen about 2.8Ga.

Chapter VI
ORIGIN OF LIFE—HUMAN RELATION

The first step in the emergence of life may have been chemical reaction that produced many of the simpler acids that are building blocks of life. An experiment in 1953 by STANLEY MILLER and HEROLD UREY showed that such molecules could form in an atmosphere of water, methane, ammonia and hydrogen with the aid of sparks to mimic the effect of lightning. Later experiments with more realistic composition also managed to synthesize organic molecule organic molecules. Recent computer simulations have even shown that extra terrestrial organic molecules could have formed in the proto-planetary disc before formation of the Earth.

The next stage of complexity could have been reached from at least three possible starting points-(i) Self replication, (2) organisms ability to produce off-spring that are very similar to itself and (iii) metabolism its ability to feed and repair itself and extend cell membranes which allow food to enter and waste products to leave but exclude unwanted substances.

6.1 IRON-SULFUR WORLD THEORY

Another long standing hypothesis is that the first life was composed of protein molecules. A series of experiments starting in 1997 showed that amino acids and peptides could form in the presence of carbon monoxide and hydrogen sulfide with iron sulfide and nickel sulfide as catalysts. Steps in their assembly required temperatures of about 100 degrees C and moderate pressures although one stage required 250 degrees C and pressure equivalent to that found under 7 KM(4.3.Miles) of rock. Hence self sustaining synthesis of proteins could have occurred near hydrothermal vents.

6.2 CLAY THEORY

GRAHAM CAIRNS claims that MONTMORILLIONITE that makes them plausible ancestors for the emergence for the of RNA world: they grow by self-replication of their crystalline pattern are subject to an analog of natural selection (as the clay "species" that grows fastest in a particular environment rapidly becomes dominant) and catalyze the formation of RNA molecules. Research in 2003 also proved that it accelerate the conversion of fatty acids into bubbles and the bubbles could encapsulate RNA attached to the clay.

Common ancestor is believed that this multiplicity of proto cells only one line survived. Current PHYLOGENETIC evidence suggests that the last Universal common ancestor (LUCA) lived during the early ARCHEAN EON perhaps lived during 3.5 billion years or earlier. This LUCA cell is ancestor of life on Earth today. Like all modern cells it used DNA as genetic code RNA. Some Scientist believe that instead single organism being last universal common ancestor, there were population of organism exchanging gene by lateral transfer.

OXYGEN REVOLUTION: The earliest revolution absorbed energy and food from environment around them. They used fermentation which can occur in ANARROBIC(oxygen-free) environment. However most of life that covers the surface of the Earth depends directly or indirectly on Photosynthesis, turns carbon dioxide, water, and sunlight into food. It captures the energy Sunlight in energy rich molecules. Among the oldest remnants of oxygen-producing life forms are fossil STROMATOLITES, WHICH APPEARED AROUND 3.2 billion years. Photosynthesis had another major impact. Oxygen was toxic, much life on probably died out as its kevel rose in what is known as the OXYGEN CATASTROPHE. Resistant forms survived and thrived and some developed ability to use oxygen to increase their metabolism and obtain more energy from the same.

6.3 SNOW BALL EARTH

The natural evolution of the sun made it progressively more luminous during ARCHEAN AND PROTEROZOIC EON's. The Sun luminosity increase 6% every billion years. As result the Earth began to receive more heat from the sun in the PROTEROZOIC EON. However the earth did not get warmer. Instead the geological record seems to suggest it cooled dramatically during the early PROTEROZOIC period. Glacial deposits found in South Africa date back 2.2 billion years at which time at which time PROTEROZOIC puts them near the equator. Thus this glaciations known as the MAKGANYENEGLACIATION, may have been global. Some Scientists suggests that this following PROTEROZOIC ICE AGE were so severe that the Planet was totally frozen from the poles to the equator, a hypothesis called SNOW BALL EARTH. The ice age around 2.3.billion years could have increased oxygen concentration in the atmosphere. When free oxygen became available in the atmosphere the concentration of methane could have decreased dramatically, enough to counter the effect of the increasing heat flow from the sun. Nitrogen Gas commonly Known as LAUGHING GAS may have brought as the great ICE AGE to an end, a new research led by MIRJAM PFIEFFER of Swiss Federal Institute of Technology in LANSANNE. (Deccan Chronicle, Hyderabad, India, Dt. July 20, 2012.)

6.4 CAMBRIAN EXPLOSION

The rate of evolution of life as recorded by fossil accelerated in CAMBRIAN period (542-488Ma). The sudden emergence of new species, PHYLA and forms in this period is called CAMBRIAN explosion. During this time development of hard body parts such as Shells, skeletons or exoskeletons in animals like mollusks, echinoderms, crinoids and arthropods developed. Some of these Cambrian groups appear complex but are quite different from modern life for example ANOMOLOCARIS and HAIKOKOVICHTHYS. During this period the first vertebrate animals like first fishes had appeared. The ancestor of fishes was PIKAIA. The colonization of new niches resulted in massive body sizes like DUNKLEOSTEUS, which could grow 7 meters long, evolved. After each extinction pulse, the shelf regions we repopulated by similar life forms that may have been evolving elsewhere.

6.5 COLONISATION OF LAND

Oxygen accumulation from Photosynthesis resulted in the formation of an OZONE layer that absorbed much of the sun's ultraviolet radiation, meaning unicellular organism that reached land were less likely to die and PROKARYOTE lineages had probably colonized the land as early as 2.6 Ga even before the origin of EUKARYOTES. For a long time the land remained barren of multi cellular organism, fish, the earliest vertebrate evolved in the oceans around 530Ma. A major Cambrian-Ordovician plants(like algae) and fungi started growing at the edge of water, then emerged out of it.

6.6 EVOLUTION OF TETRAPODS

At the end of Ordovician period, 443Ma additional extinction events occurred due to ice age. Around 380 to 375 Ma, the first tetra pods evolved from fish. It is thought that perhaps fins evolved to become limb which allowed the first tetra pods to lift their heads out of water to breath air. This would allow them to live in oxygen-poor water or pursue small prey in shallow water. They may have later ventured on land for brief periods. Eventually, some of them became so well adapted to terrestrial life that they spent their adult lives on land although they hatched in the water and returned to lay eggs. This was the origin of amphibians. About 365Ma, another period of extinction occurred, perhaps as result of global cooling. Plants evolved seeds, which dramatically accelerated their spread on land around this time (360Ma).

About 20 million years later (340Ma) the amniotic egg, which could be laid on land giving survival advantage of amniotes from amphibians. Another 30 million years saw divergence of SYNAPSIDS including mammals from the AOUROPSIDS(birds and reptiles). Other group of organism continued to evolve and lines diverged-in fish, insects, bacteria and son. Then came MESOZONIC ERA (middle life) 252Ma to 65,5Ma during which JURASSIC TRIASSIC extinction event took place and by 180Ma, PANGAEA broke up into LAURASIA and GONDWANA along with ARCHAEOPTERYX (which was considered one of the first bird)lived around 150Ma and finally CENOSOIK ERA began around 65.6Ma and subdivided into POLEGENE AND NEOGENE periods during which Mammals and birds able to survive.

DIVERSIFICATION OF MAMMALS: Mammals have existed since the late TRIASSIC but prior to the CRETAEOUS—POLEOGENE extinction event they remained small and generalized. During the period Mammals rapidly diversified to fill the niches that the Dino and other extinct animals had left behind, becoming the dominant Vertebrates and creating many of the modern orders. With many reptiles extinct, some mammals began living in the oceans and became CETACEANS. Other became fields and candid, swift and agile land predators. The dryer global climates of the CENOZOIC period lead expansion of grasslands and the evolution of grazing and hoofed mammals, such as EQUIDS and BOVIDS. Other mammals such as ARBOREAL LIVING and became the Primates of which one lineage would lead to modern humans.

CHAPTER VII
ANTHROPOLOGICALPERSPECTIVE OF HUMAN LIFE.

HUMAN EVOLUTION

A SMALL AFRICAN APE LIVING AROUND 6Ma was the last animal whose descendents would include both modern humans and their closest relatives Chimpanzees. Only two branches of its family tree have surviving descendents. Very soon after split for reasons that are still unclear, apes in one branch developed the ability to work up right. Brain size increased rapidly and by 2Ma the first animals classified in the genus HOMO had appeared. The line between different species or even genera is somewhat arbitrary as organisms continuously change over generations. Around the same time the other branch split into the ancestors of common chimpanzee and ancestors of BONOBO AS EVOLUTION CONTINUED SIMULTANEOUSLY IN LIFE FORMS.

The ability to control fire probably began in HOMO ERECTUS (or HOMO ERGASTER), probably at least 790,000 years ago, or perhaps as early 1.5.Ma. As brain size increased babies were born earlier, before their heads grew too large to pass through the pelvis. As a result, they exhibited more plasticity and those possessed increased capacity to learn and required a longer period of dependence. Social skills became more complex, language became more sophisticated and tools became more elaborate. This contributed to further cooperation and intellectual development. Modern humans (HOMOSAPIENS) are believed to have shaped around 200,000 years ago or even earlier in Africa ; the oldest fossils date back to around 160,000 years ago. The first humans to show signs of spirituality are NEANDERTHALS (usually classified as a separate species with no surviving classified as separate surviving with no surviving descendents); they buried their dead, often with no sign of food or tools.

7.1 HOMOSAPIENS

By 11,000 years ago, Homo sapiens had reached the southern tip of South Africa, the last of the uninhibited continents (except ANTARTICA WHICH REMAIN UNDISCOVERED UNTIL 1820AD). Tool use and communications continued to improve and inter-personal relationships became more intricate. Recent finding as published in Gulf News Dt. 29 June 2012(Friday) that "some stone age artists were painting red discs, hand prints, club-like symbols and geometric patterns on European Cave walls long before previously that in some cases more than 40,000 years AGO Scientists recently(lead by JOHN BOBLE WIL FORD-NEW YORK NEWS TIMES)said after completing more reliable dating tests that raised possibility that NEANDERTHALS were the artists. A more likely situation the researchers said is that the art 50 samples from 11 caves in North western Spain was created by automatically modern humans fairly soon after their arrival in Europe.

The findings seems to put an exclamation point to run recent discoveries: direct evidence from fossils that Homo sapiens populations were living in England 41,500 to 44,200 years ago or only 43,000to 45,000 years ago and that they were making flutes in German caves about 42000 years ago. Then there is genetic evidence of modern human NEANDERTHAL interbreeding, suggesting a closer relationship than earlier thought." In the new research, an international team led by QALISTAR W.G. PIKE of the

University of Bristol in England determined that red disc in the cave known as ELSILLO was part of the earliest known decorations, at a minimum of 48000 old. That makes it the earliest caves are found so far in Europe. Further as notified in Gulf News Dt. 6 July 2012 as per New York Times News service it has found that "the early man known to be meat eater but new study suggest that his menu included a range of cooked plant food". An international team of researchers led by the University AUTONOMA DE BACELONA and the UNIVERSITY OF YORK found evidence that Neanderthals not only ate a range of roasted food but also understood to have ate plants and leafs for its nutritional and medicinal qualities. Until recently Neanderthals who disappeared between 30000 and 24000 years ago were thought to have predominantly meat eaters. The researchers studied material trapped in calcified dental plaque from five Neanderthals from the North Spanish site of EISIDRON. The varied use of plants identified suggests that the Neanderthals occupants of EISIDRON had sophisticated knowledge of their natural surrounding which include the ability to select and use certain plants for their nutritional value and self medication" lead author KARN HARDY quoted. The researchers have also found evidence of cooked food consisting of carbohydrates in the roasted starch granules in dental calculus. And also proof of cooking and exposure to smoked food was found through range of chemical markers including methyl esters phenols and poly nuclear aromatic hydrocarbons. Researchers also found that one individual had eaten bitter tasting plants.

"The evidence indicating this individual was eating bitter tasting plants such as yarrow and COMMOMILE with little nutritional value is surprising "researchers said.

Further JOAO ZILLAHO, a pre historian and NEANDERTHAL specialists at the University of BARCELONA and member of Research team, made forceful defence of hypothesis in the teleconference "we have evidence to the effect that Neanderthals possessed symbolic culture" He also said "they are close enough to modern humans to have interbred with us. This is sufficient to think about Neanderthals, as fundamentally human beings with perhaps racial differences," saying that Neanderthals were "more advanced than they have been given credit for". The new research is" more important" because it introduces a significant advance in techniques for more reliable, more precise and older dating of antiquities, especially cave art.

7.2 RACE AND GENETICS

Human lineage diverged from the common ancestor with Chimpanzee about 5.7 million years ago. The genus homo evolved by about 2.3. to 2.4 million years ago. Homo sapiens, Neanderthals, which inhibited western Euro-Asia which evolved between 400000 and 250000 years ago. The dominant view among Scientists concerning the origin of automatically modern humans is the "out of Africa" or recent African origin hypothesis which argues that HOMO SAPIENS arose in Africa and migrated out of the Continents around 50,000 to 100000 years ago replacing populations of Homo erectus in Asia and Homo Neanderthals in Europe. Recent evidence, however suggested that non-HOMOSAPIENS Neanderthal genomes may have contributed about 4% of no-African heredity and recently discovered DENISOVA HOMINIM may have contributed 6% of the genome of MALANSIANS.

7.3 GENETIC VARIATION

Genetic variation comes from mutations in genetic material, migration between populations (gene flow) and reshuffling of genes through sexual reproduction. The two main mechanisms that produce evolution are natural selection and genetic drift. A special case genetic drift is the founder effect.

7.4 GENETIC DISTANCE

Genetic distance refers to the genetic divergence between species or between populations with a species. Smaller genetic distance, indicate, a close genetic relationship where as large genetic distance indicate a more distant genetic relationship. Genetic distance can be the result of physical boundaries which naturally restrict gene flow such as islands, deserts, mountain ranges or dense forests.

7.5 ANCESTRAL POPULATION

A widely cited 1994 study by CAVALLI-SFORZA et. Al evaluated the genetic distances between 42 native populations from around the world based on 120 blood polymorphisms. These 42 populations can be grouped into 9 main clusters, which CAVALLI SFORZA termed

- (i) African (sub-Saharan)
- (ii) Caucasoid (European),
- (iii) Caucasoid (extra-European)
- (iv) Northern Mongoloid (excluding arctic population)
- (v) North east Asian arctic
- (vi) Southern Mongoloid(mainland and insular South East Asia)
- (vii) Pacific Islander
- (viii) New Guinea Australian and
- (ix) American(Amerindian).

The largest genetic distance between two continents that is between Africa and Oceania was at 0.2470. The most widely used human racial categories are based on various combinations of visible traits such as color, eyes, shape and hair structure.

7.6 BLOND ESKIMOS

The first sighting of blonde haired Arctic natives Greenly, traced to 1656, when a Dutch trading Vessel travelled west from Greenland across the Davis Strait towards Baffin Island Nicholas tunes, the captain of the vessel claimed sighting two distinct races, the first being the brownish skimmed Intuit, but the second a tall fair skinned people.

CAPTAIN GROHA of Danish Royal Navy, who in 1821 reported "Eskimos he met with" complexions scarcely less fair than Danish peasantry. Greenlandic Polar Explorer KNUD RASMUSSEN in 1903 further claimed to have found blonde haired Eskimos" of a different race" in Greenland and parts of Canada In 2003 two Icelandic Scientists the genetics' and anthropologists AGNAR HELGASON and GISLI PALSSON ANNOUNCED THE RESULTS OF THEIR RESEARCH COMPARING DNA FROM 100 Cambridge Bay Institute with DNA from Icelanders and concluded that there was no match.

7.7 TYPES OF HUMAN RACES—INHIABITANTS

There are around ten types of human races or say inhabitants in the world and they are

(i)   AFARS: People who live in rocky desert terrain of Africa and Arabia(Afars comes from first two letters of Africa and Arabia)

(ii)   ALEUTS: people residing in ALEUTIAN islands (comprising 1500 islands)These islands were colonized at least 8000years ago by hunter gatherers of Asia)

(iii)   ARIZONA: South American civilization which is as old as 2000BCE.

(iv)   ARABS: Peoples living in Arabian Peninsula.

(v)   ANDORAS: Bantu speaking people lived around 2000 years ago in Angola.

(vi)   AMAZONS: Inhabitants of Amazon forest where it is learnt that 3000 varieties of fish traced in the river and lakes.

(vii)   AUSTRALIAN ABORIGINALS: People lived around 40,000 years back and who have artistic talent.

(viii) BERBERS: The people who lived in Algeria who are considered as earliest inhabitants.

(ix)   CARIB: Native of BARUNDA and ANTIGNA.

(x)   SEA PEOPLE: Sea people are one of the populations of the ancient world who vigorously shaped the cultural land. They were people or clan of Seafarers who invaded Eastern Antarctica, Syria, Palestine, Cyprus and Egypt throughout 2 millennium BCE. The exact ethnic (racial) origin, culture, and language are still unknown. However one of the well accepted theories states that sea people were number of primarily Indo-European groups that were displaced during 13 Century BCE. Further, the Sea people are portrayed in Egyptian texts of 12 and 13 century BCE with inscription and their existence.

Chapter VIII
GEOCONNECTIONS OF HUMAN LIFE

8.1 General

The idea that nature is a holistic unity has been constantly existent throughout human history. Its concrete concept is it provides fitting framework to bridge the gap between Physical and Human Geography. The earth itself is an ORGANISM. According Love Lock, the earth haves as if it were a super organism which is composed of all the living entities and material environment. Earth started out as a self regulating organism and humans were supposed to adapt to their environment. In other words the World is not a machine but an ORGANISM. In this way the making of ethics that bridges humans, ecosystem and the planet as a whole. Humans themselves are the GUARDIANS OF THE EARTH.

8.1.1 EARTH-AXIS-ROTATION-REVOLUTION

Earth has two primary motions (i) Revolution and (ii) rotation. The first refers to Earth annual orbit around the Sun which takes bit more than 365 days per year (366 das adjusted as leap year) every four years in order to catch up. As it revolves around the SUN EARTH rotates on its axis once in every 24 hours a period of time referred to as a mean Solar day. The axis of rotation is an imaginary line passes through both geographical North and South Pole. The speed of Earth's rotation varies depending on the latitudinal position of observer. The speed is the greatest at the equator where circumference of the Earth is at a maximum:

SPEED=CIRCUMFERENCE LATITUDE/24.

8.1.2 CONTINENTS

The outer most rock layer of the Earth is termed CRUST. The oceanic Crust is composed almost entirely of BASALT, a dense igneous rock. The earth's continental crust in contrast is composed largely of lighter granitic rock. It varies greatly in thickness but average about 35 miles (56KM) thick and the oceanic crust in contrast averages only about 4 miles(6KM) thick. Because of imprecision of the definition, geographers do not agree on number of Earths continents. However Geographers in U.S. commonly recognize seven continents: ASIA, AFRICA, NORTH AMERICA, SOUTH AMERICA, ANTARTICA, EUROPE and AUSTRALIA. All the continents except Australia are roughly triangular shape narrower in South than in the NORTH.

8.1.3. CONTINENTAL DRIFT

It involves large scale of horizontal movements of continents relative to another and to ocean basis during one or more episodes of geologic time. It was discovered by German HUMBOLDT and SNIDER-PALLEGRINI of France that South America and Africa were formerly connected. Scientists say about 200 millions ago Africa and North America collided then drifted apart again. Apiece of Africa broke off and became the basis of Florida deep under the ocean.

8.1.4. AURORA BOREALIS

Northern lights or Aurora Borealis are shimmering lights that shine above the Earth near Geo—metric North Pole. The lights often bright enough read by all usually green or red. The Phenomenon is caused when solar storm discharges high energy particles that channeled in to ring by Earth's magnetic field. The Solar particles energizes atoms in the thin ionosphere, which causes emission of light. Astronauts the only person who get to see the lights above have flown through auroras and report that even have flown through auroras and report that even with eye closed they see flashes of light from the charged particles pass through their eyeballs within this band about 1250 miles (2000KM) from pole the aurora borealis can be seen almost every dark night. Wegner, a German Meteorologist proposed that lighter continents are floating on the denser underlying material of Poles. Further increased knowledge discovered that magnetized materials released from parent igneous indicate that magnetic poles, South and North have separated continents which formerly joined.

8.1.5. CONTINENTAL SHELF

Continental shelf is submerged top of continental edge, lying between the shore line and the continental slope that forms a border to a continent. In other words the Surface of Earth lies at two general levels, a lower which is the floor of ocean basins and upper, the parts of which are continents.

8.1.6. DARIEN GAP

Straddling the border of republic Panama and Columbia, the Darien Gap is home to of the least exploited and diverse ecosystem in the world.

8.1.9. FORESTS

Forests cover approximately 27 % of ice free surface of the Earth. 13 Million Square Miles or 34 Million Sq. Km. The world's forests occur mainly in two broad zones: one centered in the tropical regions and the other in Northern hemisphere between 32 degrees and 45 degrees North latitude.

8.1.10 GLACIATION

The action of Glaciers has made a huge difference in appearance of the Earths' surface changes in the land from action of glaciers is called Glaciations

8.1.11. DESERT AREA

Famous deserts include SAHARA (in Africa),. Arabia., Iranian, Somali(mid Africa)Great Austria, Kalahari(Africa), Namid (North America Peruvian), Atacama(South America) Path Goninan (South Africa) Karakum, Gobi (Russia).

8.1.13. POLES (ARCTIC CIRCLE)

It is located at 66,5,degreessouth latitude or 23.5.degrees north ward of South Pole. Here sun can be seen on June 22(the Southern Hemisphere) and North most location where midnight sun visible on December 21. On June 22, 24 hours darkness and on December, 21, 24 hours Sunlight is seen. Sun reaches his Zenith (highest point) and Sun is over head at Tropic of Capricorn, of 47 degrees above horizon and its (Nadir) lowest point at midnight. Long periods of continuous Sunlight during summer months have led to the area within arctic circle being called LAND OF MIDNIGHT SUN.

8.1.15: THE GREAT BARRIER REEF

Located on the north east Coast of Australia is comprised of world's largest cluster of coral reefs. It is 1250 Miles (2012KM) long running along 10 miles (16KM) of the Eastern Australia shore in North 100 miles (161 KM) in the south. It is the key stage in Earths continuing ECOLOGICAL AND BIOLOGICAL evolution of natural phenomena.

8.1.16: GRASS LAND

Many types of Eco system throughout the world are described as grasslands because they are dominated as sub-ordinate within community. These are approximately 9,000 species within this group because there is only one leaf protecting the seed in contrast to most flowering plants which have two seed leaves and are known as DICOTYLEDONS.

8.1.17: A GREAT CIRCLE

It is defined as direction line that forms full circle of Earth. This is also called a true OZIMUTH. This circle divides the Earth in to equal halves and on the idealized surface of Earth, the shortest distance between two points lies along a great circle. The equator circle as are all meridians of longitude. It has number of considerable properties. It is the largest possible on the Globe.

8.1.18: GRID/GRATICULE

The earth is not spherical but rather on ellipsoidal shape where NORTH and SOUTH Poles are flattened and EQUATER bulges. This unique shape is called GIODE. An imaginary network of lines called GRIDGRATICULES is super imposed on the surface of EARTH to serve the purpose.

8.1.19: HUMBOLDT CURRENT

It is also known as the pure current that flows along the Western Coast of South America, affecting air temperature of Coastal CHILIE AND PERU, It is the one of the largest ocean currents in the world, bringing cold water north from the South pacific for thousands of KILOMETERS(FROM 40 DEGREES 5 DEGREES) BEFORE IT DISSIPIATES IN THE WARMER AROUND THE EQUATOR. It is named after GEOGRAPHER HUMBOLDT who discovered it.

8.1.20: INTERNATIONAL DATE LINE (IDL)

is the imaginary line on earth slicing through the center of Pacific ocean that separates two consecutive calendar days. Countries in Eastern Hemisphere to the left of the line up to the Prime meridian are always one day ahead of countries to the right line and West of prime meridian.

OCEANS AND CLIMATES

8.1.24. ANTARTICA

Remained untouched by human until 19 century. But Russian Naval Officer FABIOMCON BELLINGHAUSEN discovered some of the islands and finally the land mass was discovered by naval officer William Smith and Edward Bran field discovered land mass in 1820.

8.1.25. Arctic ocean

is the smallest and shallowest of the Earths five Oceans occupying 4% other worlds' ocean space. The arctic ocean connects with Atlantic ocean by Green land.

8.1.26. ATLANTIC OCEAN

It is the second largest ocean of the world. It occupies 22%of earths surface and the occupation area is about 106, 400,000sq. km (41,100,000 sq. miles) with a depth of 3339 to 3926 meters (10950ft. to 12880ft.)

8.1.27: MEDITERNEAN OCEAN

The translation of its Latin name (in the midst of land) indicates the sea located between land masses of Europe, Asia and Africa. The Oceans total surface is 967000 sq, miles (2.5.million KM)

8.1.28: PACIFIC OCEAN

It has an area approximately 68767,000Sq. Miles (178,106,000Sq. KM) with its adjacent seas (INDIAN SEA and BAY OF BENGAL) 65329,000Sq. Miles (165,202,000 Sq. KM). Following are the characteristic features because it is the LARGEST OCEAN IN THE WORLD.

Volume	:	160,489 cubic miles(674052000 Sq. KM)
Average depth	:	13480 Ft.(4110 Met.)
Greatest Depth	:	35798 Ft.(10911Met) in challenger deep in the Mariana Trench.
Width	:	12,300 Miles (19800KM) between Indonesia and Coast Columbia.
Coast line	:	84,300 Miles (135663 KM)

It is almost triangular in shape. The Pacific is worlds' oldest ocean. Theories of Pacific origin are related to PLATE TECTONICS where movement of land masses of the Earth are either drifting or sinking and sliding under one another

8.1.29: BLACK SEA

Black sea is a body of salt water that stretches 630 miles(1014 KM) from east to west. Turkey, Romania, Bulgaria, Ukraine and Georgia form its coastal line. The Black Sea is usually considered the boundary between Europe and Asia. It reaches depth of 7218 Ft(2200Met) below 660ft(200met) the water hold no oxygen and Black Sea is therefore the largest anoxic basin world with about 90% of its water permanently anaerobic. The sea termed Black by Turks for its storms.

8.1.30: RED SEA

The red sea connects the MEDITERRNEAN OCEAN to the Indian Ocean via Suez Canal. It lies in the Great drift valley between Africa and Arabian Peninsula. Scientists believe that it was formed 20 million years ago when the Earth crust weakened and was torn apart creating jagged rift across Africa. Volcanoes erupted on either side creating volcanic mountains. Water filled this part of salt, creating the Red sea. It is very deep sea searching depth almost 9840ft.(3000Met.) in the center. It is saltier than any other sea. SEVENTEEN SPECIES OF FISH ARE ENDEMIC TO THE AREA, meaning they are not found anywhere else.

8.1.31. DEAD SEA

It is of 390 Sq. Miles (1010Sq. KM) salt lake located on the borders of Palestine, Israel and Jordan. It is lowest water point in the world. Its coast is at 1202 ft. below sea level (395 met.), is the lowest dry point on the Earth. The Dead sea formed when two plates of Earth crust began spreading apart, creating low region, where Earth's surface has sunk and lake bottom still sinking as much as 13" (33cm) annually an incredibly fast rate. The Dead sea is located in a hot area with low precipitation, water evaporates to the degree that sea level seldom fluctuates, other than because of irrigation and what is left behind is Salt.

Once depth is greater than 300 ft.(91`met.) then 332 grams of salt per Kg which is a state of saturation. Sea supports no plant, animal or fish life. If fish swims from stream in to this lake(sea) it is instantly killed and then preserved by lake's mineral salts. The only type of life, then existing in the sea are microbes and highly specialized algae on some occasion sea bird is seen resting on the lakes surface

If the human being swims the sea and when exits the lake the body is coated with white salt and skin can become irritated chloride calcium. The water is oily appearance.

8.1.34. CLIMATE CLASSIFICATION:

Climate is an average or aggregate of daily weather conditions over period of years.(i) Coastal Zone climate: Coastal Zone is where nature breaths its essence into poets and painters. Ancient Greeks believed it was Neptune energy encounters land. BOBERT GABLER et al (of U.S.) define zone as dynamic region on land as well as areas currently submerged under water through which the Shore line boundaries fluctuate.

8.1.35. ECO SYSTEM:

The Eco system is more for conception is whole system including not only the organism complex, but also the whole complex of physical factors forming what we call the environment. Eco system comprises group of coordinated component of the environment, such components may be BIOTIC, that is relating to life such as plants, animals and humans and ABIOTIC, that is relating to the components of environment such as water, soil, climate. All ecosystems are organized and structures the BIOTIC and ABIOTIC elements and links between them can be identified and many cases quantified.

Volumes of elements especially carbon dioxide and methane forms atmosphere as climate Thus Earths biotic and abiotic components are arbiters of climatic change which in turn affects the distribution of a bio data and functions between them. Examples of such are phosphorus, calcium, sodium and magnesium. Another major function within ecosystem is energy flow. It is quite essential for life and involves the harnessing of solar system society can be achieved only by green plants(photosynthesis). The efficiency of photosynthesis depends on water, nutrient lights availability.

8.2. RIVERSAND MOUNTAINS HAVING GEOGRAPHICAL IMPORTANCE

8.2.1 RIVERS:AMAZON RIVER:

Naturalists suggest that there may be as many as 3000 different kinds of fish in the Amazon river. It is the largest river in the world. Amazons are the inhabitants in Amazon rain forest.

EVEREST MOUNT:

A peak on the crest of Great Himalayas range in Asia. Everest is the highest point on Earth. It lies in the Central Himalayas on the border between NEPAL, CHINA (TIBET). The three barren ridges, to south West, north East and West culminates in to two summits at EVEREST(29,028 Ft. or 8848Met.) and South peak 28,700 ft. 0r 8748 met. It can be directly seen from the PLATEU of Tibet.

8.5.13 PAMIR KNOT:

The 'Knot' refers to convergence of some of the world's most major mountain ranges including TIANSHAN KARAKORUM, KUNLUN and HINDUKUSH. It originates from TAJIK name for the region BOM-DUNYO or ROOF of the world. It is centered in TAJKISTAN. It is one of the least accessible areas in the world. It consists of High peak ranges consisting of 24590 ft. (7495 Met.) to 23311ft (7105Met.)

CHAPTER IX
HISTORIC AND ANTHROPOLOGICAL PERSPECTIVE OF HUMAN ANTIQUITY.

9.1 Book

The written work of GREEK Philosopher HERODOTUS was literally an enquiry written in 5 century BCE which is the first Historical account in the ancient world about the history and anthropology. Inquiry is what anthropology is about. Anthropology is a study of humans in all places and all times. Anthropologist studies modern human and their ancestors whom we refer to as HOMINIDS. It is a search, an investigation in WHAT WE ARE NOW from whence we came and how we got to be the way we are today. Scottish Scholar, Sir James Frazier, inspired a generation as an Anthropologists to go out into the world to do field work and develop methodology that has established anthropology as a rigorous Scientific endeavor.

Much our past has been learned since Darwin's origin of species was published in 1859. Neanderthal, Cro-Magnon and first PITHECANTHROPUS ERECTUS were found in succeeding decades. The TAUN child was found in 1924 and 'LUCY' by Johnson in 1974. The methodology and the number of fossil finds and the body of knowledge about human evolution has grown enormously since Darwin.

Anthropology has many branches of study which include: Physical anthropology, Study fossil, Study of Anthropology through Forensic, Dental Anthropology, Linguistic Anthropology. Medical Anthropology and finally Ethnic Anthropology.

9.1.1. Physical Anthropology

is the study of people from a biological perspective, dissection our species with all tools of anatomy. This includes Paleo Anthropology which includes study of closest relatives, the apes, gorilla, chimpanzee, orangutan and gibbon. (ii) Second study would be variation in humans like skeleton shape, bone structure, skin color, body size, and eye color which helps as vital clues to find out historic roots. Primate have also given to understand into ancestor taboo, a worldwide culture universal among human societies that restrict mating with close relatives. It was also revealed through anthropoids that many primate have inhibition against mating with close kin.

9.1.2 Another field of anthropology

is FORENSIC which is a specialized area in Physical Anthropology.

9.1.3. Most important field of Physical anthropology

is Dental Anthropology which study teeth as recorded of living mouths or as seen in the skulls of archaeological and fossil collections through Forensic assistance. Culture is believed to date back at least to the origin of earliest stone tools, 2.5.million years ago. As hominids appear closer to us in time the evidence for culture increases. This is evident as stone tools become more complex, fire is harnessed and as hominids spread out Africa into more challenging environments with the approval of Modern humans about or more than 40,000 years ago, the pace of cultural evolution over took that biological evolution.

9.1.4. Another subsidiary branch of Anthropology

is LINGUISTIC ANTHROPOLOGY, which studies contemporary human languages as well as once from the past. As the language is conservative it is retained by people when they move or migrate from one area to another.

9.1.5. One more subsidiary field of anthropology

is ETHNOLOGY which studies human behavior as it can be seen experienced and discussed with those who live in particular culture. In other words intensive study of single culture is called as an ENTHROPOLOGY. People in cultures consider it appropriate to have more than one wife (or husband) at the same time many prefer to marry a first cousin illegal here in ILLIONIS. Some people eat dogs and cats. So culture differ from one sect to another. Within cultures there are many sub-cultures. It can best described as the interaction between culture health, and disease and this is called bio-cultural evolution clubbed with Medical anthropology. Biology and culture inter act, therefore much human adaptive change is product of cultural evolution.

9.1.6: LIFE ON EARTH:

An immense amount of time was necessary for the evolution of life on Earth. Historically the great age of the Earth was slowly appreciated, when geology became a systematic science, the incredible age of the Earth was fully revealed, as discussed in earlier chapters with understanding, evolution became not just possibility but necessity in order for life on Earth to adapt a restless and changing Planet.

The great, great, great . . . . of the human race was very ugly, unattractive mammal. He was quite small, much smaller than people of today. The heat of the Sun and biting wind of cold winter had colored his skin a dark brown. His head and most of his body, his arms and legs too covered with long coarse hair. He had very thing but strong fingers which made his hand look like those of monkey. His forehead was low and his jaw was like the jaw of wild animal which uses its teeth both as a fork and knife. He wore no clothes. He had seen no fire except the flames of rumbling volcanoes which filled the earth with their smoke and Lava. (See page no. 62)

He lived in damp blackness of vast forests as then pygmies of Africa do this very day when he felt the pangs of hunger he ate raw leave and roots of plants or took away the eggs away from the angry bird and fed them to his own young. On in while after a long patient chase, he would catch a sparrow or a small wild dog or perhaps a rabbit. These he would eat raw or he had never discovered that food better when it was cooked.

During the hours of day this primitive human being prowled about looking for things to eat. When night descended upon the Earth, he and his female friend (wife) and his children in a hollow tree or behind some heavy boulder for he was surrounded on all sides by ferocious animals and when it was dark these animals began to prowl about, looking same thing to eat for their mates and their own young and they liked the taste of human beings. IT WAS WORLD YOU MUST EAT OR BE EATEN AND LIFE WAS STRUGGLE FOR EXISTENCE, as Charles titled in his book of Species "Survival of the Strongest and fittest, was the law prevailed in the forest or call it Jungle Law. In due course time he learned that he could use the guttural noise to warn his fellow beings whenever danger threatened and he gave certain little shriek which came to mean "there is lion" or "there are five elephants". Then the others responded with something back at him and their growl warn resulted as signal of danger.

Further during the course of time weather changed ice used to fall and felt the shortage of food and meanwhile people from neighbor hills or forests joined with the folk for shelter. There was no food enough for the old in inhabitants and for the new comers. When they tried to stay more than few days there was terrible battle with the claw like hands and feet and whole families were killed. The other fled back to their area and died in the next blizzard. But the people in the forest were greatly frightened. All the time they grew shorter and nights colder than they ought to have been.

Finally, in a gap of between two high hills their appeared a tiny speck of green ice. Rapidly it increased in size. A gigantic glacier came sliding down hill. Huge stones were being pushed in to the valley with a noise of dozen thunderstorms, torrents of ice and mud blocks of granite suddenly tumbled among the people of the forest and killed them while they slept. Century old trees were crushed into kindling wood and then began to snow. It snowed for months and months. All the plants died and the animals fled in search of the southern sun. Man hoisted his young upon his back and followed them.

But he could not travel as fast as wilder creatures and he was forced to choose between quick thinking or quick dying. He seems to have preferred the former for he has managed to survive terrible glacier periods which upon four different occasions threatened to kill every human being on the face of Earth. SINCE THE NECESSITY IS MOTHER OF INVENTION, he felt necessity of clothing himself and learned how to dig holes and cover them with branches and leaves and these he caught bears and hyenas, and he killed with heavy stones and whose skins, he used as coats for himself and his family. Next came shelter (housing) problem and this was simple because there are many caves available where animals were habit of sleeping. Man now followed this example, drove the animals out of their warm homes and claimed them for his own.

Further as the climate was too severe for most people and old and young at terrible rate. Then genius he thought himself of the use of fire. He remembered that he had been almost roasted to death by the flames. Thus far fire that had been an enemy, now it became a friend. A dead tree was dragged in to cave and lightened by means of smoldering branches from burning wood. This turned the cave in to cozy little room. And then a dead chicken fell into fire. It was not rescued until it had been roasted. Man discovered that meat tasted better when cooked and he then and discarded one of the old habits which he shared with other animals and began to prepare his own food. In this way thousands of years passed. Only people with cleverest brains survived. They had struggle day and night against the cold and hunger. Then they forced to invent tools and learned how to sharpen stones into axes and how to make hammers. They were obliged to put up large stores of food for endless days of winter and they found that clay could be made into bowls and jars and hardened in the rays of sun. Though glacial period which had threatened to destroy the human race, became his greatest teacher because it forced man to use his brain. These earliest ancestors of ours who lived in great wilderness were rapidly bearing new things. It is safe to say in due course of time that they have given up the ways of savage and would have developed civilization of their own. Thus there came to an end to their isolation living.

A traveler from unknown south and who had dared to cross the sea and high mountain passes had found his to the wild people of European continent. He must have come from Africa and his home was in Egypt. The valley of Nile had developed a high stage of civilization thousand years before the people of the west had dreamed of possibilities of a fork or a wheel or a house. And we shall therefore leave great grand fathers in their caves, while we visit the southern and eastern shores of Mediterranean where the earlier school of the human race.

9.1.7 CIVILIZATIONS:

The Egyptians have taught us many things. They were excellent farmers and knew all about irrigation. They built temples which were afterwards copied by the Greeks and which served as earliest models for the churches in which we worship now a days. They had invented calendar which proved such useful instrument for the purpose of measuring time has survived with few changes until today. But important of all the Egyptians had learned how to preserve speech for the benefit of future generations. They had invented the art of writing. Similarly and simultaneously one more civilization called Indus valley civilization equally fared well in the development of mankind by way of agriculture, art, worship and language.

9.1.8. EVOLUTIONARY THOUGHT:

DARWIN's theory of evolution was not just an idea routed out of bed and proclaimed it. The emergence of evolutionary theory with tenets of natural selection, common, descent, importance of variation steered research into evolutionary studies of teeth. Evolutionary theory describes any change in anything. To be more specific, definition applicable to biological evolution the origin of all species originating from pre-existing species. It is an ongoing process being the result of change produced by natural selection and genetic change.

Implicit in this is that humans are animals and themselves product of biological evolution. Accumulation of evidence reveals that humans have an evolutionary origin that is extremely ancient from life forms very unlike human today.

Geographical Periods	Climate State	Animal Life	Human Type	Cultural EPOCH	Time Estimate
Recent Historic				Neolithic new stonage	EUROPE 7000 BCE
				Copper Bronze age	EUROPE 3000-1000 (BCE) 4000-1500
				Early Iron age	Orient 1800-1000 Europe 1000-500
				Later Iron age	(BCE) 500
	Post glacial	Reinder musksheep	cromagnon	Later poeolithic OR	25000
	FIRST	LION HYENA	-	DISTANCE	-
PRE HISTORIC	INTER GLACIAL	WIND BEAR LYNX	AGE	-	475, 000
	SECOND GLACIAL	BOBBER-TOOTH-TIGER	-	-	400,000
	THIRD GLACIAL	WOOLY-MAMMOTH	-	-	150,000
	INTER GLACIAL	HIPPOPOTA MOUS-ELEPHANT-RHINOCERS			375,000
	FOURTH GLACIAL	STEPPE-HORSE-AUREUTS-NEANDERT HAL-PILT DOWN-		EARLY PALOEOTHIC AGE-OLD STONE AGE	50,000

9.1.9. RACIAL EVOLUTION:

The savage is a mere child of nature. He secure food from wild plants and animals; he know nothing of metals. He was hunting gatherer. His home is merely a cave or rock shelter or a rude bark hut. Barbarism forms a transitional stage between savagery and civilization. Barbarian has gained some control of nature. He learned to sow and reap the fruits of the Earth, instead of depending entirely on hunting. He started to domesticate animals and started using metals for routine use. Barbarous tribes at the time include North American Indians, the Pacific islands and the most American Negros.

Three primary varieties of man are distinguished the BLACK(NEGROID)race, The YELLOW(MONGOLID) race and the WHITE(AUCA SIAN).

RACE	PEOPLES LINGUISTIC PEOPLE
BLACK	NEGROS—BANTU-DWARF-PYGMIES-HOTTONTOTS—BUSHMAN—DRAVIDANS—VEDDAS(CEYLON)—PAPUANS(Malaysian-new guinea)-AUSTRALIA
YELLOW	MONGOLIANS(Chinese, Japan) KOREANS-BURMESE—SIAMESE—MANCHUS-MANGOLOID TATARAS—TURKS—BULGARIANS—MAGHYARS OR HUNGARIANS—ESTONIANS. FINNS (Lapps)—MALAYS(In Formosa)-PHILLIPINES-(Malay ARCHPOLEGO) (NICOBAR ISLANDS) (MADAGACAR)—POLYNESIAN(MARY-New Zealand)—TON TONGANS—SAMOANS—HAWAIANS—AMERICAN INDIANS.

| WHITE (CAUCASIANS) | HEMATIC (Libyans, Egyptians, Eastern Hamitians)—SEMETIC (Babylonian)Assyrians, Phoenicians, Hebrews Armenians, Arabs, Abyssinians) INDO EUROPEANS(Hindus, Medes, Persians, Hittites, Armenians, Scythenians) GREECO LATIC(Albanians, Greeks, Helenians, Spaniards, Portuguese, French, (Walloons, Rumanians) CELITIC (Britons, Welsh, Irish, Highland Scots) TUTANIC(Germans, Frisians, Dutch, Swedish, English, Low land Scots. LETTES, SLAVIC,(South Serbians)Slovenes, mountaineering Slovenes) WEST SLAVES(Czechs, Slovaks, Poles,) EAST SLAVES(Great Russians or Lutherans, White Russians) |

9.1.10 LANGUAGES OF MANKIND:

The different kinds of languages also took place during the prehistoric period. The first language must have been simple enough. Man, doubtless, eked out of his imperfect speech with expressive gestures and cries of alarm or passion, such as lower ANIMAL MAKE. The language of even lowest savage thus indicating complex in structure and copious in vocabulary, thus indicating how far they have developed in course of time.

Thousands of languages and dialectic now spoken thought out the world belong to one another three groups: (i) AGGULUTINATING language show grammatical relations by adding (gluing) sounds ex: Turkish) (II) ISOLATING LANGUAGE: show grammatical relations chiefly by the orders of words(ex. Chinese) (iii) INFLUENTIAL LANGUAGE regularly employ conjugations and declensions etc. to set forth the relations of words to one another. These three linguistic groups have fairly definite association with the races of man.

Human language is among life forms of earth because of its complex structure affects as much wider range of possible expression and use than any known system of animal communication with limited functions and mostly genetically rather than socially transmitted. The Brain is the coordinating center of all linguistic activity. It controls both production of linguistic cognition and meaning and mechanic of speech production.

The Earth's population of 7 billion people speaks roughly 7000 of which 2050 languages were already extinct and around 2500 are in the stage of endangered extinction. Only 100 languages are popularly spoken which include:

LANGUAGE	NATIVE SPEAKERS(IN MILLION)
Mandarin	845
Spanish	328
Arabic	221
Hindi	182
Bengali	181
Portuguese	178
Russian	144
Japanese	122
German	91

9.1.11 River Valley civilizations:

Earlier river valley civilizations arose in Mesopotamia, Egypt, Indus and China Earlier Agricultural Societies (8000 to 13000Years ago) were largely substance cultures. The river valley civilizations had enough to provide for class and mass of the people other than just farmers. These societies all used agriculture surpluses to establish civilizations with cities and trade and to create greater sophistication in the arts, sciences government and even a leisure class. Cities enabled societies much more sophisticated than primitive that agriculture allowed. The first beginning of higher level urban rural society began in MESOPOTAMIA about 4000 BCE. The other civilizations appeared shortly.

i)   The Second Major civilization is Egypt(5000-3000BCE
ii) The third is Indus valley civilization(3000-2500BCE) and
iii) The Fourth is China Civilization(2800-2600BCE)

Though PALEOLITHIC COMMUNITIES HAD EXISTED 200000 years ago, NEOLITHIC communities from 8000-5000 BCE and finally complex societies as mentioned above arose 3000-2500BC.

The Region between Mediterranean and Arabian desert contained in antiquity three small countries: Syria, Phoenicia and Palestine. The inhabitants spoke SEMITIC languages and probably come from Northern Arabia. They are known as Armenians OR Syrians; Phoenicians and Hebrews. None of these people overplayed a leading part in Oriental History (like Egyptians) but each made important contributions to oriental civilization. Hebrew as the ordinary speech in Palestine some parts of Old Testaments are written in ARAMAIC. The chief center of Armenians was DAMASCUS, one of the oldest(like Cairo) cities in the world and still a thriving place.

9.2. HIST0RIC AGE

9.2.1. History

which begins in near East for the last 2500 has entered Europe. We learnt in earlier chapters that Europe was inhabited by man during PALAEOLITHIC times and that with exception of certain invading people who came from Asia in antiquity Middle ages, the present inhabitants of Europe belong to white race. They can be represented in to three types (i)the Baltic or NOEDIC TYPE found in Scandinavia (ii) Mediterranean (south type) and (iii)Alpine (central type)about 60 district languages are spoken in Europe.

9.2.2 AEGEANS:

The first civilization to arise in Europe was the AEGEAN as early as 3000 Years back, It gave up stone and began to use copper and Bronze and this lasted for about thousand years. The Aegean's had passed from picture writing to sound writing. They probably denote syllabus and indicate a decided advance over both Egyptian and Babylonian scripts.

9.2.3: GREEK:

The invaders who plunged the AEGEAN once into barbarianism were tall light complexion fair handed, blue eyed, probably OF THE BALTIC(NORDIC) racial type. Their language was Greek which belong to Indo-European. They lived nomadic life as hunters and herdsmen. When the grass lands became insufficient to support their sheep and cattle these hunters began gradually move southward into the DANUBE VALLEY and hence through many passes of the Balkans into Greece. The invaders and the locals slowly intermingled thus producing the one GREEK people which found at the down history. The beginning of historic times in the Greek world about 750 BCE and this period is usually known as HOMERIC age whose epic poems called ILLIAD and ODESSY which were composed in IONIA and thereby Greeks were attributed to blind bared named HOMER.

Greek believed in communications from God were received at certain places called ORACLES. It was honored till the close of 4th century ADE when Roman emperor after adoption Christianity silenced forever. The Olympic games started at OLYMPIA in ELLIS. The city state arose and eventually combined into kingdom. Each state had a king who did not possess absolute authority as in orient, he was more or less controlled by council of Nobles and both king and Nobles shall consult common people on matters of great importance such as making wars or declaring peace. The citizen would be summoned to meet in the market place where they shouted ASSENT to the proposals laid before them. Thus people ruled people directly and every citizen took active part in politics, however, citizenship was awarded only to ATHENEANS and foreign traders only.

Philosophers like SOCRATES, THALES, PLATO, ARISTOTLE and HERACLETUS lived during this period. Human civilization in modern shape of society existed. ALEXANDER, The great whose Master was Aristotle, almost dominated half of the world and spread Greek civilization. He was considered as one of the foremost, perhaps the first of the great captain of antiquity.

9.2.4. ROMANS:

After his death old Greece period came to an end and new great power ROME took birth. Rome began LATIN settlement on the PALATINE MOUNT. Rome thus became the city of SEVEN HILLS. ROMULUS was the founder after whom the city called Rome came to exist. Romans also exerted the same history as that of Greece. JULIUS CEASER was noted ruler of the time. After his death ANTONY and his Egyptian queen CLEOPATRA fled Egypt on account of OCTAVIAN invasion. The advent of three great religions like JUDAISM, CHRISTIANITY and ISLAM who while propagating Monotheism, countered some divine figure who was regarded as redeemer from SIN and EVIL and offered devotees happier existence beyond grave.

Thus the Golden age of ATHEAN (during Socrates, Plato and Socrates)also called the period of REASON was buried into the grave yard for a period about thousand years. Later empire established by CONSTANTINE, sole ruler during 324-337AD established another capital for Roman world which is named as CONSTANTINOPLE or NEW ROME. Old Rome itself passed into barbarous hands. Thus imperial system collapsed due to the reason that Empire made no local self Government. Ordinary people were subjected only for payment of Tax, Noble posed as rulers and kings became puppets in the hands of clergymen.

9.2.5: MIDDLE AGES:

The period called middle ages is not well defined either as its beginning or its close. The Roman Empire had now been dismembered and barbarian kingdom destined to became in later centuries the national states of Western Europe and had been formed into ITALY, SPAIN and BRITAIN. For concluding dates we may take those of inventions of Printing (1450AD) the capture of CONSTANTINOPLE by TURKS(1433) the discovery of America(1402) and opening of sea routes to the East Indies(1498). Such significant events of all falling with in the second half of 15 century seem mark the end of Medieval and beginning of Modern times.

The change from antiquity of Middle ages and again from Medieval to Modern world was in each case a gradual process extending over several centuries. The fact is that the social life of man forms continuous growth and mans history, an uninterrupted stream. The medieval period falls into divisions of about equal length. The first, or early middle ages, formed in Western Europe an era of turmoil, ignorance and decline consequent upon barbarians invasions. The process of absorption of TENTONIC people with Romanized provisions was practically completed by the end of tenth century.

Western Europe then entered upon middle ages an era more settled Government, increasing knowledge and steady progress in almost every field of human activity. The medieval period thus presents to the historical eye not a level stretch of thousand years with mankind, stationary but rather first a down ward and then upward slope. CRUSADES (1095-1291) in their widest, as may be regarded as the renewal of the long contest between East and West. The contest assumed a new character when Europe had become Christian and Asia Islamic.

It was not only two contrasting types but also two rival world religions which in the 18 century faced each other under walls of Constantinople and battle field of tours. Throughout this period (from eleventh century to eighteenth century) there was an almost continuous movement of Crusades to form Moslem possession in Asia minor, Syria and Egypt.

THE CRUSADES WERE FIRST AND FOREMOST SPIRITUAL ENTERPRISE. THEY SPRANG RELIGIOUS PILIGRIMAGE ONE SIDE CHRISTIANS TO JERUSALEM WHERE CHRIST BORN AND CRUCIFIED AND ANOTHER SIDE MUSLEMS TO MECCA WHERE ISLAM HOLY PLACE MECCA LOCATED. THE CHRISTIANS MANAGED TO KEEP JERUSALEM FOR SOME WHAT LESS THAN HUNDRED YEARS TILL THEIR LAST POST IN SYRIA DID FALL TO MOSLEM IN 1291 AN EVENT COMMONLY REGARDED AS AN END OF

CRUSADES. AFTER CENTURIES OF CONFLICT AND AFTER A GREAT EXPENDITURE OF WEALTH AND HUMAN LIVES THE HOLY JERUSALEM FELL INTO THE HANDS OF MOSLEM. THIS RESULTED IN TENDING DEATH OF FEUDALISM.

THE CRUSADES ALSO CONTRIBUTED TO INTELLECTUAL AND SOCIAL PROGRESS. THEY BROUGHT THE INHABITANTS OF WESTERN EUROPE IN TO CLOSE RELATION WITH THEIR FELLOW CHRISTIANS OF BYZANTINE EMPIRE AND WITH NATIVES OF ASIA MINOR SYRIA AND EGYPT. COMMERCE AND TRADE DEVELOPED THROUGH SEA ROUTES.

9.2.6. CRUSADES OPENED UP A NEW WORLD:

China, Russia, nomadic tribes like MONGOLIANS Huns in north of the Black Sea came in contract with European voyages of Asia. The genius leader of MONGOLIA, JENGIZ KHAN, Great wall of China (constructed all about 1500 miles) were identified. During middle ages, History, rather than race or even language explains the present grouping of European states. When the Christian era opened all the region between the north sea and Black Sea and from Mediterranean to Rhine and Danube belonged to Roman Empire. This Romanized Europe under the influence of Germanic invasion began to split up into number of separate, independent states. Three strongest in Europe at the end of medieval period were ENGLAND, FRANCE and SPAIN. During these periods royalty triumphed over Feudalism which advanced civilization. Only strong kings could keep the peace, punishment and foster industry and trade. The kings were generally despotic.

9.2.7: CITY LIFE:

The great economic feature of the later middle ages was the growth of cities. Developing of trade commerce and manufacturers led to the increase of wealth, growth of markets and substitution of money payments for those in produce or service. Flourishing cities arose in the days of Roman empire freed themselves from the control of nobles and became homes of Liberty and democracy. The free city had no room for either SLAVES OR SERBS. All servile conditions ceased inside its walls. Thus proverb or a famous saying TOWN AIR RENOERS FREE found expression in common folk.

There came into existence of MIDDLE CLASS of city people between the clergy and Nobles on one side and peasants on the other side—what French call BOUGEOSIC. The crusades brought east and West face to face, greatly increased the trade, the Mediterranean lands first felt stimulating effects of intercourse with orient but before the long commercial revival extend to other parts of Europe.

Before the discovery of the CAPE GOOD HOPE the spices, drugs, incense, carpets, tapestries, porcelains and Gems of India, China and the East Indies, reached west by three main routes—PERSIAN GULF, TIGRIS RIVER OF BAGHDAD, CAIRO and ALEXANDRIA, by way of Red Sea and the Nile.

LANGUAGE: LATIN CONTINUED TO BE AN INTERNATIONAL LANGUAGE THROUGH OUT THE MEDIVAL PERIOD. However, each European country during the middle ages had also its own national languages including FRENCH, ITALIAN, SPANISH, PORTUGUESE, and RUMANIAN derived from LATIN SPOKEN BY THE ROMANIZED inhabitants of lands now, after Nationalism. Gradually each country new and vigorous language related to, yet different from old classical Latin in pronunciation grammar and vocabulary, TEUTONIC language and then Anglo-Saxon(English) took birth

9.2.9. RENAISSANE:

The French word Renaissance means rebirth or revival. It is most convenient term for all the change in the society, law and Government, in Science, in Philosophy, religion, literature and art which transformed medieval civilization into modern times. The change was transitional in character but not as revolution. The language and literature, philosophy and scientific thought of Greece and Rome opened up a new world thought of HUMANISM. Revival of learning was immensely stimulated when books printed on linen paper invented by china and Arabs, A German John Gutenberg set up practical printing press with movable type about 1450 from it issued the first Book—BIBLE.

Printed books could be multiplied far more rapidly than manuscripts copied by hand. Universities and educational institutions adapted this revolutionary printing mechanism due to which popular education made accessible to common man. Library, and ultimately cheap news papers thus became force for emancipating mankind from the BONDAGE OF IGNORANCE.

9.2.10: SOCIAL AND GEOGRAPHICAL RENAISSANCE:

First place among renaissance must be given to COPERNICUS (1473-1543) for the founder of Modern Astronomy whose findings erased the Social and geographical thought and awakened a new perspective of human life.

He could dare enough to proclaim the fact that EARTH TURN UPON ITS OWN AXIS AND TOGETHER WITHPLANETS REVOLVED AROUND THE SUN. To add fuel 0f prevailing dogmas GALILIOGALILI made one of the first telescope—it was powerful as an opera glass and turn it on the heavenly bodies and declared that SUN is moving unmistakably on its own axis Venus showing phases in relation to the Sun, Jupiter accompanied by revolving moon or the satellites and the MILKY WAY composed of multitude of separate stars which are far bigger than Sun.

The revival of exploration brought about the discovery of ocean routs to the far east and America and the result is commerce was vastly stimulated and two continents hither to unknown were opened up civilization. Thus Renaissance cooperated with other movements of age in bringing about transition from Medieval to Modern times.

Thoughtful men like Martin Luther criticized the worldliness of Church and demanded wholesale change in Catholic belief and worship. WYCLIFF and HUSS assisted for laying foundation for REFORMATION.

DOGMATISM was BOMBSHELLED by the colonization of strong countries over weak countries. The result was that vanity selfishness or ambition of individual rulers and dynasties plunged Europe in one after another.

HENCE NATIONAL AGGRANDIZMENT BEGAN TO REPLACE RELIGIOUS DISSENSION. ABSOLUTISM AND DEVINE RIGHT KINGS PROCLAIMED THEMSELVES TO THE SOLE SOURCE OF AUTHORITY IN SEVENTH CENTURY RELINQUISHED OF THEMSELVES OF THE TITLE. Their title I AM THE STATE became the SERVANT OF STATE.

RUSSIA under the rule of PETER THE GREAT (1689-1725) became free from MONGOLE and SCANDINAVI A and BYZANTINE EMPIRE AND DRESSED WITH MODERN TEXTURE.

After 1683 the boundaries of European Turkey gradually receded. Russian Merchant ship receive right of free navigation in the Black Sea and access through the BOSPOROUS AND DARDEMELLES CATHERINE TO THE MEDITERRNEAN. By this, PETER opened another window on Europe.

9.2.11 ECONOMICS:

Most European statesmen at this time accepted the principles of mercantile system, which was economic doctrine enlightening the importance of manufacturers and foreign trade. Large and flourishing colonies seemed essential to the success of mercantile system. Colonies were viewed simply as estates to be worked for the advantage of the country fortunate enough to them.

In 16 and 17 century French and English besides Portugal, Spain and Holland became principal competitors for Indian Trade and control of region half large as Europe. The conquest of India was made possible by the decline of MOGHUL (or MONGOL) which had been founded by Turkish Chieftain BABER in 16 century.

English men under Tudors colonized the New World—AMERICA. Dutch colony of New Netherland soon passed in the hands of English and became New York.

9.2.12. AMERICAN REVOLUTION:

Restrictions on colonial manufacturers and commerce, heavy taxation on colonies gave birth to GREAT REVOLUTION by local Americans. The American War of Independence enabled to form itself as UNITED STATES IF AMERICA in 1776. And this settling for the UNALIENABLE RIGHTS OF MAN as against federal oppression provided an ardent spirit in France with a formula of LIBERTY and thus gave birth of another great revolution called FRENCH REVOLUTION, in 1789.

Early in 19 century still another revolutionary movement stripped SPAIN and PORTUGAL of all their continental possession in the World. All these are the brain children of American Revolution.

Great Britain soon found least partial compensation for the loss of 13 colonies in the colony of Australia and islands of the PACIFIC. The vast ocean covering more than one third of the Globe, remained little known to Europeans until later part of 18 century.

Magellan's voyage, Thomas cooks discovery of HAWAIIAN ISLANDS established a regular commercial route between Mexico and Philippines gradually discovered ARCHEPELAGOES which stood intervening seas. Two such discoveries were Great South land, NEW HOLLAND, VANDIEMENS LAND, TASMANIA, NEWZEALAND, HAWAII ISLANDS AND ALASKA respectively. These Geographical discoveries of Newlands made 18th century as an age of ENLIGHTENMENT. THE AGE OF DOGMAS ENDED AND REBIRTH OF CONSPICUOUSLY AN AGE OF REASON AND ENLIGHTMENT TOOK PLACE.

Rationalization also invaded politics. To say that all government exists or should exist by the CONSENT OF THE GOVERNED is to set up the DOCTRINE OF SOVERIGNITY. PHILOSOPHERS LIKE VOLTAIR, MONTESQUE, ROUSSUE (1762) CHANGED OR SAY REMOVED THE ARTIFICIAL MASK FROM THE FACES OF PEOPLE IN GENERAL AND RULERS IN PARTICULAR BY THEIR REVOLUTIONARTY SLOGAN—EQUALITY—FRATERNITY—LIBERTY.

If VOLTAIR WAS THE DESTROYER OF THE OLD, ROUSSE WAS THE PROPHET OF NEW. He loved a picture what supposed once the STATE OF NATURE before Government had arisen before the STRONG BEGUN OPPRESS THE WEAK, when nobody owned the land and when there were no taxes and no wars. BACK TO THE NATURE WAS THE ROUSSEU'S CRY. In his book SOCIAL CONTRACT he states that MAN WAS BORN FREE AND EVERY WHERE HE IS IN CHAINS. He wanted to describe purely ideal state of society in which CITIZENS ARE RULED NEITHER BY KINGS NOR BY PARLIAMENT, BUT THEMSELVES MAKE LAWS DIRECTLY. The only way to form the world according to ROUSSEE was to restore the SOVERIGNITY OF THE PEOPLE WITH LIBERTY AND EQUALITY.

9.2.13. FRENCH REVOLUTION:

ROUSSEU, VOLTAIR and MONTESQUIEU were among the contributors for famous ENCYCLOPEDIA a work in 17 volumes which appeared after the middle of the 18 century. The Encyclopedia took measures to secure religions toleration to relieve poverty to encourage scientific research. The immediate effect of this Encyclopedia in all over Earth including Russia, Australia, Europe and Spain despotism became BENEVELANT and Even Despotism finally culminated in French Revolution (1789-1799). French Revolution affected Globally and the result was of Revolt of Nations (1808-1814) which were under British control and finally ended into DEMOCRATIC MOVEMENT IN EUROPE (1815-1848), Dynasties became victims of Democracy and National constitutional assemblies formed in the world. PEASANTS BECAME PARLIAMENTARIANS. American War of independence ended in becoming first Democratic country. United Kingdom of England and its empire was liquidated in to individual nations during 19 century.

CONSTITUTIONS, CHARTERS were formed for administration for local self Governments. FRENCH REVOLUTION CREATED HISTORY WITHIN THE HISTORY OF THE WORLD. Democracy prevailed all over the world except in certain Islamic countries where Monarchy still exists. However in these countries like Egypt, Syria, Yemen, Libya etc. recently revolts have been started for common man getting himself converted in to parliamentarian. Balkan wars (1912-13) released Greece from the control of Turks, became free under the treaty of Paris.

Russia and China became Socialists and communist under the influence of KARLMAX. The dismemberment of Ottoman Empire, the powers of Sultan gave grudging consent and new State of RUMAANIA came into existence.

Further the treaty between Russia and Turkey gave birth to the creation of Greater Bulgaria stretching from the Danube to AEGEAN including MACEDONIA. In the year 1908 saw also revolution in sultans dominations. The work of YOUNGTURKS, a group of Patriotic reformers who aimed to modernize OTTOMON EMPIRE. They were not only

Nationalists but also democrats. Just as Russian policy was one of RUSSIFICATION so also that young Turks was of OTTAMANISATION.

The Great Britain, France, Dutch. And Spain also granted independence to their colonies and opened scope to become Independent Nations like RHODESIA, SOUTH AFRICA, and many AFRICAN COUNTRIES. Opening up and partitions in Asia also left a gate way for the countries like India, China, Japan, Myanmar etc. for becoming politically Independent. However China became Communist while India became a democratic and secular country after giving birth to new countries like Pakistan, Bangladesh, Nepal from its womb. China and India are becoming super powers in the forth coming period despite their over populous in kind. The great wonders of GREAT WALL OF CHAINA AND TAJ MAHAL MADE CHAINA AND INDIA left their signature on the Historical heritage of the WORLD MAP

Similarly CANADA, LATIN AMERICA, NEW ZEALAND, PHILLIPPINES, FORMOSA, MALASIA, MICRONESIA, POLYSIA, declared themselves AS SEPARATE NATIONS after getting DECHAINED from European clutches. Simon de BOLIVAR WHO REVOLTED AGAINST SPAIN AND FREED VENIZULA, BOLIVIA and PERU ONE BY ONE ALL COLONIES IN South America together with central America and Mexico threw the SPANISH YOKE and TRANSFORMED BRAZIL in to republic. This revolt produced seven independent states in South America, URUGUAY, Great Columbia, Brazil, Argentina and Peru. All these republics formed democracy along with MIXICO in 1821.

Further, the expansion of United States beyond the limits fixed by Treaty of PARIS in 1738, began to purchase of the LOUSIANA, territory between MISSISSIPI river and Rocky mountains during 1803 for sum of 15000,000 dollars. ALASKA which was a province of Russia was also purchased by U.S. for 7200000 dollars in 1867. In the last decades of 19 century the HAWAIIAN Islands lying about two thousand miles off the coast of COLUMBIA were annexed by 1898. After the MANROE DOCTRINE America for Americans became the slogan of Americans and declared that American continents were hence forth NOT TO BE CONSIDERED BY ANY EUROPEAN POWERS. The water way PANAMA CANAL was bought for 40 million dollars.

THUS THE END OF COLONIAL EXPANSION AND WORLD POLITICS.

Chapter x
SOCIAL AND ECONOMIC PERSPECTIVE

10.1 Introductory:

Man is by nature a social animal. His primitive life was dependent mainly on his basic needs like procurement of food, resorting to shelter to spend leisure life, satisfying of his sexual demand, accommodate himself for a suitable accommodation depending upon the weather conditions, to get himself saved from natural calamities, to invent accessible armaments to hunt animals whenever he deem fit to meet food shortage or in occasions of competition to struggle himself either for the sake of his survival or for the sake of his spouse and children. Thus his prehistoric life passed through only to meet these goals and not for anything else. To be short he struggled for HIS Survival only. This is similar when compared with his subordinate animals. But, however, his life never stood on that point only because he is surrounded by many other fellow beings competition to meet his basic needs generated both between himself and his family but also with others. Population of human beings multiplied and naturally inter-dependability started among themselves, and inter-dependability raised occasion for social existence. As social existence is a child of herd instinct. Herd instinct necessitated a leader for governance, and this governance gave birth to dictation and the dictator must be stronger enough to overrule others. Here where the competition, ambition, greed rivalry started and this gives birth to another struggle, struggle not for existence but struggle for supremacy. Mean while craze after wealth and faith in unknown being entered the arena and divided the societies in to groups and groups became cultures and traditional sects. Thus cultures and sects turned into races and ethnics. Humanity masked with ideals of Good and evil which further divided human society in to tribes and tribes into civilizations and civilizations into sects and sects into state and finally shaped into countries. Capitalist Countries with their entrepreneur skills intended to expand their trade colonized other countries with an intention of market their products and gain commercial dictation. Again one more struggle waged among human kind for the survival of commercial growth. Thus societies, cultures, states, countries and even continents became battle field for gaining supremacy among humans. That is what we have studied in historical perspective in the earlier chapter. Human intelligence also has cold war among its possessors hence study of various fields of Knowledge of both Social and Physical sciences is necessitated hereunder and also to know how to eradicate and wipe out this cold war among mankind itself. Let us begin with the very fundamental subject i.e. SOCIAL SCIENCE AFTER WHICH HUMAN BEING CALLED AS SOCIAL ANIMAL:

10.1.1: SOCIOLOGY:

Sociology is the study of Society and human social actions. Sociology derived from Greek and the term "Soci" which is from the Latin word 'Socious' meaning companion or society in general. Sociology was originally established by AUGUST COMPTE (1798-1857) in 1838. COMPTE endeavored to unify history, Psychology and economics through descriptive understanding of social realm. He proposed that social life 'ILLS' could be remedied through Sociological positivism, an epistemological approach. Though COMPTE is generally regarded as "father of Sociology" EMILE DURKHEIM (1858-1917) developed positivism as foundation to practical social research. At the turn of 20 century the first wave of German Sociologists including MAX WEBER and GEORGE SIMMEL developed sociological anti positivism, Marxist historical materialism and conflict theory. Sociology evolved as an academic response to the challengers of Modernity, such as industrialization, urbanization secularization and received process of enveloping rationalization. The field generally concern the social rules and processes that bind and separate people not only as individuals but as members of associations, groups, communities and institutions and includes the examinations of organization and development of human Social life.

10.1.2. ECONOMICS:

Economics is a social science that seeks to analyze and describe the production, distribution and consumption of wealth. The Economics is from Greek word 'IKOS' family household and estate, and 'NOMOS' "custom, law and means house hold management or the management of the State. The classic brief definition of economics, set out by LIONEL ROBBINS in 1032 is the "Science which studies human behavior as a relation between scarce means having alternative uses. Without scarcity and alternative uses there is no economic problem. To sum up it is "the study of how people get to satisfy needs and wants and "the study of financial aspects of human behavior".

Economics has two broad branches "Micro economics" where unit of analysis is the individual agent such as house hold or firm, and "Macro Economics" where the unit of analysis is an economy as a whole. Economic reasoning has been increasingly applied in recent decades to other social situations such as politics, marriage and family life, law, history, psychology, religion and other social interactions.

There are some heterodox schools of thought such as Institutional Economics' "Green economics' 'Marxist Economics' and 'Economic sociology'. For example Marxist economics assumes that economics primarily deals with the exchange value and labor (human effort) is the source of value. The expanding domain of economics in the social science has been described as economic imperialism.

10.1.3: PSYCHOLOGY:

Psychology is an academic and applied field involving the study of behavior and mental process. Psychology differs from Anthropology, economics, political science and sociology in seeking to capture explanatory generalization about mental function and OVERT behavior of individuals. Psychology differs from biology and neuroscience in that it is primarily concerned with interaction of mental process and behavior and overall process themselves though the subfield of neuropsychology combines the study of actual neuro processes with a study of the mental effects they have subjectively produced. In reality, Psychology has myriad specialties including social psychology, Developmental psychology, cognitive psychology, mathematical psychology, neuropsychology and quantitative Analysis of behavior to name only few. The Word 'psychology comes from ancient Greek PSYCHE (soul or Mind) and 'ology' means study. Although some sub-fields encompass a natural science base and a social application, others can be clearly distinguished as having little to do with social science or having lot do with social sciences.

10.1.4 INDUSTIAL REVOLUTION:

The year 1776, the year of declaration of Independence and Adam smith' "WEALTH OF NATIONS" also marks approximately the commencement of Industrial revolution. No other word except revolution so well describes the wholesale change in manufacturing, Transportation and other Industries which within a century and half transformed Modern life. This revolution in Great Britain, spread after 1815 to the continent and United States and now extends throughout civilized world. Improvements in Means, Transportation, Rail Roads, canals, steam navigation, by facilitating travel permitted into other continents.

The Industrial Revolution also created numerous body of wage earners, moved from rural districts and villages into factories, sweat shapes and tenements of great cities. There they learned gradually the value of organization. They formed trade unions in order to secure higher wages and shorter hours. They read news papers and pamphlets listened to speeches by agitators, see Televisions and began to press laws which would improve their lot. Then they want further and demanded the right to vote, to hold office, to enjoy all the Liberty and equality and Fraternity which the BOURGEOSIS or Middle class had won from the monarchs and aristocrats. The Industrial revolution furnished much of driving power for the democratic movement which has been so marked in Europe during 19century.

It thus reinforced the new ideas of democracy introduced into the world by American and French Revolution. The Industrial Revolution fostered national movement in Europe during the last century. Rail Roads, Air routes, voyage routes telephone and telegraph Televisions, cell phones Computers and internets have been compared to a net work of VEINS AND ARTERIES CARRYING THE BLOOD OF NATION

FROM CAPITAL TO THE REMOTE PROVINCE, COUNTRIES TO CONTINENTS such as increased facilities for travel and communications inevitably caused the disappearance of local prejudices and provincial limitation along with cultural, traditional and religious barriers. It was now for easier for the people of each country to realize their common interest then when they lived isolated.

10.1.5. FACTORY SYSTEM:

The workers on the other hand to accept wages and labour upon such conditions as he was willing to offer. The separation of labor and capital, which thus begun under domestic system became complete under the factory system. The capitalist employer now not only provided the raw material and disposed of finished product, but he also owned machinery and the workshop. The word MANUFACTURER no longer applied to the hand worker but to the person who employed other to work for him.

10.1.6 DIVISION OF LABOR:

The factory system introduced a minute division of labor into industry. Thus there are forty operations involved in the manufacturer of ready-made clothing, nearly one hundred in the manufacturing the shoes and over thousand in the construction of fine watch. Many men working together may turnout in a few minutes an article which one man formerly required week or months to provide. Machinery, the factory system and the division of labor made it possible to manufacture on a large scale and the enormous qualities for the worldwide market. It is, however the advent of computers would lessen the number of labors in the modern day.

Improvement of transportation and communication made further reduced the supply of manufactured goods to place with the consumer. Another important improvement in this system of production is commerce. Exchange system banking shareholding sole and partnership business, rendering interest system payment of wages developed.

10.1.7 AGRICULTURE:

Improvement in agriculture have now extended to every progressive country. Machinery replaced the ancient SCYTHE, SICKLE, FLAIL and other implements. One machine of American invention, not only reaps the grain, but threshes it, winnows it and delivers it into sacks at single operation Introduction of cheap artificial fertilizer make profitable cultivation of poor lands formerly allow to lie idle.

10.1.8 Labor movement:

disappearance of craft guilds, rise of trade unions, prohibition of trade unions, labor laws, regulation of Industry by Government, public entrepreneurship, local self government Municipality) enterprise, state enterprise and defining LAISSEZ-FAIRE allowed mankind to improve their life style.

10.1.9 KARL MAX (1818-`1883):

Mean while new socialism, more systematic and practical than old began to be developed by German thinkers. Its' chief architect was KARL MAX whose famous work 'Das capita' profoundly influenced human thought and action. To put in its simple form "MARXISM asserts that while labor is the source of value, laborers receive in fact only a fraction of what they produce and all the rest goes to the Capitalist BEURGEOSIE or middle class who produce nothing except investment or Agency" Capitalism however is the inevitable result of factory system. Like feudalism it forms a necessary stage in the development of MANKIND.

10.1.10 POLITICAL SYSTEM:

SOCIALISTIC TYPE: To erase the title "peasant or common man or labor or mass" a socialist movement clubbed with communism started whose demand include:

(i)   The state shall own and operate the instrument of production that island and capital where personal income would disappear;

(ii) The leisure class shall be eliminated by requiring everybody to perform useful labor either physical or mental;

(iii) the income of state shall be distributed as wages and salaries among workers, according to some fairer principle than practiced at present.

Socialism is the byproduct of Industrial revolution. The gulf between the Capitalism and wage earning PROLETRIAT became wider. The contrast between and rich poor became sharper, than ever before. Though wealth was now produced than earlier ages, but it was still unequally distributed. THE FEW HAD TOO MUCH, THE MANY HAD TOO LITTLE. Radical reformists distressed by this inequality and began to proclaim wholesale reconstruction of Society. This resulted in COOPERATION MOVEMENT which is a child of Socialism. National workshop began to provide Capital by state.

THE SOCIALIST DEMOCRATIC PARTY: Under the rule of BISMARK, Germany prohibited Socialist literature. He implemented strict fines imprisonment for Socialists. However, prosecution failed to check the movement which grew phenomenally. In this context, the SOCIALIST DEMOCRATIC PARTY PROVIDED A MODEL for similar organization of Marxism, in Britain, France, Italy, Australia, Russia and other European countries as well as United States and China and Japan. In 1914 the Socialist through out the world polled about eleven million votes and elected over seven hundred represented to the various parliaments.

10.1.11 POLITICAL SICENCE:

Aristotle a great Philosopher asserted that man is a POLITICAL ANIMAL in his book 'POLITICS' Political Science is an academic and research discipline that deals with the theory and practice of politics and descriptive analysis of Political systems and political behavior. Fields and sub-fields of political Science include positive political economy, political theory and political civics and comparative politics, theory of direct democracy, APOLITICAL governance, participatory democracy, national systems, cross-national political analysis, political development, international relations, foreign policy, international law and politics, public administrative behavior. Political Science also studies Global relations and theory of Great super power. HERBERT BAXTER ADAMS is credited with coining the phrase "Political Science" while teaching history at Johns Hopkins University. There are empirical methods include Survey, research, Statistical analysis, econometrics, case studies, experiments and model building.

Types of Regimes: Political Scientists refer regimes using different terms. Which term political Scientists use often depends on two factors—the number of people with political power and the amount of power the Government itself exists.

P O L I T I C A L G O V E R N A N C E
(TYPES, REGIMES, AND HOLDER OF POWERS)

Type of regime	Number of people hold power	Example
MONARCHY	ONE	Saudi Arabia, Brunei, Oman, UAE etc.
DICTATORSHIP	ONE	Libya, Cuba, North Korea
ARISTOCRACY	A few casually small ruling class	Ancient Sparta.
OLIGARCHY	A few usually, wealthy	Renaissance Venice.
DEMOCRACY	Many or all	United States, India, European countries old Athens.
TOTALITARIAN	Absolute power by all citizens	Soviet union(present Russia) North Korea Nazi Germany.
AUTOCRATIC	Less powerful than Totalitarian regime still arbitrary control of citizens under single ruler.	Iraq before 2003
CONSTITUTIONAL	Limited specific rulers such as citizens' right or freedom of religion	United States United Kingdom, India, Germany, Japan,
ANARCHIST	No power or no Government	somalia.

DEMOCRACY:

The word Democracy comes from the Greek word 'demo' means The people and 'cracy' means "rule by". Today we call a regime a democracy when many or all its people share political power. There are two types of democracies: (i) Direct democracy: citizens make all decisions. They gather frequently to vote on Laws regulations and appointments. They are all representatives. Direct democracy was common in ancient Greece; today at all local level in town hall meetings held throughout the United states (ii)Representative democracy: citizens elect officials to act on their behalf. If the Office holders disappoint or anger them, citizens can choose new officials at the next election. A regime that runs by representative democracy called as REPUBLIC. In republic citizen hold power. Again there two types of Democracies (a) PARLIAMENTRY DEMOCRACY: Citizen elects legislators. The legislature then elects the executive (frequently called Prime minister) from its members. Example, Many European democracies use parliamentary system. One advantage of this type of democracy is ability quickly respond to public opinion. If the Prime Minister loose the confidence of voters, new election can be held immediately. But parliamentary governments can be unstable perhaps the classic example is ITALY, which changed Government about once a year for fifty years following World war II (b)PRESIDENT TYPE OF DEMOCRACY: Citizen elect officials to act as legislatures. The Legislature then directly elect Executive.: Example: The U.S. is presidential type of democracy. Although a presidential system can be slow to respond to change in public opinion it is likely to be more stable than Parliamentary system. All democracies in theory should provide four basic things: SECURITY, LIBERTY, and POLITICAL EQUALITY AND POPULAR SOVERGNITY.

10.1.12 PUBLIC ADMINISTRATION:

Public Administration though, is one of the branches of Political Science, can be broadly described as the development and study of branches of Government policy. The pursuit of public good by enhancing civil society and social Justice is the ultimate goal of the field. It is the Government protocol to solve a public problem and also the making of public policies including the enforcement of such and the tools given to the institutions to do so.

The Public administrators find themselves serving as parole officers, Secretaries, note takers, paperwork processors, record keepers, notaries of the public, cashiers and managers. Indeed, the discipline coupled with many vocational fields such as information Technology, finance, law and engineering where public Administrator involved necessarily.

10.1.13 EDUCATION AND LAW AND OTHER FIELDS:

Education encompasses teaching and learning specific skills and also something less tangible but more profound the imparting knowledge, positive judgment and well developed wisdom. To educate means to draw out from the Latin 'EDUCARE' or to facilitate the realization of an individual potential and talents. The education of an individual human beings at birth and continues throughout life.

(ii) LAW: Unlike the rule of ethics, law in common concept means rule which is capable of enforcement through Institution. It has been defined "as a system of rules" as an imperative concept to achieve justice, as an authority to mediate peoples interests as well as the command of Governance, backed by the threat of sanction. Laws are politics since politicians create them. Law is philosophy because moral and ethical persuasions shape their ideas. The noun LAW derives from the old English 'LAGU' meaning something laid down or fixed and the adjective legal comes from LATIN word 'LEX'

OTHER FIELDS OF SOCIAL SCIENCES:

ARCHAEOLOGY: It is the Science that studies human culture.

BEHAVIORAL SCIENCE: Is a term that encompasses all the activities and interactions among organisms in the natural world.

COMMUNICATION SCIENCE: It studies with process of communication, commonly defined as the sharing of symbols over distance in space and time to create meaning.

DEMOGRAPHY: is the statistical study of all population.

DEVELOPMENT STUDIES: A multidisciplinary branch of social science which addresses issues of concern to developing countries.

ENVIRONMENTAL SOCIAL SCIENCE: is the transdisciplinary study of interrelation between humans and natural environment.

JOURNALISM: Is the craft of conveying news descriptive material and comment via widening spectrum of media.

LEGAL MANAGEMENT: Is a social management that designed for students interested in the study of State and legal elements.

LIBRARY SCIENCE: is an interdisciplinary field that applies the practices, perspectives and tools of management, information technology, education and other areas of libraries, the collection and organization preservation and dissemination of information sources and the political economy of information.

MATHEMATICS: arithmetic, geometry and algebra had been studied in the schools and universities of middle ages. It remained to create higher mathematics including analytical geometry, logarithms, the theory of probabilities and infinitesimal calculus. Knowledge of calculus deals with quantities infinitely small has been immense service and even formed base for engineering and other applied science. Calculus was discovered by German LEIBNIZ (1646-1716) and ISSAC NEWTON (1642-1727)

LINGUISTICS: Linguistic investigates the cognitive and social shape of human language. The field is divided into areas that focus on aspects of linguistic signals such as SYNTAX(the study of rules that govern the structure of sentences), SEMANTICS(the study of meaning) MORPHOLOGY(the study of the of the structure of words) PHONETICS(the study of speech sounds) PHONOLOFY(the study of abstract sound system of particular language), EVOLUTIONARY LINGUISTICS(the study of the origins and evolution of language) and PSYCHO LINGUISTICS(the study of psychological factors in human language)

FERDINAND DE SASSURE recognized as the father of modern linguistics. NOAM CHOMSKY has further influenced for aiming at formulating theories of cognitive processing of language. However, language does not exist in vacuum or only in the brain and approaches like contact linguistics, social international linguistics and socio linguistics explore the language in its social context.

Science is intellectual activity carried on by humans that is designed to discover information about the natural world in which humans live and to discover the ways in which this information can be organized into meaningful patterns. A primary aim of science is to collect facts (data). An ultimate purpose of science is to discern the order that exists between and amongst the various facts.

Fiction is about the suspension of disbelief;

Science is about the suspension of belief.

Science is the most subversive thing that has been devised by man. It is a discipline in which the rules of the game require the under mining of that which already exists, in the sense that new knowledge always necessarily crowds out inferior antecedent knowledge . . . This is what is patent system is all about . . . The history of the physical Science is replete with episode after episode in which discoveries of science, subversive as they were because they undermined existing knowledge, had a hard time achieving acceptability and respectability. Galileo was forced to recant; Bruno was burned at the stake; and so forth. An interesting thing about the physical science is that they did achieve acceptance. Certainly in the more economical advanced areas of the western world, it has become common place to do everything possible to accelerate the undermining of existent knowledge about physical world. The underdeveloped areas of the world today still live in a pre-newtounianian universe. They are still resistant to anything subversive, anything requiring change, resistant even to that would change their basic concept of the physical world.

Philip Morris Hauser—1909

Chapter XI
NATURAL SCIENCES: HUMAN PRIDE

SCIENTIFIC METHOD: It is a technique for investigating acquiring new knowledge. Or correcting and integrating previous knowledge. To be termed SCIENTIFIC a method of enquiry must be based on empirical and measurable evidence subject to specific principle of reasoning.

Oxford English Dictionary says that "Scientific method is a procedure that has characterized natural science since 17 century consisting of systematic observation, measurement and experiment and the formulation testing and modification of hypothesis"

Scientific inquiry is generally intended to be as objective as possible in order to reduce biased interpretations of results. This practice is called" Full disclosure" and also allows statistical measures of reliability of these data to be established.

As noted by William Whew ell (1794-1866) "invention", "sagacity" "genius" ARE REQUIRED AT EVERY STEP. Following are steps adopted in Scientific method to establish a fact:

(i) formulation of a question;
(ii) Hypothesis;
(iii) Prediction (inference);
(iv) Test;
(v) Analysis.

Further four basic elements of Scientific method are illustrated by the following example from the discovery of the structure DNA(DEOXY RIBO NUCLEIC ACID); (i) DNA characterization(observation, definition, measurement); (ii) DNA Hypothesis(theoretical, hypothetical explanation of observation); (iii) DNA experiment(tests of all the above)

The examples are continued in evaluations and iterations with DNA iteration.

The Scientific process also include other components required even when all the iterations of the steps above been completed (i) Replication (ii) External review (Data recording and sharing)

For essential elements of Scientific method are further elaborated into:

(i) Define a question; (ii) Gather information and resources(observation) (iii) form an explanatory hypothesis; (iv) Test the hypothesis by performing an experiment and collecting data in a reproducible manner; (v) analyze the data (vi) Interpret the data and draw conclusions that serve as starting point for new hypothesis (vii) Publish results and (viii) Retest.

11.1.1 BIOLOGICAL Science:

Biology literally means "the study of life" It is a such a broad field, covering the minute working of chemical mechanics inside our cells, broad scale concepts of echo systems and global climate change. Biologists study innate details of human brain, the composition of our genes and even functioning of reproductive systems. Biologists recently all but completed the deciphering of human 'genome' the sequence of DNA bases may determine much of our innate capabilities and predispositions to certain forms of behavior and illness. DNA sequences have played major roles in criminal cases. (O.J. Simpson, President of US Bill Clinton and N.D. Tiwari, Former Governor of A.P India were detected as criminals on account of DNA and there are several cases to spell out). The central dogma explains the influence of heredity (DNA) on the organism (proteins). Modern biology on several great ideas or theories which include:(i) The cell theory; (ii) The theory of evolution by natural selection (iii) Gene theory and (iv) Homeostasis.

THE CELL THEORY: Robert Hooke (1635-1703) one of the first Scientists to use microscope to examine pond water, cork, and other things to the cavities he saw in cork as "CELLS". MATTIAS SHHLEIDEN (in 1839) concluded all plant tissues consisted of cells. RUDOLF VIRCHOW in 1858 combined ideas and added that cells come from preexisting cells, formulating the cell theory. The theory states that all organisms are composed of one or more cells.

American Scientist James Watson and British Scientist Francis Crick developed the model for DNA. Further information from DNA "language" is converted into RNA(ribonucleic acid) language and the language of proteins.

DEVELOPMENT OF THEORY OF EVOLUTION: HISTORY: Ancient Greek philosopher ANAXIAMENDER (611-547BCE) coined the concept that all living things related and they have changed over time. Another Greek Philosopher Aristotle developed his SCALA NATURAE or ladder of life.

MODERN VIEW OF EVOLUTION:

(I)   George-Luis Lecleric comte de Buffon(1707-1839) proposed that species could change,

(II)   (ii) Swedish Botanist Carl Linne(1753) attempted pigeon-hole all known species and conceptualized that now evolution is underlying in growth of species.

(III) (iii) William "STRATA" Smith (1769-1839) fathered the science of statigraphy, the correlation of rock layers based on their fossil contents and also stated that life changed over time.

(IV) (iv) Jean Baptist Delamarck (1744-1829) developed one of the first theories on how species changed.

(V) Iv) Charles Darwin's Theory evolution: In his book on the 'origin of species' by means of natural selection, published in 1859 considered a major breakthrough and guiding theory for modern biology which provide us the basis for the interrelation of all living organisms.

(VI) Scientists have completely identified all world coniferous plants. Biologist have yet to describe many species of plants and lichens. So the number of species known to Science increased substantially every year. However, plants identified by biologists as on date are as listed below:

PLANTS	SPECIES
(i) Flowering plants(angiosperms)	281,821
(ii) Conifers (gymnosperms)	1,021
(iii) Ferns and horsetails	12,000
(iv) Mosses	16,236
(v) Red and green algae	10,134

OTHERS:	
(vi) Lichens	17,000
(vii) Mushrooms	31,496
(viii) Brown algae	3,067
GRAND TOTAL	**372,775**

11.1.2 CHEMICAL SCIENCE:

The word CHEMISTRY COMES FROM THE ALCHEMY. The Word 'alchemy' is derived from Arabic "al-kimia" This term was borrowed from Greek and later Chemistry is defined as study of Matter and changes it undergoes (CHANG 1998).

Chemistry is the Science of matter, especially chemical reactions, but also composition, structure and properties. Chemistry is concerned with atoms and their interactions with other atoms and particularly with the properties of chemical bonds. Chemistry is some time called "THE CENTRAL SCIENCE" because it connects with other natural Sciences, such as geology and biology. Though chemistry is a branch of Physical science but distinct from Physics.

HISTORY OF CHEMISTRY: Ancient Egyptians pioneered the art of Synthetic "wet" chemistry up to 4000 years ago. By 1000 BCE ancient civilization using technologies that formed basis of various branches of chemistry such as—extracting metal from their ores, making pottery, fermatic beer and wine, making pigments for cosmetics and painting, extracting chemicals from plants for medicine, making cheese, dying clothes, tanning leather, rendering fat into soap, making glass and making alloys like bronze.

The genesis of chemistry can be traced to the widely observed phenomenon of burning that led to metallurgy, the art and science of processing ores to get metals. The greed to gold led to the discovery of process for its purification, even though the underlying principles were not well understood. However ancient schools believed that there exists, means for transferring cheaper (base) metals into gold. This gave to alchemy and the search for the Philosophers stone which was believed to bring about such transformation by mere touch.

Chemistry as Science was almost created by Muslims of whom Jabir Ibn Hayyan (GEBER-815AD), Al-kindi (873AD) Al Razi(925) Al Biruni (1048) and Al Hazen (1039AD). The contribution of Indian Alchemist and Metallurgists in the development of chemistry was also significant.

Similarly in Europe the influence of Philosophers such as Francis Bacon (1561-1626), RENE DECARTES(1596-1650) demanded more vigor in mathematics and in moving bias from scientific observations led to scientific revolution, In chemistry, this began vigor with Robert Boyle(1627-1691) who came with equation known as BOYLE's Law about the characteristic of gaseous state.

Chemistry indeed came to its age when Antoine Lavoisier (1743-1794) developed the theory of conservation of Mass in 1783 and the development of Atomic Theory of John Dalton around 1800. Lavoisier's Law of conservation of Mass, resulted in the reformation of chemistry along with "Oxygen Theory of Combustion" for which he can be well said as "FATHER OF CHEMISTRY'. The later discovery of FRIED RICH WOHLER that many natural substances, organic compound, can indeed synthesized in a chemistry, laboratory also helped the modern chemistry to mature from its infancy.

BASIC CONCEPTS:

ATOM: An atom is the basic unit of Chemistry which consists of (atomic nucleus) protons and neutrons and which maintain number of electrons to balance the positive charge in the nucleus.

ELEMENT: A chemical element is specially a substance which is composed a single 'atom'. A chemical element is characterized by particular number of protons in the nuclei are atoms of the chemical element. Carbon and all atoms with 92 protons in their nuclei are atoms of the element Uranium. Ninety four different chemical elements or types of atoms based on the number of protons are observed on Earth naturally having one ISOTOPE stable or has a very long half-life. A further 19 elements have been recognized by IUPAC (International Union of Pure and Applied Chemistry) after they have made the laboratory.

COMPUND: A compound is substance with a particular ratio of atoms of particular chemical element for example Water is a compound containing hydrogen and Oxygen in ratio of two to one, and angle 104.5 degrees between them.

SUBSTANCE: A chemical substance is a kind of Matter with definite composition and set of properties. This is set by IUPAC.

MOLECULE: A molecule is the smallest indivisible portion of pure chemical substance that has its unique set of chemical properties, that is potential to undergo a certain set chemical reactions with other substance. One of the main characteristic of molecule is its GEOMETRY often called IS ITS structure.

IONS AND SALTS: An ION is charged species, an atom or molecule that has last or gained one or more electrons.

ACIDITY AND BASICITY: A substance can often be classified as an acid base. According to BRONSTED-LAWRY's acid-base theory acids are substances that donate a positive hydrogen ION to another substance in chemical reaction; by extension.

PHASE: In addition to specific chemical properties that distinguish different chemical classifications chemicals can exist in several PHASES. A PHASE is set of states of a chemical system that have similar bulk of structural properties, over a range of conditions such as pressure or temperature. Less familiar phases include PLASMAS.

BONDING: Atoms sticking together in molecules or crystals are said to be bonded with another.

REACTION: When a chemical substance is transformed as a result of its interaction with another or energy, chemical reactions said to have occurred. Chemical reaction can result in formation or dissociation of molecules. During chemical reactions bonds between atoms break down and form resulting in different substance with different properties. In a blast in furnace, iron-oxide, a compound reacts with carbon monoxide to form iron, one of chemical elements and carbon dioxide.

EQUILIBRIUM: It is possible, in the context of chemistry it arises whenever a number of different states of chemical composition are possible. Chemicals present in biological systems are invariably not at equilibrium; rather they are from equilibrium.

ENERGY: Chemically speaking, energy is an attribute of substance as a consequence of its atomic, molecular or aggregate structure. The speed of chemical reaction (at given temperature-T) is related to the activation of energy-E by the BOTZAMANN population factor e—E/KT that is probability of molecule to have energy than equal to E at the given temperature T.

11.1.3 PHYSICAL SCIENCES:

Physics is often described as the study of matter and energy how both relate to each other; and how they affect each other over time through space.

Physicists may be roughly divided in to two groups: Experimental Physics and Theoretical Physics. Experimental Physicists design and run carefully investigations on a broad range of phenomena in nature, often under conditions which typical of everyday lives. They may for example investigate what happens to the electrical properties of materials at temperature very near absolute zero(460 degrees) or measure the characteristics of energy emitted by hot gases.

Theoretical Physicists proposes and develop models and theories to explain mathematically the results of experimental observations. They have a broad overlap.

Let us distinguish classical Physics and modern Physics. Classical Physics has its origins approximately 400 years ago in the studies of GALILIO and NEWTON on mechanics in the work of Ampere, Faraday and Maxwell 150 years ago in the fields of Electricity and Magnetism. This Physics handles objects which neither too large nor too small which move at relatively slow speeds(at least compared to the speed of light 186,000 miles per second)

The emergence of modern physics at the beginning of 20 century was marked by three achievements.

THE FIRST, in 1905 was EINSTEIN's brilliant model of light as a stream of particles (photons).

THE SECOND was the revolutionary theory of relativity which described objects moving at a speed of close to the speed of light.

THE THIRD breakthrough came in 1910 with Rutherford's discovery of nucleus of the atom. This was followed by BOHR's model of atom which in turn stimulated the work of BROGILE, HEINSBERG, SCHROE-DINGER, BORN, PAULI, DIRAC and others on the QUANTUM THEORY. The avalanche of exciting discoveries in Modern physics continues today. The distinction with in the field of Physics, experimental theoretical, classical and modern has subdivided physics into various disciplines including-astrophysics, atomic-physics and Molecular physics, biophysics, solid physics, solid-state Physics, optical physics and laser physics, fluid and plasma physics nuclear physics and particle physics.

11.1.4 ZOOLOGY:

Zoology is a branch of biology that relates to kingdom including the structure, embryology, evolution, classification and distribution of all animals, both living and extinct. The term is derived from Greek ZO on Means animal(logos "knowledge). Zoological sciences emerged from natural history reaching back to the works of Aristotle and Galen in the ancient Greek-Roman world. The ancient work was further developed in to the middle ages by Muslim Physicians and Scholars such as Albert Magnus. Europe by renewed interest in empiricism and the discovery of many novel organisms. Prominent in this movement were VESALIUS and WILLIAM HARVEY. CARL LINNAAESUS and Buffon who began to classify the diversity of life and the fossil record as well as the development and behavior of organisms. Microscopy revealed the previously unknown world of micro organisms, laying the ground work of cell theory. Over the 18 and 19 centuries, Zoology became an increasingly professional Scientific discipline. Explorer Naturalists such as Alexander Von Humboldt investigated the interaction between organisms and their environment and the way this relationship depends upon geography, thus laying foundations for Bio-Geography Ecology and Ethnology.

CELL THEORY PROVIDED A NEW PERSPECTIVE ON THE FUNDAMENTAL BASIS OF LIFE.

In 1859, Darwin placed a theory of organic Evolution on a new footing, by his discovery of a process by which organic evolution can occur and provided observational evidence that it had done so.

Darwin gave new direction to morphology and physiology by uniting them in a common biological theory, The THEORY OF ORGANIC EVOLUTION. The result was reconstruction of classification of animals upon a genealogical basis, fresh investigation of the development of animals and early attempts to determine their genetic relationship.

SYSTAMATICS: Scientific classification in Zoology is a method by which Zoologists group and categorize organisms by biological type, such as genus or species COROLUS, LINNAEUS grouped species according to shared physical characteristics which was proposed by Darwin. Classification of each animal kingdom connotes Domain Kingdom; PHYLUM; CLASS; ORDER; FAMILY; GENUS; SPECIES. The Scientific name of organism is generated from its genus and Sapiens the species. For example humans are listed as HOMO SAPIANS. Homo is the genus and Sapiens the species.

The dominant classification system is called the LINNAEAN TOXONOMY, which is coded and administered by International code of Zoological Nomenclature (ICZN) and

International Code of Nomenclature of BCTERIA(ICNB) for animals and bacteria respectively. The classification of VIRUSUS, VIROIDS, PRIONS AND ALL OTHER SUB-viral agents that demonstrate biological characteristics are conducted International Code of virus classification and nomenclature (ICVCN).

11.1.5 ETHNOLOGY:

Ethnology studies animal behavior. They are concerned with evolution of behavior and the understanding of behavior in terms of theory of natural selection. The first Modern Ethnologist was Charles Darwin himself whose book THE EXPRESSION OF THE EMOTIONS IN MAN AND ANIMAL, influenced many ethnologists.

Thomas Henry Huxley is modern zoologist and who explained comparative anatomy to include the following disciplines:

(i) Zoology also known as descriptive zoology that describes animals and their habits.

(ii) Comparative anatomy studies the structure of animals—Animal Physiology.

(iii) Behavioral ecology;

(iv) Ethnology (study of animal behavior);

(v) Mamma logy herpetology, ornithology, and entomology are taxonomical oriented disciplines.

(vi) Evolutionary biology;

(vii) Molecular Biology; and

(viii) Paleontology

(ix) Scientist have described over 1,7 million of world s species of animals, plants and algae as of 2010. The list below gives the number of species known in the world for each major categories of animals, birds insects etc.

CATEGORY	SPECIES	TOTAL
Mammals	5,490	
Birds	9,998	
Reptiles	9,084	
Amphibians	6,433	
Fishes	31,300	62,305
Invertebrate Animals:		
Insects	1000,000	
Spiders and Scorpions	102,248	
Mullusecs	85,000	
Crustaceans	47,000	
Corals	2,175	
Others	68,827	1305,250
		1367,555

These species totals do not include domestic animals such as sheep, goats, cows, dogs and single celled organisms.

11.1.7 HUMAN GENETICS:

Human Genetics is the study of inheritance as it occurs in human beings. Human genetics encompasses variety of overlapping fields including:

* Classical Genetics
* Cytogenetic
* Molecular genetics
* Biochemical genetics
* Genomics
* Population genetics
* Developmental genetics
* Clinical genetics and Genetic counseling.

Genes be common factor of the qualities of most inherited traits. Study of human genetics can be useful as it can answer questions about nature, understand the diseases and development of effective disease treatment and understand genetics of human life. The article describes only basic features of human genetics.

Inheritance of are based upon GREGOR MENDEL' MODEL of inheritance. Mendel deduced that inheritance depends upon discrete units of inheritance, called factors or genes.

AUTO SOMAL DOMINANT INHERITANCE: Autosomal are associated with a single gene on an auto some(non-sex chromosome) they are called "dominant" because single copy inherited from either parent—is enough to cause this trait to appear.

X-LINKED AND Y-LINKED INHERITANCE: X linked genes found on the X-Chromosome in X-linked genes just like autos mol genes have both dominant and recessive types. Recessive X-linked disorders are rarely seen in females and usually affect males. This is because male inherit X-chromosome and X-linked genes will be inherited from maternal side. Fathers only pass on their Y—chromosome to their sons, so no X-link trait will be inherited from father to son.

Female express X-linked disorders when they are homozygous for the disorders and became carriers when they are heterozygous. X-linked dominant inheritance will show the same Phenotype as heterozygote and homozygote. Just X-linked inheritance, there will be a lack of male-to male inheritance which makes it distinguishable from autos mol traits. One example of a X-linked trait is Coffin-Lowry Syndrome which is caused by a mutation in ribosomal protein gene. This mutation results in skeletal Craniofacial abnormalities, mental retardation and short stature.

X-chromosomes in female undergo a process known as X-inactivation is when the two X-chromosomes in female is almost completely inactivated. The mechanism for X-inactivation will occur during the embryonic stage. For people with disorders like TRISOMY X, where the genotype has three X-chromosomes, X-inactivation will inactive all X chromosomes until there is only one X chromosome active. X-chromosome active X inactivation is only limited to female, males with KLINE FELTER SYNDROME, who have an extra X-chromosome will also undergo X-inactivation to have only one completely active chromosome.

Y-linked inheritance occur when a gene trait or disorders is transformed through Y chromosome. Since Y chromosome can only be found in Males. Y linked traits are only passed from father to son. The test is determining factor, which is located on the Y chromosome, determines the maleness of the individual. Beside maleness is inherited in Y chromosome then there are no other found Y-linked characteristics.

PEDIGREES: A PEDIGREE diagram showing the ancestral relationship and transmission of genetic traits over several generations in a family.

KARYOTYPE: IS VERY USEFUL tool in Cytogenetic. It is a picture of all the chromosomes in the METAPHASE stage arrange according to length center mere position. It is also useful in clinical genetic, due to its ability to diagnose genetic disorder.

GENOMICS: It refers to the field of genetic concerned with structural and functional studies of genome. A genome is all the DNA contained within an organism or cell including nuclear and MITOCHONDRIAL DNA. The human genome is the total collection of genes in a human being contained in the chromosome composed of over three million nucleotide. In April 2003 the HUMAN GENOME PROJECT was able to sequence all the DNA in the human genome and to discover that human genome was composed of around 20,000 protein coding genes.

POPULATION GENETIC: It is a branch of evolutionary biology responsible for investigating process that cause changes in ALLELE AND GENO TYPE frequencies in population based upon MENDEELIAN INHERITANCE. Four different forces can influence to frequencies. (i) Natural selection(ii) mutation (iii) gene flow and (iv) genetic drift. A population can defined as a group of interbreeding individual and their off spring. For human genetics the population will consist only the human species. The HARDY-WEINBERG PRINCIPLE is widely used principle to determine allelic and genotype frequencies.

HARDY-WEINBERG PRINCIPLE: The principle states that no evolution occurs in population, the allele and genotype frequencies do no change from one generation to he next, no natural selection and genetic drift.

X-LINKED TRAITS: Sex linkage is the phenotypic expression of an allele related to the chromosomal sex of the individual. This mode of inheritance is the contrast to the inheritance of trait on autosomal chromosomes, where both sexes have the same probability of inheritance. Since both sexes have the same probability of inheritance. Since human have many more genes on the X than Y, there are many more X-linked traits than Y-linked traits. However females carrying two or more copies of the X chromosome resulting in potentially toxic dose X-linked gene. To correct this imbalance, Mammalian females have evolved unique mechanism of dosage compensation. In X-Chromosome interaction female mammals transcriptional silence one of their two Xs in complex and highly coordinated manner.

11.1.8 BLOOD TYPE:

A blood type is also called a Blood group which is a classification of blood based on the presence or absence of inherited antigenic substance on the surface of red blood cells(RBC). These antigens may be proteins, carbohydrates, glycol-proteins or glycolipids, depending on the blood group system. Some of these antigens are also present on the surface of other types of cells of various tissues. Several of these red blood cell surface antigens can stem from allele(or closely linked genes) and collectively form a blood group systems. Blood types are inherited and represent contributions form both parent. A total of 30 human blood group systems are recognized as on date by the INTERNATIONAL SOCIETY OF BLOOD TRANSFUSION (ISBT)

CHAPTER XII
HUMAN CREDENTIALITY
(Medical Science)

12.1 MEDICAL SCIENCE:

In ancient times medicine and religion were closely connected. The priests were the custodians of public health since the propriety of human sickness regarded as diving retribution and God could affect the cure. Great demands were made by the priests to maintain ethical standards to prevent illness. The main contribution of pre-medical period lied not much in treatment of illness rather in the prevention of disease and the care of community health. The hygienic measures advocated were of practical as well as of religious. A principal which recur number of times is that "bodily cleanliness leads to spiritual cleanliness". Hygienic regulation applied among other things to town planning, climatic conditions, social community life, family life and care of the body. The importance of medicine and physicians among Jews and Europeans even Indians is best seen in the long line of rabbi-physician, Jewish physician translator that medical knowledge of the East and much ancient Greek medical lore preserved and transmitted to the west.

12.1.1 HUMAN BODY:

It is entire structure of human organism and consists of HEAD, NECK, TORSO, ARMS AND LEGS. By the time human reaches adulthood the body consist of close to 100 trillion cells, the basic unit of life. These cells are organized biologically to eventually form the whole body.

The organ system of the body include the MUSCULO SKELETAL SYSTEM, CARDIOVASCULAR SYTEM, DIGESTIVE SYSTEM, ENDOCRINE SYSTEM, INTEGUMENTARY SYSTEM, URINARY SYSTEM, LYMPHATIC SYSTEM, IMMUNE SYSTEM, RESPIRATORY SYSTEM, NERVOUS SYSTEM AND REPRODUCTIVE SYSTEM.

THE SKELETAL SYSTEM(Bones): There are 206 bones in skeletal system of an adult. Bones of hands and feet alone constitutes 50% of total bones in the human body:

(i)   a new born baby has 300 bones, out of which 94 bones fuse together as it grows;

(ii) The largest bones of human body is the femur in the thing which constitutes about 27.5% of a person's stature, average length of this bone about 50 cm; and

(iii) The shortest bone in the human body is the stirrup bone in the middle ear.

COMPOSITION OF BONE

Organic matter———————	33.30%
Phosphate of lime———————	51.04%
Corborate of lime———————	11.30%
Florida of calcium———————	2.00%
Phosphate of Magnesia————	1.16%
Soda chloride of sodium————	1.00%

HUMAN SKELETON AND LIST OF BONES OF HUMAN SKELETON

HUMAN BODY	NUMBER BONES
SPINE AND VERBRAL COLUMN	26
CRANIUM	8
FACE	14
UPPER EXTREMITIES	70
LOWER EXTREMITIES	62
Total	206

CARDIO VASCULAR SYSTEM:

It contain heart, Veins, arteries, and capillaries. Primary function of heart is to circulate blood and through blood oxygen and vital minerals are transferred to the tissues and organs that comprise the body. The left side of main organ (left ventricle and left atrium) is responsible for pumping blood to all parts of body, while the right side (right ventricle and right atrium) pumps only to the lungs for re oxygenation of the blood. The heart itself is divided into three layers called the ENDOCARDIUM, MYOCARDIUM and EPICARDIUM (liquidation) which vary in thickness and function.

DIGESTIVE SYSTEM:

The digestive system provides the body means of processing food and transforming nutrients in to ENERGY. The digestive system consists of the buccal cavity, ESOPHAGUS, STOMACH, SMALL INTESTINE, LARGE INTESTINE ending in the RECTUM AND ANUS. These parts together are called the ALIMENTARY CANAL (Digestive track)

CONSTITUENTS HUMAN BODY

CONSTITUENT	WEIGHT	ATOMS PERCENTAGE
OXYGEN	38.8.Kg	25.5%
CARBON	10.9.Kg	9.5%
HYDROZEN	6.0.Kg	63.0%
NITROZEN	1.9.Kg	1.4%
CALCIUM	1.2.Kg	0.2%
PHASPHROS	0.6.Kg	0.2%
POTASSIUM	0.2.Kg	0.07%

INTEGUMENTRY SYSTEM:

This is the largest organ system in human body and is responsible for protecting the body from most physical and environmental factors. The largest organ in body is SKIN. The integument also includes:

APPENDAGES:

Primarily the SWEAT and sebaceous glands, hair, nails and ARRECTORE PILI(tiny muscles) at the root of the hair that cause GOOSE LUMPS.

LYMPHATIC SYSTEM:

The main function of LYMPHATIC SYSTEM is to extract, to transport and metabolize LYMPH the fluid found in between cells. The lymphatic system is very similar to the circulatory system in terms of both its structure and its most basic function (to carry a body fluid)

MUSCULOSKELETAL SYSTEM:

The human muscular—skeletal system consists of the human skeleton made by bones attached to other bones with joints and skeletal muscle attached to the skeleton by tendons.

(i) There are about 630 important muscles in the human body which normally for 40% of body weight and the largest and bulkiest muscle in the body is GLUTEUS MAXIMUS or buttock Muscle and the smallest is in the middle year which measures less than 1/20 of an inch.

REPRODUCTIVE SYSTEM:

Human reproduction takes place as internal fertilization by sexual intercourse. During the process the ERECT PENIS of the male is inserted into the female vagina until the male ejaculates semen which contain Sperm in to the female vagina. The sperm travels through the Vagina and cervix into the uterus or fallopian tubes for fertilization process. The Primary direct function the male Gamete or Spermatozoa for fertilization of ovum

The major reproductive organs of the male can be grouped into the three categories:

(i) First Category—Sperm production and storage production takes place in the testicles which are housed in the temperature regulating SCORUTUM, immature sperm then travel to the EPIDIDYMIS for development and storage;

(ii) second category are ejaculatory fluid producing gland which include the SEMINAL VESICLE, PROSTRATE and VAS DEFERENS. The final category are those used for capulation and deposition of the SPERMATOZA ((Sperm) within the female, these include PENIS, URETHRA, VAS DEFERENS and COWPER' Gland

The human female reproductive system is a series of organs primarily located inside the body and around the pelvic region of a female that contribute toward the reproductive process. The human female reproductive system contains three main parts, VAGINA which acts as the respectable for the male's sperm, the Uterus which holds the developing fetus and the ovaries which produce the female's OVA. The breasts are also an important reproductive organ during the parenting stage of reproduction.

The Vagina meets the VULA which also includes the LABIA, CITORIS and URETHRA during the intercourse this area is lubricated mucus secreted by the BARTHOLIN's Glands. The Vagina is attached to the uterus through the CERVIX while the uterus attached to the ovaries via fallopian tubes. At certain intervals, typical and approximately every 28 days, the ovaries releases an OVUM which passes through the fallopian tube into the uterus. The lining of the uterus, called ENDOMETRIUM and unfertilized OVA are shed each cycle through a process known as MENSTRUATION.

SPERM DIAGRAM:

Generally a man is considered to have normal sperm when it has 20million sperm per millimeter of semen. (b) Human female typically has about 400,000 potential eggs all formed before birth. Only several hundred (about 480) of these "eggs" will actually ever be released during her reproductive years. Normally in humans after onset of puberty due to the stimulations of FOLLICULAR-STIMULATING-HORMONE(FSH). "One egg" per cycle matures and is released from its ovary. One month the left Ovary will release a potential egg and the next month the right ovary will release a potential egg.

DETERMINATION OF GENDER:

Chromosome X sperm make female and Chromosome Y and determines male. Normally human male will have XY chromosome and where as human female has both XX Chromosomes, as detailed in Genetic title of earlier chapter.

LUNGS:

A pair of spongy organs consisting of elastic tissues situated in the chest cavity. There are two lungs, the right lung is larger than the left. Together they weigh between 1.18 and 1.19 Kg in healthy adult. Their main function is to purify blood and supply oxygen to it. The entire blood supply (4.5 to 5 liters) washes through the lungs about once a minute.

KIDNEYS:

The two kidneys are situated in upper posterior of abdominal cavity, one on each side of the vertebral column. Each kidney is approximately 10cm long and 5cm wide and 2,5 cm thick. They filter nitrogenous waste of the body from the blood and throw it out in the form of urine.

HUMAN BRAIN:

It consists of two parts: the brain located in the skull and the spinal card located in the vertebral column. The weight of the average human brain triples between birth and adult hood. The final weight of the brain in adult male is about 1.4.kg (and 1.3kg in case of woman) which averages about 3% of the body weight. The brain uses 20% of the oxygen a man breaths, 20% of calories a man takes in and about 15% of body blood.

CENTRAL NERVOUS SYSTEM:

THE brain along with spinal card constitutes the nervous system. The brain consists of,

* CEREBRUM:

the largest part of brain consisting of two hemispheres which control voluntary actions and these are the seat of INTELLIGENCE, memory assocassociation, imagination and will.

* CEREBELUM:

The large mass having ridges and furrows attached to cerebrum, which regulates muscular movement of locomotion;

*MEDULLA OBLONGATA:

The lower most part of brain which continues as the spinal card in the Vertebral columns. It controls involuntary actions. GLANDS OF HUMAN BODY: Organs human body which manufactures some liquid products which are secreted from cells are called glands.

There are two types of glands:

DUCTED GLANDS AND DUCTLESS GLANDS.

(I) DUCTED GLANDS: These glands secrets their product through well defined ducts e.g. LIVER: produces Bile; LACHRYMAL-secrets tears in the eyes; SALIVARY—secrets saliva in the mouth; and SWEAT GLANDS IN THE SKIN: Secrets sweat.

(II) DUCTLESS GLANDS: These are also called "endocrine" glands or internally secreting glands. They secret hormones directly into blood-stream in response to the instructions from the brain: The list of Ductless glands include:

* THYMUS	:	In early child hood it plays some part in building resistance and growth;
*THYROID	:	Regulates metabolism;
*PROSTRATE	:	Regulates blood pressure and sexual potency;
*GONADS	:	Relates to reproductive system and secrets sex hormones;
*ADRENAL	:	Causes acceleration of breath, heightens emotions, increases in physical strength during fear anger,
*PANCREAS	:	Aids in digestion of proteins, carbohydrates and fats, it secrets insulin,
*PITUTORY	:	It is called master gland as it controls the other ductless glands and influences growth and metabolism.

Chapter XIII
HUMAN CREDENTIALITY
(Engineering & Technology)

13.1.1 General

From the metallurgists who ended the Stone age to the Ship builders who united the word' people through travel and trade, the past witnessed many marvels of engineering powers. As civilization grew it was nourished and enhanced with the help of increasingly sophisticated tools for agriculture, technologies for producing textiles and inventions transforming human interaction and communication. Inventions such as Mechanical Clock and Printing press irrevocably changed civilization. In the modern era, Industrial Revolution brought engineering influence to every niche of life, as machines supplemented and replaced human labor for countless tasks improved systems for Sanitation enhanced health and the steam engine facilitated mining, powered trains and ships and provided energy for factories.

In the century just ended ENGINEERING recorded its grandest accomplishments. The wide spread development and distribution of electricity and clean water, automobiles and airplanes, radio and televisions, spacecraft and lasers, antibiotics, cinematography and medical imaging and computers and internets are just some of the highlights from a century in which engineering revolutionized and improved virtually every aspect of human life.

For more about the great engineering achievements of 20th century from separate National Academy of Engineering (NAE) who as reported by astronaut/engineer NEIL

ARMSTRONG who leaped his first step on the MOON through LUNAR MODDULE launched by NASA through APOLLO 11in 1969 announced 20 Engineering achievements that had greatest impact on the quality of life in 20th century, which include such as:

(1) ELECTRIFICATION: The vast net work of electricity that power the world developed; (2) AUTOMOBILE: Revolutionary manufacturing practices made the world major mode of transportation making cars more reliable and affordable to the masses;

(3) AIR PLANE: Flying made more accessible spurring globalization on a grade scale;

(4) SAFE AND ABUNDANT WATER: Preventing the spread of diseases, increase life expectancy;

(5) ELECTRONICS: Vacuum tubes and later transistors that underline nearly all modernity;

(6) RADIO AND TELEVISION: dramatically changed the way the world received information and e Entertainment;

(7) AGRICULTURE MECANIZATION: Leading vastly larger, safer, affordable food supply to masses

(8) COMPUTERS: The heart of numerous operations and systems that impact our lives;

(9) TELEPHONE AND CELLULAR PHONES: Changing the way the world communicate personally and in business and the entire world A GLOBAL VILLAGE;

(10) AIR CONDITIONING: Refrigerators—beyond convenience. It extends the shelf life of food and medicines, protects electronics and plays an important role in health care delivery;

(11) INTER-STATE HIGH WAYS: Connected distant places/towns states in the vast countries U.S. India, China and Russia;

(12) SPACE EXPLORATION: Going outer space vastly expanded humanity's horizons and introduced 60,000 thousand new products on Earth;

(13) INTERNET: A global communications and information system of unparalleled access;

(14) IMAGING TECHNOLOGIES: Revolutionized diagnostics;

(15) HOUSE HOLD APPLIEANCES: Eliminated strenuous, laborious tasks especially for women;

(16) HEALTH TECHNOLOGIES: Mass production of antibiotics and artificial implants led to vast health improvements stimulating longtivity of individual life span;

(17) PETROLEUM AND GAS TECHNOLOGY: The fuels that emerged 20 century;

(18) LASER AND FIBRE OPTICS: Applications are wide and varied including almost stimulated worldwide communications, non-invasive surgery and point of scale scanners;

(19) NUCLEAR TECHNOLOGY: From splitting the atom, we gained new source of electric power;

(20) HIGH PERFOMANCE MATERIAL: Higher quality, lighter but stronger and more adaptable.

National Academy of Engineering was established in 1964 under charter of NATIONAL ACADEMY OF SCIENCES, as a parallel organization of outstanding engineers, NAE has specialized in water and wastewater environmental management, transportation, telecommunication, industrial facilities and related infrastructure.

13.1.2 Engineering and Technological challenges— Human Security—Audit Report.

Foremost among the challenges are that must be met to ensure the future itself. The Earth planet with finite resources and its growing population currently consumes them at a rate that cannot be sustained. Widely reported warnings have emphasized the need to develop new source of energy at the same time as preventing or reversing the degradation of the environment. Foremost and important challenges include:

(I)   Sunshine has long offered a tantalizing source of ENVIRONMENTALLY FRIENDLY POWER BATHING THE EARTH with more energy each hour than Planet's population consumes in A YEAR. But capturing that power converting into useful forms, especially storing it for a rainy day, poses, and provokes engineering challenges.

(II)   Another popular proposal for long term energy supplies is nuclear fusion, the artificial re-creation of Sun's source of the power on Earth. The quest for fusion has stretched the limits of engineering ingenuity which is yet attainable.

(III)   Chief among concern in this regard is the quality and quantity of water which is seriously short supply in many regions of the World. Both for personal use— drinking, cleaning, cooking and removal of waste— and large scale use of irrigation for agriculture, water must be available and sustainably provided to maintain quality of life. New technologies for desalinating sea water may be helpful, but small scale technology for local water purification may even more effective for personal needs.

(IV)   One goal of biomedical engineering today is fulfilling the promise of personalized medicine. Recent cataloging of human genetic endowment and deeper understanding of the body's complement of proteins and their biochemical interactions, offer prospects of identifying the specific factors that determines sickness and wellness of any individual. An important way of exploiting such information would be the development of methods that allow Doctors to forecast the benefits and side effects of potential treatments or cures. REVERSE-ENGINEERING "The Brain", how it performs its magic should offer the dual benefits of helping to treat diseases while providing clues for new approaches to computerized artificial intelligence. Advanced computer intelligence, in turn, should enable automated diagnosis and prescriptions for treatment. And computerized catalogs of health information should enhance the medical system is ability to tract the spread of diseases and analyze the comparative effectiveness of different approaches to prevention and therapy. Another reason to new medicines is growing danger of attacks from novel disease-causing agents. New virus arises with the power to kill and spread more rapidly than prevention systems are designed to counter act.

(V)   The violence of terrorists for which biomedical engineering solutions are badly in need to counter the violence and the destructiveness of earth quakes, hurricanes and other natural dangers. Technologies for early deployment counter measures (such as vaccine and viral drugs) rank among the most urgent of today's engineering challenges. Even terrorist attacks epidemics and natural disasters represent acute threats to the quality of life, more general concerns pose challenges for the continued enhancement of living. Engineers face the grand challenge of renewing and sustaining the aging infrastructures of cities and services, while preserving ecological balances and enhancing aesthetic appeal of living spaces.

(VI)　And the external world is not the only place where engineering matters, the inner world of mind should benefit from improved methods of instructions and learning, including ways to tailor the minds growth to its owners. Propensities' and abilities some new methods of instruction such as computer created virtual realities will no doubt also be adopted for entertainment and leisure, furthering engineering contributions to the joy of living.

(VII)　The spirit of curiosity in individual minds and in society as a whole can further be promoted through engineering endeavors enhancing exploration at the frontiers of reality and knowledge by providing new tools for investigating the vastness of the cosmos or the inner intricacy of life and atoms.

All these examples merely scratch the surface of the challenge that engineers will face in the coming centuries. The problems described here mere illustrate the magnitude and complexity of the tasks that must be mastered to ensure the sustainability of civilization and health of citizens, while reducing individual and societal vulnerabilities and enhancing the joy of living in the modern world.

13.1.3 AUDIT OBSERVATION

None of these changes will be met however without finding ways to overcome the barriers that block their accomplishment. Most obviously engineering solutions must always be designed with economic considerations in mind—for instance, despite environmental regulations, cheaper polluting technologies often remain preferred over more expensive, clean technologies.

Engineers must also face formidable political obstacles. In many parts of the world, entrenched groups benefiting from old systems wield political power that blocks new enterprises. Even where no one group stands in the way of progress, the expenses of new engineering projects can deter action, and meeting many of the century's challenges will require unprecedented levels of public funding.

13.1.4 ENGINEERS MUST JOIN WITH SCIENTISTS:

Engineers must join with Scientists, Educators and others to encourage and promote improved Science and Technology, Engineering Maths (STEM) Education in the schools and enhanced flow of technical information to the public at large-conveying not just the facts of Science and engineering, but also an appreciation of the ways that Scientists and Engineers acquire the knowledge and tools required to meet Societies needs. Teachers must revamp their curricula and teaching styles to benefit from electronic methods of personalized learning. Doctors and hospital personnel will have to alter their methods to make use of health informatics system and implement personalized medicines.

Another example where such barrier exists in the challenge of reducing vulnerability to assaults in cyberspace, such as identity theft and computer virus designed to disrupt internet traffic systems for keeping cyber space secure must be designed to be compatible with human users. Part of the engineering task will be discovering which approaches work best at ensuing user cooperation with new technologies.

13.1.15 SOCIO—PHILOSOPHIC ANALYSIS

In sum, Governmental and Institutional, Political and Economic and personal and social barriers will repeatedly arise to impede the pursuit of solutions to problems. And all Society's members must be interpreted literally at least to be away with unsocial and unnatural calamities like fundamentalism, fanatism, pseudo ethnical, terrorist attempts, criminal approach with fellow being, secular in religious beliefs and should not riches when some sects of society are suffering from poverty or incurable diseases. Attempts to solve their poverty and try to tend yourself "yours' faithful citizen"

So in pursuing the humanity's great challenges engineers, Doctors, Scholars particularly artists, privileged classes must frame their work with ultimate goal of universal accessibility in mind. Just as Abraham Lincoln noted that house divided against itself cannot stand, a world divided by wealth and poverty, health sickness food and hunger, cannot long remain a stable place for civilization to thrive. The world has become bigger to small and small to smaller and smaller to smallest, more inclusive and more connected hence these challenges are not isolated locales, but of the PLANET AS A WHOLE and all the planet's people. Meeting all those challenges must make the world not only a more technologically advanced and connected place but also a more sustainable or religiously Spelled "HEAVEN" is in this planet itself and nowhere else, soul will live peacefully here itself and not after death.

NOBLE AND NOBEL HUMANS

Chapter XIV
NATURAL CALAMITY.

A natural disaster is major adverse event resulting from the EARTH'S NATURAL HAZARDS; for example floods, tsunami, hurricanes, cyclones, volcanic eruptions heat waves, and fall of meteorites, Asteroid, Comets or landslides that causes DAMAGES, DISASTERS, INJURIES, DEATHS TO LIVING CREATURES ON EARTH. The severity of the losses depends on the ability of the affected population to resist hazards also called their resilience. The understanding is concentrated in the formulation:" disasters occur when hazards meet vulnerably."

Thus an event will not constitute a natural disaster if it occurs in an area without vulnerability for example an earthquake in uninhibited area. The term NATURAL has consequently been disputed because the evens are not purely natural but result from interaction between natural forces and the human race in particular and earthly being in general. A concrete example of the division between a natural hazard and natural hazard is that the 1906 San Francisco earthquake was a disaster, where as earthquakes are a hazard. However, this article gives an introduction to notable natural disasters, refer to the list of natural disasters.

14.1.1 10,000-11,000 BCE

The earliest disaster we know from our historical or mythic records is of course, the legendary Deluge of Atlantis. The description of the end of Atlantis given by Plato in the TIMAEUS and CRITIAS dialogues bears striking resemblance to what many Scientist are now agreed would be the inevitable result of an oceanic impact by disintegrating comet or large asteroid. This is very likely the event discussed by Firestone, West and Warwick-Smith in "THE CYCLE OF COSMIC CATASTROPHE: HOW STONE-AGE COMET CHANGED THE COURSE OF WORLD CULTURE." This event is very likely that the even that led to the extinction of about 30 species of large mammals about 12,000 years ago was the source of the legends of Atlantis and probably the legends of a global deluge. Just North of Siberia entire islands are formed of the bones of Pleistocene animals swept northward from the continent in the freezing Arctic Ocean. It is also suggested that some ten million animals may be buried along the rivers of northern SIBERIA. Thousands upon thousands of tusks created a massive ivory trade for the master carvers of China, all from the frozen mammoths and mastodons of SIBERIA. The famous Beresovka mammoth first drew attention to the preserving of being quick-frozen when buttercups were found in its mouth. This terrible event took millions creatures in a single day and this event suggests an enormous tsunami raging across the land, tumbling animals and vegetation together, to be finally quick-frozen for the next 12000 years. But the extinction was not limited to the ARCTIC, even if the freezing at colder locations preserved the evidence of Nature's rage. This event was global since the mammoths of Siberia became extinct at the same time as the giant rhinoceros of Europe; the mastodons of Alaska, the bison of Siberia, the Asian elephants and American camels. "The Pleistocene period ended in death. This was no ordinary extinction of a vague geological period, which fizzled to an uncertain end. This death was Catastrophic and all inclusive." (Quoted from THE SECRET HISTORY OF THE WORLD) Now a question would arise how many human deaths ought to have taken place? As Firestone, et al discuss it was global in effect and the evidence of sharply reduced population of not only animals, but also humans, is there in the geological DEBRIS.

PRE-HISRTORICAL DISASTERS:

- ☐ 9100 BCE: Extinction of the wooly mammoths.
- ☐ 7500 BCE: Brings ice to an end.
- ☐ 5900 BCE: Metals smelted naturally, bringing of Homeric"
- ☐ 3195 BCE: Eco-disaster as shown in tree rings.
- ☐ 3123 BCE: 29 June—Germany The clay tablet showed an asteroid destroyed Sodom 5000 years ago 2345 BCE-Eco-disaster focused in the Levant shown in tree.

HISTORICAL DISASTERS.(ILLUSTRATIVE)

- ☐ 60-70 BCE-destruction of Jerusalem on account of acute famine.
- ☐ 476 ADE-I-his and Chin-ling, China—Thundering chariots "like granites" fell to ground and vegetation of scorched.
- ☐ 526 ADE—Great Earthquake.
- ☐ 536-545-Reduced sun-light, mists of "dry fogs, cop failures, famines plagues in China.
- ☐ 540ADE—In Yemen, the Great Dam of Marib began collapsed thousands migrated.
- ☐ 1321-1368AD-O-Chia district, China-iron rain kills people, animals, and damages houses.
- ☐ 1348ADE-Earthquake in Carinthia, 16 cities destroyed, fire fell 40,000 dead.
- ☐ 1490-Ch'ing-yang, Shansi, China-Stones fell like rain more than 10,000 people killed.
- ☐ 1889-Johnstown-Due to flood over 2200 people— lost their lives—when South Dam holding back lake Conemaugh broke.
- ☐ 1900—India—draught killed between 250,000 to 3.25 million.-

An ear piercing "whistling" sound which might be understood as manifestation of the electrophonic phenomena which have been discussed in WGN over the past few years; the sun appearing to be blood-red before the explosion. The event occurred at about 8 hour local time, so that the bolides probably came from the sunward side of the earth. If the objects were spawning dust and meteoroids—that is, it was cemetery in nature-then, since low-inclination, eccentric orbits produce radiant's close to the sun, it might be that the solar coloration (which, in this explanation, would have been witnessed elsewhere) was due to such dust in the line of sight to the sun. In short, the earth was within the tail of the small comet. There was a fall of fine ash prior to the explosion, which covered the surrounding vegetation with a blanket of white.

- 1931-The Great Flood of The Huang He ((yellow river)in China caused 4,000,000 deaths.
- 1928-30-North west China famine caused over 3 million deaths
- 1936—1941—Sichuan Province China—famine caused 5 million and 2.5.million deaths.
- 1959-The AIDS pandemic beginning.
- 1970-Bhola cyclone which struck East Pakistan (now Bangladesh) killed thousands of people.
- 1972—In Iran blizzard resulted in approximately 4,000 deaths and lasted 7 days.
- 1975-Typhoon NINA which struck China.
- 1984-July 12-Hail storms are falls of rain drops that arrive as ice, rather than melting before they hit the ground. A particularly damaging hailstorm hit Munich, Germany, causing about 2 billion dollars in insurance claims.
- 1984-Cameroon—a limbic eruption in Lake Monona caused 37 deaths nearby residents
- 1986-Lake Nyos whereby much larger eruption killed between 1700-1800 by asphyxiation.

- □ 1989—The Daulatpur-Saturia Tornado killed roughly 1,300 people in Bangladesh.
- □ 1993-United States—Great flood was one of the costliest debacle in the history of U.S
- □ 1998—China-YANGZE River floods left 14 million people homeless.
- □ 2000-Mozambique flood covered much of the country for three weeks thousands of deaths.
- □ 2005—Mumbai floods which killed 1094 people.*2005-Hurricane in New Orleans.
- □ 2008-Afganisthan blizzard. *2009-Victorian bush fire in Australia.
- □ 2004-Ao-Nang, Thailand Indian ocean Earthquake—called Tsunami created disaster.
- □ 2010-Sumatra Indonesia-Tsunami occurred on October 26. *2010-Hini influenza Swine Flu
- □ 2011-Fukushima, Japan Tsunami occurred in Pacific.
- □ 2011 Cyclone Tasi struck Australia.

14.1.2. SOLAR FLARES:

- □ An X20 event in August 16,1988 ;(ii) A similar flare on April 2, 2011
- □ 2003-Most powerful flare ever recorded on November, 4 estimated X40 and X45.
- □ 1859-The most powerful flare in the past 500 years is believed to have occurred in September.

14.1.3 Gamma ray burst.

They are, most powerful explosions that occur in the Universe and they release an enormous of energy in milliseconds or as long as ten seconds. They release as much or even more energy than the Sun will in its whole life. Gamma rays burst are not rare events. They occur about once every day and are detected by telescope both on Earth and space. Mostly large masses of stars, bigger than the Sun, produce a GRB. A GRB of distance nearer that 8000 light years may cause a concern to life on Earth, Mainly Wolf-Rayet Stars WR 104 can produce GRB. Astronomers do believe that the Ordovician-Silurian extinction, the third most destructive extinction on earth might have been due to a GRB.

Cruelty has a human heart and jealously face,

Terror the human form divine, and secrecy the human dress,

The human dress is forged iron, the human form a fiery forge,

The human face a furnace sealed, the human heart is hungry George

—William Blake.

Chapter xv
HUMAN MADE CALAMITY—DEMOCIDES

15.1 Unnatural calamity

It is a deliberate and systematic destruction of human life on account of an ethnic, racial, religious, regional or national motive by human himself. It can be best termed as GENOCIDE. As per the article of the Convention on the prevention and punishment of the Crime of genocide(CPPCG)" any of the following acts committed with intent to destroy, in whole or in part a national, ethnical, racial or religious group as such killing members of the group; causing serious bodily or mental harm to members of the group, deliberately inflicting on the groups conditions of life, calculated to bring about his physical destruction in whole or part, imposing measures intended to prevent births within group; (and) forcibly transferring children of the group to another group.

The preamble to the CPPCG not only states that "genocide is crime under international law, contrary to the spirit and aims of United Nations and condemned by the civilized world", but that "at all periods of history genocide has afflicted great losses on humanity. An act of genocide is certainly not to be taken lightly and will almost always liable to be condemned. Following list of genocide and alleged genocide is illustrative but not exhaustive, and still it will throw light on the ghastic crimes that a human being exercised with his fellow human being. He has HUMANNESS WHICH WAS acquired after leaving back his primitive life of jungle where in struggle was the threshold of lively hood. Even after DRESSED HIMSELF WITH CIVILIZATION committed and going on committing genocides is nothing but unnatural calamity imposed on other human who is similar to him in all aspects. THIS IS NOTHING BUT ABUSING HIMSELF. Nature has created man, man has created God and thereby he became into religionist, regionalist, racist, ethnic and what not, which have aliened himself into verities of RITUALISTIC ASSEMBLIES.

Adam Jones explains in his book Genocide: a comprehensive Introduction that the people throughout history have always had the ability to see other groups as a alien; he quotes Chalk and Jonassohn "Historically and anthropologically peoples have always had a name for themselves. In a great many cases, that name meant 'the people' to set the owners of that name off against all other people who were considered of lesser quality in some way. If the difference between the people and some other society were particularly large in terms of religion, language, manners, customs and so on, then such others were seen as less than fully human; pagan, savage, or even animals" He also asserts that "the difficult is that such historical records exist are ambiguous and undependable. While history to day is generally written with some fealty to 'objective' facts, most previous accounts aimed rather to praise the writer's pattern (normally the leader) and to emphasize the superiority of one's own gods and religious beliefs." Further Scholars differentiate between genocide and gendercide, in which males were killed but the children (particularly girls) and women were incorporated in to conqueror's society. Chalk and Jonassohn provide a wide-ranging selection of historical events such as the Assyrian empire, root-and branch depredations in the first half the first millennium BCE, and the destruction of Melos by Athens during Peloponnesian War (fifth century BCE), a gendercidal rampage described by Thucydides in his 'Malian Dialogue' Jared Diamond has suggested that genocidal violence may have caused the NEANDERTHALS TO EXTINCT.—beginning of genocide. In his Book "DEATHA BY GOVERNMENT" R.J. RUNNEL, who has exhaustively compiled the DEMOCIDE(A term used for the deaths on account of governments)statement of deaths innocent people who were massacred through gruesome acts and the list include

(a) pre twentieth century genocides on account of Government wars:

CASE	YEARS	DEMOCIDE NUMBER
(i) In china	221 BC-119AD	33,519,000
(ii) By Mongols in China		29,927,000
(iii) Slavery Africans	1451-1870AD	17,267,000
(iv) Thirty years	1618-1648AD	5,750,000
(v) In India By Sultans-Tughlak . . .	13-c-19c	4,511,000
(vi) In Iran	5c-19C	2.000.000
(vii) Ottoman empire(crusades) . . .	12c-19C	2,000,000
(viii) In Japan(Boxers wars)	1570-19C	1,500,000
(ix) In Russia Czar wars	10C-19	1,007,000
(x) In Christian crusades in Israel-. . .	1095-1272C	1,000,000
(xi) By Aztecs	early century	1,000,000
(xii) Spanish	16C-17C	350,000
(xiii) French revolution	1793-94AD	263,000
(xiv) Albigensian	1208-1249	200,000
(xv) Witch hunt	15 C—17-C	100,000
(xvi) Plague Deaths	541C	109,000
(xvii) Inter related war deaths	Century	10,634,000

Total	133,147,000*
30-BCto AD hypothetical figure	625,716,000
Plague death	102,070,000
Grand total	860,933,000

(b) TWENTETH CENTURY GENOCIDE

(i) The Soviet Gulag State 61,911,000
(ii) The Communist Chinese Anthe hill 35,236,000
(iii) The Nazi genocide State 20,946,000
(iv) The Depraved National Regime 10,214,000
(v) Japan Savage Military 5,964,000
(vi) The Khmer Rogue Hell State 2,035,000
(viii) Turkey Genocide Purges 1,883,000
(ix) The Vietnam War State 1,670,000
(x) The Poland's Ethnic cleansing 1,585,000
(xi) The Pakistani Cut Throat State 1,503,000
(xii) Marshal Tito's Slaughter House 1,072,000
(xiii) Orwellian North Korea State 1,663,000
(xiv) Barbarous Mexico 1,417,000
(xv) Feudal Russia 1,066,000

	Total of (b)	148,165,000
Pre-Twentieth century genocide	Total of (a)	133,147.000
	GRAND TOTAL	281,312,000

(**Source-"DEATHS BY GOVERNMENT" by R.J
RUMMEL-Translation Publication 1997**)

15.2 DOMESTIC& GEOCIDE:MEGA MURDERS

MEGAMURDERS1900-87(D) 116,380,000
and Genocide:33,476,000 (for 1900-87) . . . . A
DEKA-MEGA MURDERS (USSR, China,
German) 102,842,000 and Genocide 16,690,000 . . . . B
(U.S.S.R, China, Germany, China (KMT) for 1900-87

LESSER MEGA MURDERS For Domestic
12,237,000 and Genocide 6,184,000 (1900-87 Japan,
China, Cambodia, Turkey Vietnam, Poland
Pakistan, Yugoslavia) C
SUSPECTED MEGA MURDERS: Domestic:
3,301,000 and 602,000 (North Korea, Mexico,
Russia,.(For 1900-87) .... D
CENT-KILO MUDERS: (1900-87) Domestic:
10,812,000, Genocide: 4,071,000 (China (war lords),
Turkey U.K. Portugal, Indonesia,)I .... E
LESSER MURDERS:(1900-87) Domestic:
2,355,000 and Genocide:1,019,000 .... F

Grand total 1900-87AND PRE20 CENTURY WORLD
FIGURE==318,169,000

(Source: John Rummel Deaths by Government-New Bruns
wick N.J. Transaction publishers 1994)

15.3 COMMUNIST DEMOCIDE:

State	Year	Genocide	STATE	Year	Genocide
			Afghanistan	1978-87	703,000
Albania	1944-87	150,000	Angola	1944-87	200,000
Bulgaria	1975-87	322,0	Cambodia(RK)	1975-87	3,035,000
Cambodia(KRQ)	1975-79	462,000	Cambodia	1979-87	382,000
China	1923-49	11,692,000	China(PRC)	1949-87	102,671,000
Cuba	1959-87	141,000	Cuba	1952-59	1,000
Czechoslovakia	1948-68	181,000	El-Sal(GLS)	1979-87	1,000
Ethiopia	1974-87	1,285,000	Ethiopia(ETA)	1974-87	2,000
Germany	1948-87	70,000	Guatemala	1954-87	23,000
Hungary	1948-87	27,000	Indonesia	1948-48	2,000
Korea(north)	1948-87	3,549,000	Laos(pathet)	1960-75	55,000
Laos(PDR)	1975-87	70,000	Mongolia	1926-87	200,000
Malayan	1946-51	3,000	Mozambique	1975-87	350,000
Mozambique(f)	1964-75	3,000	Nicaragua	1979-87	7,000

Peru	1980-87	5,000	Philippines	1972-86	5,000
Poland	1948-87	54,000	Romania	1948-87	920,000
USSR	1917-87	126,891,000	Vietnam(28)	1945-87	3,664,000
Yemen(South)	1967-87	1,000	Yugoslavia(P)	1941-44	150,000
Yugoslavia(Tito)	1944-87	2,130,000			

TOTAL 259,432,000

15.4 Total DEMOCIDE UPTO 19th CENTURY:

MAO'sfamine	76,702,000
New World Old Total	174,000,000
New from China	38,000,000
New Colonies	50,000,000
GRAND TOTAL	338,702,000

15.5 COMMUNIST CHINESE ANTHILL: DEATH TOLL (%indicate country population)

TOTAL ITARIAZATION	2,785,000,000—1949-53	0.30%
COLLECTIVZATION	25,000,000—1954-58	0.25%
CULTURAL REVOLUTION	563,000,000—1964-75	0.08%
RETRENCHMENT	26,000,000—1959-63	0.33%
LIBERALIZATION	42,000,000—1967-87	0.01%
GRAND TOTAL	3,440,000,000—1949-87	0.12%

Maotse Dung has ruthlessly certifies his motivated killing of innocent HUMANS BY SAYING "Apart from their other characteristics, Chinese 600 million people have two remarkable peculiarities; they are, first of all, poor and secondly blank. That may seem like a bad thing, but it is really good thing, poor people want to change, want to do things, want revolution. A clean sheet of paper has no blotches, and so the newest and most beautiful words can be written on it, the newest and most beautiful pictures can be painted on it." This shows how sadist attitude he possessed of.

15.6 THE WORST GENOCIDED OF THE 20 AND 21 CENTURY:

Table below: BY INDIVIDUAL DESPOT

(i) Maoze Dong China-1958-61 and 1966-69—Tibet-1949-59:	49.78.000,000
(ii) Adolf Hitler Germany—1943-45-Concentration camps and civilians deliberately killed in World war II plus "LET TO DIE":	15,000,000
(iii) Joseph Stalin(USSR-1932-39	6,000,000
(iv) Hideki Tajo (Japan)—1941-44	5,000,000
(v) Ismail Enver Turkey: 1915—Armenians	1,200,000
1920—Greek Pontoons	350,000
19122Analtolian Greek	480,000
1915-20 Assyrians—500,000	2,530,000
(v) Kim II Sung North Korea 1948-94	1,600,000
(vi) Polo Pot Cambodia—1975-79	1,700,000
(vii) Mengistu-Ethopia—1975-78	1,500,000
(viii) Yakubu Gowon—Biafra 1967-70	1,000,000
(ix) Lionid Brezhnev—Afghanistan—1979-82	900,000
(x) Jean Kamabanda—Rwanda 1994	800,000
(xi) Saddam Hussain—Iran-KURDISTAN-1987-90	600,000
(xii) Marshal Tito—Yugoslavia 1945-87	570,000
(xiii) Sukarno-Communisim-1965-66	400,000
(xiv) Fumimaro Konev—Japan 1937-39 Chinese civilization . .	500,000
(xv) Mullah Omer Taliban-Afghanistan—1986-2001	400,000
(xvi) Idi Amen—Uganda—1969-79	300,000
(xvii) Yahiya Khan—Pakistan—1970-71—Bangladesh	300,000
(xviii) Benito Mussolini—Ethopia—1936-Libya-1934-35	300,000
(xix) Mobotu Sese Seko—Zaire-1965—97	300,000
(xx) Charles Taylor—Liberia—1989-96	220,000

(xxi) Foray Sankoh, Sierra Leo net—1991-2000 200,000

(xxii) Suharto Aceh, East Timor-New-Guinea—1975098 200,000

(xxiii) Hochimin—Vietnam—1953-56 200,000

(xxiv) Slobodan Miloaevic—Yugoslavia-1992-99 100,000

(xxv) Richard Nixon—Vietnam—1969-74 70,000

(xxvi) Efrain rio Mont—Guatemala 1982-83 70,000

(xxvii) Papa Doc Duvalier Haiti 1957-71 60,000

(xxviii) Rafael Trujillo—Dominion Republic—1930-61 50,000

(xxix) His sane Habra—Chad. 1998-90 40,000

(xxx) Chiang Kai-Sheik—Taiwan 1947-Popular Uprising 30,000

(xxxi) Vladimir Ilich Lenin USSR—1917-20—Dissidents executed 30,000

(xxxii) Francisco Spain—Dissidents executed after civil war . . . 30,000

(xxxiii) Fidel Castro—Cuba—1959-99 30,000

(xxxiv) Lyndon Johnson—Vietnam—1963-68 30,000

(xxxv) Maximiliano Hernandz Martinez El Salvador 1932 30,000

(xxxvi) Robert Mugabe—Zimbabwe—Ndebele Minority 20,000

(xxxvii) Ayaothulla Khomeini—Iran—1979-89 20,000

(xxxviii) Hafez Al Assad—Syria 1980-2000 25,000

(xxxix) Basher Assad—Syria—2012 14,000

(xL) Raffle Vidalia—Argentina. 1976-83 13,000

(Xli) Herald Mc. Millan—Britain—1952-56-Kenya Man rebellion 10,000

(Xlii) Paul Kormas—Sierra—Leone 1997 6,000

(Xliii) Osama Bin Laden Taliban leader-1993-2001 3,500

(Xliv) Augusto Pinochet—Chili-1973 3,000

(Xiv) Alzarqawi—Iraq—2004-2006 2,000

(Main Sources: Chaney 1988-Genocide-article Bibligrophy: Review (ii) Stephen Curtois Black book On communism; 1995 (iii) Matthew warfare and Armed conflict 1992; (iv) Clodefelter(warfare and armed conflicts 1992; (v) Eliot twentieth century Book of Dead 1972; (vi) Bouthoul: A list of 366 Major Armed conflict of the period ; R.J. Rummel Democide of Governments and Mass Murders Matt white website (vii) Wikipedia list of Massacres)

15.7 HUMAN SACRIFICES:

(This section lists notable individual episodes of mass suicide or human sacrifice. For tolls arising the systematic practice suicide)

Highest Lowest

(i)	88,000	80,000	Mass suicide Battle of Okinawa Japan	1945
(ii)	8,000	8,000	Battle of Sapiens Mariana Island	1944
S(iii)	3,000	8,000	Reconstruction of great Pyramid	1487
(iv)	960,	960	Seize of Masada Jewish Judea	73 AD
(v)	300	1,000	Reconstruction of ten Commandments of God Uganda March 2000	2000
(vi)	913	913	Johnstown peoples temple Guyana	1978
(vii)	53	53	Order Solar Temple Switzerland & Canada	1994
(viii)	39	39	Heaven's—Gate-California—	1997
(ix)	16	16	Order of Solar Temple France	December 1995

15.8 DEATHS DUE TO RIOTS AND POLITICAL DEMONSTRATIONS (Table)

VICTIMS	EVENT	COUNTRY	CITY	YEAR
300,000	Partition of India	India	Punjab-Bengal	1947
86,000	Tibetan uprising	Tibet	Lhasa	1959
300,000	La Violence	Columbia	Country wide	1948-60
30,000	Nika-riots		Constantinople	532
30,000	La See Maine Sang ante	France	Paris	1871
30,000	228 Incident	Taiwan	Taiwan	1947

14,000	Juju Uprising	South Korea	Juju Island	1948
13,000	August uprising	Soviet Socialists Georgia		1924
12,000	Salvadoran peasant uprising		Elsalvador	1932
11,000	Rumanian Peasant revolt	Romania		1907
10,000	KROONSTAD Rebellion	Russia	Kroonstad	1921
8,000	1984-Anti Sikh Riots	India	New Delhi	1984
7,500	March first Movement	South Korea	Seoul	1919
3,800	Pitchfork Uprising	Russia		1920
60,000	Iranian Revolution	Iran		1979
3000	8888-Uprising	Burma Myanmar		1988
2000	Santa Maria School	Chili Cinega		1928
2000	Basra March		Columbia	1928
1526	Jallan wala Bag	India	Amritsar	1919
3000	Tiananmen Square Protest	China	Beijing	1989
2976	Taliban Attack	U.S.A.	WTC Pentagon Virginia	2001
796	Yezdi	Iraq	Adnaniyah	2007
422	Cinema Rex	Iran	Abad	1978
329	Air India Flight-182		Atlantic ocean	1985
309	1983-Beirut Barracks	Lebanon	Lebanon	1983

15.9 RELIGIOUS WARS:

DEATHS	EVENT	LOCATION	BETWEEN	PERIOD
11,500,000	Thirty years war	Holy Roman Empire	Protestants and Catholics	1618-1648
400,000	French war of Religion	France	Protestants and Catholics	1562-1598
300,000	Crusades	Holy land Europe	Islam-Christians	1095-1290
200,000	II Sudan War	Sudan	Islam-Christians	1983-2005
250,000	Lebanese Civil War	Lebanon	Shiite-Sunni-Christians	1975-1990

(Even attacks, Human-Bomb attacks are being going on even in 21 century)

(II) Mythological wars: Devas and Asuras(God and Demons) Wars in Ramayana between Rama and Ravana Battle of Zholu about 2500 BC War of Kurukshetra between Kouravas and Pandavas in India—1200BCE Wars prior to 1 century BCE numbering to 85 occurred and Wars after first century ADE innumerable wars accounting not less than 100 wars were fought among racial groups, ethnic groups and political group. Even during the current period(20012 attacks, group fighting is still going on in the countries like Pakistan, Afghanistan, Syria, Egypt, India, Myanmar, Jordan, Israel, Iraq etc.

CHAPTER XVI
HUMANITARIAN CRISIS

Humans (homo sapiens) as we have reviewed earlier, are primates of the family HOMINIDAE, and the only living species of the genus HOMO. The human lineage diverged from Chimpanzee, some millions years ago. The first Homo species to move out of Africa was Homo erectus. Homo sapiens proceeded to colonize the continents arriving EUROSIA 60,000 years ago; Australia around 40,000 years ago; to America around 15,000 years ago and remote islands such as Hawaii, Newzealand between the years 3000 and 1280.

As early as 12000 years ago human began to practice agriculture, domesticating animals and plants which allowed the growth of civilization. Humans subsequently established various forms of Government, religious and culture around the world, unifying people within a region and leading to the development of States and Empires. The rapid advancement and scientific and medical understanding in the 19 and 20 centuries led to the development of fuel driven technology, improved health causing human population to raise exponentially. With individuals wide spread in every continent except Antarctica, human are a cosmopolitan species and by 2012 their population was estimated to be around 7billion.

Humans are characterized by having a large brain relative to the body size, with a particularly well developed NEOCORTEX, PREFRONTAL CORTEX and TEMPORAL LOBES, making them capable of abstract reasoning, language introspection, problem solving and culture through social learning. The analysis of THE BRAIN includes:

STRUCTURE AND FUNCTION OF THE HUMAN BRAIN.

The brain has three main parts, the CEREBRUM, the CEREBELLUM and the BRAIN STEM. The brain is divided into region s that control specific functions.

THE CEREBRUM—Frontal Lobe: (i) Behavior (ii) Abstract solving (iii)problem solving (iv) attention (v) creative thought (vi) some emotion (vii) Intellect (viii) reflection (ix) Judgment (x) Initiative (xi) Inhibition (xii)Coordination of movements (xiii) Generalized and mass movements (xiv) Sense of smell (xv)Some eye movements (xvi) Muscle movements (xvii) Skilled movements (xviii) some motor skills (xix) Physical reaction and (xx)Libido (sexual urges).

OCCIPITAL LOBE: (i) Vision and (ii) Reading.

PARIETAL LOBE: (i)Sense of touch (tactile sensation) (ii) Appreciation of form through touch(Stereo gnosis) (iii) Response to internal stimuli (procrioception) (iv) Sensory Combination and comprehension (v) some language and reading functions (vi) Some visual functions);

TEMPORAL LOBE: (I) Auditory memories (ii) some hearing (iii) Visual memories (iv) Some vision pathways (v) Other memory (vi) music (vii) fear (viii) some language (ix) Some Speech (x) Some behavior and emotions and (xi) some identity.

RIGHT HEMISPHERE (The representational hemisphere): (i) The right hemisphere controls the left side of the body (ii) Temporal and spatial relationships (iii) Analyzing nonverbal information and (iv) Communicating emotion;

LEFT HEMISPHERE (the categorical hemisphere): (i) The left hemisphere controls the right side of the body (ii) Produce and understand language;

CORPUS COLLASUM: Communication between the left and right side of the brain;

THE CEREBELLUM: (I) Balance (ii) Posture and (iii) Cardiac, respiratory, and vasomotor centers;

THE BRAIN STEM: (I) Motor and sensory pathway to body and face (ii) Vital centers: cardiac, respiratory, vasomotor;

HYPOTHALUMUS: (I) Moods and motivation (ii) Sexual maturation (iii) Temperature regulation and (iv) Hormonal body processes;

OPTIC CHIASM: Vision and the optic nerve;

PITUTURORY GLAND: (I) Hormonal body processes (ii) Physical maturation (iii) Growth (height and form) (iv) Sexual maturation and (v) Sexual functioning;

SPINAL CORD: Conduct and source of sensation;

VENTRICLES AND CEREBRAL AQUEDUCT: Contains the cerebrospinal that bathes the brain and spinal card.

Human left behind Anima city—Developed Enmity among Humans

This mental capability combined with an adaptation to BIPEDAL locomotion that frees the hands for manipulating objects has allowed humans to make far greater tools than any other living species on Earth. Humans are the only extant species known to build fires and cook their food as well as the only known species to clothe themselves and use numerous other technologies and arts created by himself. The study of humans is the Scientific discipline of anthropology.

Humans are uniquely at utilizing systems of symbolic communication such as language for self-expression, the exchange of ideas and organization.

Human create complex social structure composed of many cooperating and competing groups from families and kinship, networks to states. Social interactions between Norms and rituals, which together form the basis of human society. Humans are noted for their desires to understand and influence their environment, seeking to explain and manipulate phenomena through his own inventions like SCIENCE, PHILOSOPHY, MYTHOLOGY AND RELIGION Until 10,000 years ago humans lived as hunter gatherers. They generally lead in small nomadic groups known as BRAND SOCIETY. The advent of agriculture prompted the Neolithic revolution, when access to food surplus led to the formation of permanent human settlements, the domestication of animals and the use of metal tools for the first time in the history. Agriculture encouraged trade and cooperation and led to complex Society. Because of the significance of this date for human society, it is the epoch of Holocene Calendar or HUMAN ERA.

About 6000 years ago the first proto state developed in Mesopotamia, Egypt Nile and Indus Valley. Military forces were formed or protection and government bureaucracies for administration. States cooperated and competeted for resources, in some cases waging wars. Around 2000-3000 years some states such as Persia, India, China, Rome and Greece developed through conquest into the first EXPANSIVE EMPIRES. Ancient Greece was the Seminal Civilization that laid the foundation of western culture being the birth place of Western Philosophy, democracy, major Scientific and mathematical advances, Olympic Games, Western literature and historiography as well as drama including tragedy and comedy. Influential religions such as Judaism originating in West Asia, and Hinduism originating in South Asia rose to prominence at this time.

The late middle ages saw the rise of evolutionary ideas and technologies an advanced and urbanized society promoted innovations and science, such as printing and seed drilling. In India major advancement were made in mathematics, philosophy, religion and metallurgy. The Islamic Golden age saw major Scientific advancements in Muslim empires. In Europe rediscovery of classical and inventions such as the printing press led to renaissance, in 14 and 15 centuries. Over the next 500 years exploration and colonization brought great parts under the European control, leading to larger struggles for independence. The Scientific revolution in 1700 CE and Industrial revolution in 18-10 centuries promoted major innovation such as railway and automobile, energy development such as coal, fossil fuel and electricity and Government such as reprersentive democracy and communism. With the advent of information age at the end of 20 century, MODERN HUMANS live in the world has become increasingly globalized and interconnected. As of 2012 6 Billion (around 95 percent of world population) are able to communicate with each other via Internet and Mobile phone subscriptions.

Although interconnection between human has encouraged the growth of science, are and information technology it has led to culture and religious clashes and the development and use of weapons of mass destruction. Human civilization has led to environmental destruction and pollution significantly to the ongoing Mass construction of other forms of life called the HOLOCENE EXTINCTION EVENT.

The humans are only of several species to have self-awareness to recognize themselves in mirror. The human brain perceives the external world through the senses and each individual human influenced greatly by his /her experiences, leading to subjective views of existence and the passage of time. They are said to possess CONSCIOUSNESS, SELF-AWARENES and THOUGHT (mental process).

MOTIVATION AND EMOTIONS: Motivations is the driving force of DESIRE behind deliberate actions of humans. Motivation is based on emotion-specially on the search for satisfaction and the avoidance of conflict. Positive and negative is defined by individual brain state which may be influenced by social norms: a person may be driven to self-injury or violence. Within psychology conflict avoidance and the libido are seen in primary motivations. Within economics motivation is often seem to be based on incentives; there may be financial, moral or coercive. Religious generally pose it divine and demonic influences. Happiness or the state of being happy, is human emotional conditions. The happiness is common philosophical; some define it as the best condition that human can have—a condition of mental and physical health. Others define it as freedom from want and distress consciousness of the good order of thing, assurance one's place in the Universe or Society.

In modern scientific thought, certain refined emotions are considered a complex neutral trait innate in variety of domesticated and non domesticated mammals. These were commonly developed in reaction to superior survival mechanism and intelligent interaction with each other and the environment such as REFINED EMOTIONS is not in all cases as discrete and separate from natural neural functions as was once assumed. However, when human function in civilized tandem, it has been noted that uninhibited acting on extreme emotions can lead to social disorder of crime.

SEXUALITY AND LOVE: For humans sexuality has important social functions; it creates physical intimacy, bondage and hierarchies among individuals besides ensuing biological reproduction. Humans are only one of two primate species, the other being the BONOBO, that frequently have sex outside of female fertile period and that also often engage in sexual activity for no other purpose than pleasure and enjoyment, something very rare among animals. Sexual desires or libido is experienced as bodily urge often accompanied by strong emotions such as LOVE ECSTASY and JEALOSY.

Human choices in acting on sexuality are commonly influenced by cultural norms which vary widely. Restrictions are often determined by religious beliefs or social customs. The pioneering researcher SIGMUND FREUD believed that humans are born POLYMORPHOUSLY PERVERSE which means that any number of objects could be source of pleasure. According to Freud human then pass through five stages of psychological development and fixate on any stage because various traumas during the process. For Alfred Kinsey, another influential sex researcher, people can fall anywhere along a continuous scale of sexual orientation with only small minorities fully hetero-sexual or homosexual. Research studies of neurology and genetics suggest people may be born predisposed to various sexual tendencies. Sex related illness are most common in humans which include: 99% breast cancer, Ovarian cancer, Osteoposis, bi polar, auto immune disease as scleroderma, sjogren's syndrome, clinical depression, histrionic personality disorder or borderline are mostly common in women. Prostrate cancer, X-linked recessive inheritance such as color blindness, abdominal aortic aneurysm, autism and anti social personality disorder mainly seen in men. Besides these HIV/AIDS, Syphilis are common illnesses to humans.

CULTURE: Humans are highly social beings and tend to live in large social groups. More than any other communications for self expression, the exchange of ideas and organization and as such have created complex SOCIAL STRUCTURE composed of many cooperating and COMPETETING groups. Human groups range from families to nations. Culture is defined here as pattern of complex symbolic behavior i.e. all behavior that is NOT INNATE but which has to learned through social interaction with others such as the use of distinctive material and symbolic systems, including LANGUAGE, RITUAL, SOCIAL ORGANIZATION, TRADITION, BELIEFS AND TECHNOLOGY.

LANGUAGE: The human capacity to exchange information and ideas through speech(and recently writing) is paralleled in other species. The faculty of language is defining feature OF HUMANITY AND A CULTURAL. Universal language is central to communication between humans and the sense of identity that unite nations, cultures and ethnic groups. The invention of writing system at least five thousand years ago allowed the preservation of language on material objects and was a major technical advancement. There are about 6000 different languages currently in use including SIGN LANGUAGE and many thousand more that extinct. At this point also human clashes, cold wars have become common among humans about the honor and greatness of their language in particular.

GENEDER ROLES: the sexual division of humans into male and female has been marked culturally by corresponding division of roles norms, practices, dress, behavior, rights, duties, privilege, status and power. Cultural difference by gender have been believed to have arisen naturally out of division of reproductive labor and the biological fact that women give birth led to their further cultural responsibility for nurturing and caring children.

ETHNICITY: Humans often form ETHNIC GROUPS such as group tend to be larger than kinship net works and be organized around common identity defined variously in items of shared ancestry and history, shared cultural norms and language or share biological phenotype. Such ideologies of shared characteristics are often perpetual in the form of POWERFULL, COMPELLING, NARRATIVES that gives legitimacy and continuity to get the shared values. Ethnic groups often correspond to level of political organizations such as bond type, city or nation. Although ethnic groups appear and disappear through history members or ethnic groups often conceptualize their groups as having histories going back into the deep past, which has also become one of the major social crisis of HUMANS. This ethnic propriety of ethnicity has closely tied to rise the NATION-STATE as the predominant form of political organization in 19 and 20 century.

SOCIETY-GOVERNMENT—AND—POLITICS:

Society is the system of organization and institutions arising from interaction between and external Sovereignty. Recognition of State's claim to independence by other states enabling it to enter into International agreement is often important to the establishment of its Statehood. As conceptualized by Max Weber "a state is a human community that successfully claims the monopoly of LEGITIMATE use of physical force within given territory.

GOVERNMENT can be defined as the political means of creating and enforcing laws typically via BUREAUCRATIC HEIRARCHY. Politics is the process by which decisions are made with groups; this process often involves CONFLICT as well as compromise. Politics is also observed in all human group interactions including corporate academic and religious institutions. Many different political systems exist which include MONARCHY, COMMUNIST STATE, MILITARY DICTATORSHIP, THEOCRACY AND LIBERAL DEMOCRACY. DEMOCRACY is dominant to day. And all the issues have a direct relationship with ECONOMICS.

WAR: War is a state of widespread conflict between states or other larger groups of humans, which is characterized by use of LETHAL VIOLENCE TO ASYMMETRIC WARFARE TO TOTAL WAR AND UNCONVENTIONAL WARFARE. Technique include HAND TO HAND COMBAT, THE USE OF RAGED WEAPONS, NAVAL WARFARE AND more recently AIR AND NOVAL SUPPORT. Satellites in LOW EARTH orbit, have made out space factor in warfare as well as it is used for detailed intelligence gathering, however no known aggressive have taken place from space. Already we acknowledged in an earlier chapter **HUMAN MADE CALAMITY—DEMOCIDE** that millions to millions have lost their lives due to warfare among themselves just on the norms of ethnic and religious supremacy.

ABUSE OF HUMANITY

Evidence of slavery has existed in many cultures slavery rare among hunter gatherer population as slavery is system of stratification. Economic surpluses and high population density is viable. Due to these factors the practice of slavery would have only proliferated after invention of agriculture during Neolithic Revolution about 11,000 years ago slavery was known in civilization as old as SUMER.

It was prevalent in every civilization as almost every ancient civilization including Ancient Egypt, China, Assyria and Columbian America. Such institutions were a mixture of Debt slavery, punishment for crime, enslavement of prisoners of war, child abandonment and a birth of slave children to slaves.

It continued upto middle ages, particularly in Islamic world, even though Islamic agenda prohibits it.

In Netherland, Britain, Ireland, Germany, U.S, slavery trade continued upto 19th century. In this trade particularly African Black were the main targets for this gruesome act. Surprisingly slavery was legalized in New York and New Jersey. Salavery was legal in most of Canada upto 1833. Around 2,532,300. African across Atlantic equality 41% of the total transport of 6,132,900 individuals used to be packed in gunny bags and transported to different countries even as of 1928.

Chapter XVII
CLASHES IN HUMAN CIVILIZATIONS—AN AUDIT REPORT

The clash of civilizations has become realistic analysis of current international situation. It is sad to acknowledge that clash of civilization is here to say we have learn with it willingly or unwillingly. Since the end of cold war between U.S. and Russia, Capitalism and Communism, the main global conflicts have not been ideological or economic, but between civilizations divided from each other by culture and religion language and history. Samuel HUNTINGTON in his book 'Clash of civilization' mentions "the West was the world by organized violence. Even today the West is trying to maintain its dominance over world through organized violence.

The raise of Mujahedeen in Afghanistan against U.S.S.R. (former Russia) is an example of proxy war that the U.S. fought, putting guns on the shoulders of defiant Afghans. It was planned, sponsored and executed in the Pentagon. The difference now is that the West is not able to push other cultures as it used to instead its actions will inevitably lead to conflict. Today many Muslim countries are busy amassing military might to fight an enemy in future, and Israel is always there, confident in its backing from its US patron. Even civilizations do not want to plunge in to such war, the threat is there. The West may be forced to clash due to unavoidable political compulsions. As different example of civilization can be found in Sri Lanka, where two civilizations in one country refuse to intermingle between Buddhists, Sinhalese and Hindu Tamils whose armed wing is the Liberation of Tamil Elam.

Similarly is the recent case with Myanmar where there is clash between two civilizations in one country refuse to intermingle between Buddhists and Muslims. The case of India, is already known since 1947', where two civilizations of Muslims and Hindus are unable adjust among them.

The Clash of Civilizations is not a myth but reality that is taking shape in the minds of people through discussions, news, education, books and religious teachings. Though the west is allowing many of its citizens to accept Islam, Christianity does not grown in Muslim countries, resulting in frustration of ranks of missionaries' who collect millions of dollars from rich Christians in the name of spreading message of Christ. Similarly is the case with Islam expansion through Zamath (missionaries), duly backdoor funded by Islamic countries.

Conflict between Islam and the West is shown through disputes over religious practices, such as banning Hijab in French Schools and attempts to control the teaching of religious institutions. The opposition of many Europeans to the idea of allowing Muslim Turkey into European Union demonstrated that they see Islam to be something un-European an unacceptable "other".

The idea that there is a clash of civilization does not claim that there is culture block are monolithic. Nevertheless groups of nations sharing religious and cultural traditions have much more in common than dividing them, and these shared interest are radically opposed to those of other civilizations. For example, as long as Palestinian problem exists, the threat of terrible clash of civilizations beginning looms over the world. Uncritical American support for Israel helps to explain, why Muslims all over the world see themselves as an opposition to the West. They ask why is the U.N. so lazy in sending its army to arbitrate in Palestine when world saw the marching of armies from scores of Western countries to free Kuwait from Saddam? Why do they think it is a fine for Israel to acquire nuclear weapons but Iran must be punished for merely trying to develop civilian nuclear power? Even Israeli citizens are fed up of war, yet their leaders are not willing to compromise on the security of Israel. The conflict between Islam and the West is not only source of conflict between civilizations today. Many civil conflicts stem from major cultural divisions within countries. For example, the reservation of the backward casts in India has not brought fruits as expected and tensions continues to grow as more and more Indian citizen choose Buddhism, and Christianity over Hinduism, news papers carry stories of mass conversions as rebellion against high cast.

Ukraine is split between European learning West, and orthodox, Russian-speaking east. Most violently Shia, Sunni and Kurdish Iraqis are bitterly divided. Such internal divisions often drawn in other countries on behalf of their cultural brethren, for example Iran with Shia in Iraq or Russia wishing to bounce back in the political field as heavy weight in Ukraine.

There may not be any might in the Muslim but suicidal tendency is always there. Their frustration could be forced upon blaming the Western could lead crises to flare up. It just requires another spark like 9/11, and the whole world would be in the midst of a clash. It could happen any moment anywhere.

In addition, the threat to global peace is not only from Islamists and westerners, but also from bloody local fights between various factions. The Shia-Sunni fight is growing dangerously, rifts between the USA and South American States are increasing with their rulers and people coming out openly to mock America. Is there any single country in the world a powerful country, which can enforce peace amid such mass killing? Is the UN fit and courageous? No then, wait for Dooms day.

Those who bet upon the Popes for world peace should know that there is a new Pope and we know that his remarks about Prophet Muhammad have sparked frictions in the already strained relations between the Muslims and Christians. On the other hand Kuwait parliament has proposed a bill to lay capital punishment to those who write against Islam and their prophet. Those who blame only the Islamists for the decaying peace, should also blame the Pope and the missionaries too for their big contributions in disturbing peace, in fact they have acted as catalysts. There is a tribe of people like Pat Robertson and Jerry Fall Well who go on T.V. shows and split venom against Islam, thus promoting Islamic retaliations.

There is also a prophecy of Armageddon in the books of Christian and 'a mother of all battles' in the Muslim books in which there is the mentioning of an anti-Christ and big war between Christians and non-Christians. Some preachers have been saying that the Prophet Muhammad is the Anti-Christ, indicating that Christians must mentally prepare for a war that is approaching the World faster. Wishing for peace is one thing but threat to conflict is far real but not a myth. How many people choose to understand their religion in correct manner? And that is the key reason to fear that the world will be unwillingly plunged into war when the Doom is near, even intellectuals fail to judge correctly, and that is what we see around us.

It would be rather unwise to argue that the world is now at peace. The collapse of Soviet Union was followed by emergence or reemergence, of many serious conflicts in several areas that had been relatively quiescent during the cold war. Some of these new conflicts have been taking place within the former Soviet Union, such as war between Armenia and Azerbaijan over Nagorno-Karabakh and fighting in Chechnya.

Ethiopian conflicts aside, there have been threats to international order that are needed beyond the full control of major powers, even the US the victor of cold war. The most notable ones include religious militancy terrorism, North-South conflict and severe completion over scare resources. Thus the end of cold war can be said to have brought about the solidarity and instability to international relations.

With the collapse of Communist regime in Eastern Europe and disintegration of the Soviet Union the BIPOLAR international system dominating the cold war period disappeared leaving basically its place a UNIPOLAR system under the leadership of US, speaking especially from military/political point of view. Other countries have to seek American protection. The "American Empire" may best be seen operating in the Persian Gulf, Iraq and Middle East in general where the armed forces of the U.S. have established a semi permanent foothold and thousands of soldiers deployed at bases keep a watch on Iran, Syria and other potential enemies.

American Military power in Japan does only protect Japan against foreign enemies. It indirectly protects China and other Asian States against the consequences of that might flow heavily re-armed Japan. More over American Military power serves as an organizer of Military coalition, both permanent (such as NATO) and an adhoc (such as peace keeping Mission).

In the same way, the European Union expanded towards Eastern Europe, symbolizing once again. Western dominance, particularly with 2004 expansion of eight formerly countries, LITHUNIA, LAVITA, ESTONIA, HUNGARY, SLOVENIA, SLOVAKIA and CHECK REPUBLIC joined the union in 2007.

Despite contrary expectations, however a fresh cycle Ethiopian movements have reemerged recently in Eastern Europe (including Balkan), Central Asia African and many other countries of world.

18.1 INSANITY OF EXTREMISM

Religious-driven violent intolerance can also be connected to terrorism in many cases. In fact, some of the World's most dangerous terrorist organization to day like "Islamic Jihad" and "El-Kaida" are ideologically fed by religious fundamentalism. Most people in such organization strongly believe that use of violence in the name religion is obligatory. They are also convinced that if they die in their "holy struggle" they will be rewarded in the next life, which is permanent one and which will be in heaven. This belief removes fear or guilt feeling, making killing and dying much easier consequently (see YILMAZ-2002).

IN HUMAN AND BRUTAL TORTURE ON WOMAN FOLK

(i) Recently a group of Al-Kaida Terrorist fired against school going woman children in Pakistan of whom a girl named MALALA YOUSUF ZAI was shot at in September 2012 and seriously injured and got operated in London. The sin she committed is she is school going girl. During the encounter, she being a 12 year old girl vehemently criticized the heinous act with thunderbolt words that "we are being forced to keep guns in fingers when we are supposed to hold pen in them" and for this statement almost all the world population praised her and demanded her to award NOBEL prize for peace. (Gulf News 10 November 2012). Even more heinous acts of killings are taking place in Pakistan-Afghanistan border where Al-Kaida Terrorists have camped. Blasting mosques in Pakistan during praying hours and massacring through human-bomb lethal, has become a common incidents occurring for the past few years. The reason behind this was that the Pakistani is friendly with United States

(ii) An innocent family whose outing on 7 July 2012 to a local park at ALBAHA (Saudi Arabia) turned into a bloody night mare when they were terrorized by fanatics concealing their own extreme beliefs behind the official badges, Commission for the Promotions of Virtue and prevention of Vice, (Hai'a) which has a government sanction. A man who is a husband and father of two innocent children was put to death. His pregnant wife's right arm was amputated and one child is in critical condition and hanging between life and death, and is under treatment in I.C.U. The sin they have committed is they were listening songs from their car sterio on an outing in a week end in a park beyond the border of the city of ALBAHA, Saudi Arabia.

(iii) In most of Islamic countries even in modern times, women's role are notably considered as inferior to men. They are considered deficient in mind and body and classified as "second class human being" women are being treated as a property or toys of men. Here a person wealth includes female slaves to whom the owner can put to sale and used sexually, since there activity has religious sanction.

(iv) Girls aged below 12 and above 9 are used for nuptial after marriage. It is also has religious sanction since their prophet Muhammad who was in his 50's married a six year old girl, Aisha and had nuptial at the age of 9.

(v) Another gruesome practice is when a woman is gang raped, the convict will be the woman her self and not the rapists.

In 2002, a woman named MUKHTAR MAI, hailing from village in Pakistan Punjab was gang raped and local religious clerics acquitted the rapists and ordered punishment awarded to MUKHATAR MAI. Her appeal was nullified on the grounds that the incidence of rape was not certified by four male witnesses. This is so because their Shari'a an Islamic Law doesnot permit without sufficient witness.

(vi) In another case, in Iran, 17 year old Nazanin was gang raped. Her cousin who was below 12 years was also raped by the same people. On seeing this Nazanin stabbed one of the rapist with knife. However, the Iranian court without heeding testimonies, sentenced her to be hanged.

(vii) In one more case capital punishment was awarded by religious clerics, when a women proved by two male witness to have had an extra martial affair, by burying the woman upto her waist and stoned until death.

Besides in these religious culture, male can marry four or more wives at a stretch by paying nominated amount, which is legally called as Mehar. Male has also authorized to give divorce to his wives on simple reason that "She has not wear hijab properly, or she has seen or has a talk with a person other than husband, and the divorce can verbally given by saying Talaq thrice.

These are instances of EXTREME BELIEF in religious and this is a culture termed as Sunnath / obligatory for Muslims.

(viii) FEMALE CIRCUMCISION: Female circumcision or what is globally known as female genital Mutilation (FGM) involves partial or total removal of external female genital for non medical reasons. It is internationally recognized as a violation of women's rights.

However this practice of circumcision or Khetan (as it is known in Arabic) is still wide spread among girls between the ages of nine and 12. Christians in North Africa, the Muslims in Middle East and Europe and Egypt practice FGM.

During January, 2012 the first conference on FGM in Middle East revealed that the practice is carried out in Iraq, Iran, Syria, Saudi Arabia, Yemen and Qatar. A report by Wafa AL Marzouqui exploring the tradition and prevalance of FGM in the UAE revealed that FGM is being performed in private clinics or resorting to midwives. Desires for sex will be mutilated and thus the women folk would be deviated with sex desire. It is an inhuman practice, one that brutalizes societies and reinforces medieval perceptions that women need to be considered purified or Tahra. It reflects deep rooted inequalities between sexes and represents one extreme form of discrimination against woman. This was in practice since prophet Mohammads time when men were away at war and their wives bear long absence of their husband

(ix) In countries like India, where in some cultures young widows are not allowed to remarry and more so prohibited to wear colorful dresses and ornaments and not even allowed in auspicious functions. In same cultures of Rajasthan and Uttar Pradesh wife is put to in the pyre of her husband's death.

Bride grooms are paid huge sums in the shape of dowry by the parents of a bride for marrying her by to get rid of her rights for life time. Daughter is considered as an outsider and burden over the parent.

Another gruesome act came to lime light through a programmed called "Satyameva Jayate" relayed through T V serial during July, 2012 that as many as 3 Million cases of female foetus are aborted annually in India.

All these are only few cases of social evils which has inherited from their savage cultures web.

Terrorism, whether it is fed by religious fundamentalism or not, it became a serious threat to peace in post cold war era. Terrorism became more serious problem after the end of cold war, especially after 9/11. UNITED STATES defined Terrorism as "the calculated use of unlawful violence or threat to unlawful violence to inculcate fear, intended coerces or to intricate governments or Societies in the pursuit of goals that are generally political, religious or ideological". At the same time U.N. defined 'terrorism, for instance "as anxiety inspiring method of repeated violent actions employed by clandestine individual, group or state actors for idiosyncratic criminal and political reasons when in contrast to assistance— the direct targets of violence are not the main targets"

In addition to these activities of "clash-civilization" several conflicts since World War II, which could or did lead to war between countries tended o moderate when countries became democratic. The controversies, between countries like Britain and Argentina, Guatemala and Spain over the remnant empire, Greece and Turkey leaves the signature of clash of civilizations.

* In a 2003 survey, 500 English people living in Scotland one quarter said they had been harassed or discriminated against by Scots.

*A 2005 Study by Hussein and Millar of the Department of politics at the University of Glasgow examined the prevalence of Anglophobia in relation to Islamic phobia in Scotland.

*In 2009 a woman from England was assaulted in an allegedly anti-English racially motivated attack.

* In 2000, the Chairman of Swansea Bay Race Equality Council said that anti-English behavior citing three women who believed that they were being discriminated against in their careers because they could not speak Welsh.

* Northern Ireland-during the trouble, the IRA exclusively attacked in northern Ireland and England not on Scotland or Wales.

* In 2011-tension and anti-English or Anti-British feeling flared in relation to the proposed visit of Elizabeth II, the first British Monarch to visit Ireland in 101 years.

* A wide spread stance consisting in light-heartedly making of Britishers in similar manner that the French are made fun in Britain.

FRANCO-PHOBIA:

* Anti-French sentiments in Australia and New Zealand.

* Anti-French sentiment in U.S. and Ireland.

* Fury at French leaders to consideration of cut in Corporation Tax.

CHINES PHOBIA

Chinese hold negative influence world wide as per the following result of 2012 BBC world service Poll.

Country	Negative in %	County	Negative in %
United States	46	Spain	48
Canada	36	Russia	21

France	49	S. Korea	64
United Kingdom	32	Japan	50
Germany	47	India	31
Indonesia	26	Pakistan	7
Mexico	37	Australia	29
Chili	18	Australia	16
Nigeria	7	Ghana	10
*In china itself	5		

(Ref: The Democratic "Zone of peace"—dramatic historic phenomena. & Drennan John dt,2011-05-22)

*SINO-INDIA WAR: Fifty years ago on October 29, 1962, when the world's terrified gage fixed on the US and Soviet Union nuclear Standoff in Cuba, China attacked India, Provoked by a territorial dispute and tensions over Tibet. The war was brief and China emerged victorious. However, the war still casts a long shadow over Sino-India relations— the border war has instilled deep mistrust and strong sense of rivalry between two sides. The war erupted just a month later after an agreement (Panchseela) between two countries by Pundit Jawaharlal Nehru and Maose Dung prime leaders of India and China respectively. In the agreement the main agenda was for the maintenance of peace and cooperation between two countries. That was how the agreement was violated by China.

ISRAEL-ARAB WARS:

* 1948—Arab forces from Egypt, Jordan, Iraq, Syria and Lebanon occupied in southern Eastern Palestine not apportioned to Jews by UN. While Partitioning Palestine and Israel, and the capture of Jerusalem, including small Jewish

quarter of the old city, in an effort to forestall creation of Jewish State in Palestine.

* 1949—Israel managed to reoccupy all the occupied area by Arabs and in addition it occupied all the Niger up to former Egypt except Gaza strip. In December 1957, an agreement after the joint Anglo—French intervention, and UN Emergency force Stationed.

* 1967—Six-day War (or June War) Syria intensified bombing over Israel from Golan Heights and Israel retaliated the assault and destroyed Egypt air-force on ground. Israel units drove back Syria forces.

* 1973—Six day war developed into full scale war inn 1973. On October 6, the Jewish Holy day of YOM KIPPUR (YOMKIPPUR WAR) Israel was attacked by Egypt, across Suez Canal by Syria on Golan Heights. Though Israel forces suffered lot, it reversed early losses and pushed its way into Syrian territory and encircle Egyptian third Army by crossing Suez Canal and established forces on West Bank.

* 1982—Israel bombed Beirut of Palestine and Southern Lebanon where Palestine Liberation Organization (PLO) had number of strong holds. Following day Israel invaded Lebanon.

* On 11 November, 2012, Six Palestinians killed and 32 injured in Israeli air attack in the Gaza strip as per World news column of Gulf News dated 12,Nov.2012.

* Israel threatens to freeze funds as subscription to U.N. if the President Mahmud Abbas continues to seek observer state membership of United Nations in West backed Palestrina

INDO-PAK WARS:

*Since partition in 1947 Pakistan and India, the two south Asian countries involved in many wars.

*1965—Indi Pak War ran for 15 days and ended after intervention of Soviet Union and USA at Tashkent agreement.

*1971—Indo-Pakistan war, when conflict originated due to turmoil in erstwhile East Pakistan (now Bangladesh).

*1999—Indo Pak war known as Kargil War in which India gained upper hand.

*Competition grew among these two nations by denoting 8 Kiloton nuclear device at Pokhran (Smiling Buddha) test Range by India thus becoming first nation in Nuclear capable country outside five permanent members of UN Security council (US, USSR, China, UK and France) during May 1974.

* In retaliation Pakistan conducted 24 different cold tests in KHURANA in 1980 by Pakistan Atomic Energy commission and a tunnel between Pak and Changai (China Border) was constructed during 1979-83.

* India again operated OPERATION SHAKTI-at Pokhran II by detonating 5 kilo nuclear devices test range.

* Changai II—on 30 May 1998—6 Nuclear device completing its series underground test with it being last test carried out by two nations out to date.

* Minor conflicts termed Indian Integration of Junagadh 15 sep,48,Kashmir Conflict during 1947,Siachin conflict during 1984,1985,1987 and 1995, Operation Brass Tacks 1986, Sir Creek conflict, India Pakistan standoff in 2008,

India-Pakistan tress passing and borders shooting every since 2000.

All these inhuman clash of Civilization demands a strong UN global governance to stop inviting dooms day on EARTH.

SOLUTIONS PROPOSED TO ERADICATE SOCIAL EPIDEMIC OF CLASH OF CIVILIZATIONS

Global stability is prerequisite for Global survival. That is the plat form on which every nation stand today. By the same token global stability needs global tolerance, understanding and acceptance of each other's value.

To be able to appreciate other's values, one needs to study them. Cross cultural understanding should be promoted through education and societal exchanges among nations. Educators and religious and community leaders need to meet more often to bridge difference and promote mutual aspect and understanding. UN member governments need to facilitate such efforts.

Concerned intellectual organization, such as the Washington-based Brooking Institute, which cooperates with the Government of Qatar, need to conduct more such conferences in Muslim majority countries such as Indonesia, Pakistan and India.

There must be dialogue between Muslim religious leaders and western thought leaders because these are the two most powerful groups of opinion makers in the world.

On one hand religious norms of the Muslim world cannot be applied to democratic norms of free and secular society, on the other hand Muslim world believes that religious norms are

God inspired while democratic norms are man inspired. That is why Muslim majority countries are demanding—in spite of the fact that freedom of expression must be protected and neither Islam nor any religion is against it—that one person's free expression should not violate another's freedom.

Your freedom ends when you begin to destroy another's. Otherwise lawlessness and winner-take-all attitude reign and chaos will be the outcome. That would vindicate 'Jungle Law' but not democracy. That is to say that the limit of your free speech is where other's freedom is encroached upon.

Free speech therefore is not absolute. It has a limit. Free speech guided by conscience. Even the legal umbrella that protects free speech is guided by conscience. Without conscience, free speech is total madness in a legal sense.

Angry expression and reactions will not stop freedom of expression it will make things worse. But better understanding of each other's value will help the situation. Western Ambassadors in capital cities of Muslim Majority countries need to propose to their respective governments the establishment of special cross-cultural understanding programs to facilitate exchanges between religious thought and community leaders from different cultures. This could be good way to tame radicalism and extremism. While educating various elements of society to become more tolerant towards each other is very essential part of negotiation.

SETTING EXAMPLE: Likewise, the Muslim world needs to approach denigration issues, not with an explosive emotions, which only send the wrong signals about this esteemed religion, but with smart response, however hard it may seem under present circumstances. Right way to teach the world to accept our values is not to convey our message in a violent manner but to do so elegantly because Islamists say that their religion is of peace and violent teaching will not serve any desired purpose.

India is home to the second largest Muslim population, but reactions to the controversial video (video film on mock ring prophet Muhammad telecasted through Google during September 2012) have not been as lethal as what has happened in neighboring Pakistan. The Nakoula's (who is supposed to have prepared the video) head is priced at 204,000USD for anybody who can bring it to the Pakistan Transport Minister (and for this announcement made his name deleted by Al-Qaida Terrorist from their hit list). Hindu culture of harmony is believed to be stabilizing foundation that has prevented the Video from triggering chaos here. Similarly was the case with Salman Rushdie for writing a mock novel on Prophet Muhammad titling "Satanic Verses" against whose head Khomeini, Imam of Iran announced 1billion US dollar. Radical Islam, sometimes called Islam, is the problem, but moderate Islam is the solution for all the causes of conflict of civilizations.

PROBLEM II: THE THREAT OF GEO-POLITICAL CATASTROPHE.

This is brought about the clash of the Christian, Muslim and Jews civilization forces each of them to guard itself by preventing the others expansion. The rational West and irrational East consider each other wrong and we are unwilling to understand one another. The East does not accept the ideas of Western civilization (democracy, equality and freedom) which essential requirements for a human being. Islam believes that the KORAN dictates the world's proper structure and that only the Islam is the Nation of God. In Muslim world politics and religion are united and hence even purely political change is perceived as a threat to religion and way of life. Salvation lies in complementing one another rather than eliminating each other. It is impossible to achieve, the there is no solution.

Eventually, it is an open truth that these three religions—Islam, Christianity and Judaism are all the products of one Man that is Abraham who is considered as their ANCESTOR and that is why all the three religions are called Abrahamic religions.

SIMILARITIES BETWEEN these three religions summarized as follows.

(i)   **Creation of World: Earth, Sun, Moon, Stars, Day and Night, animals, plants, birds, Water and creatures in water were all created by God within SIX DAYS:**

*JUDAISM(Religion of Jews): Hebrew Bible Genesis 1:3, 1:6-7,1:9.10, 1:14-15,1:24-25 and 1:26-28.

*Christianity: Old Testament: 1:3, 1:6-7, 1:9-101:14-15, 1:24-25 and 1:26-28.

*Islam: Koran-Surath Al-Araf 7:54.

(ii) **After creation of the world God takes rest and occupies suitable throne:**

*Hebrew Bible Having completed the creation of heaven and earth YEHWEH (Jews God) rests from his work and blesses and sanctifies the seventh day(Gensis2:1-3)

*Christian Old testament Genesis 2:1-3

*Islam-Indeed your Lord is Allah who created the heavens and earth in six days and then rose over ISTAWA(

the throne) really the manner that suits his majesty (Surath-Al-Araf 7-54).

(iii) God who created is ETERNAL, OMNICIENT INVENTOR OF ALL THINGS and HE alone deserves for WORSWHIP.

* (Old Testament)—Judaism-Genesis 1:1

*Genesis 1:1 of old Testament of Christianity.

*Koran—Surat Al-Nasr 59:23-24 of Islam.

(iv) Creation of Man (Adam in Islam and Christianity)

* God forms the Man (Ground) Genesis 2: 4b and 25. As per Hebrew Bible.

* Lord created 'admah' Old Testament 2:7.in Christianity.

* Allah created Adam-Koran-Surath Arm rum 30:20-26 In Islam.

(v) Man Was created from the dust and breathed life into him:

* God created Man out of Dust—Hebrew Bible-2.4b

* God Created Ad-amah out of dust Old Testament 2.7.-Christianity.

* Allah created Adam of from dust and breathed into him of His spirit(S.32:7-9). Islam.

(vi) God made Man in deep sleep and removed one of his rib and FASHIONED into Woman (EVE)

* Genesis 2: 25 of Hebrew Bible—as per Judaism (Jews)

* Genesis 2.7. of Old Testament—as per Christianity.

*Koran-Surath 30:20-26—As per Islam.

(vii) God ordered Man and Women not to eat the fruit of the Tree of knowledge.

* Genesis 2:4b-25—As per Judaism (Jews).

* Genesis 2.7. of Old Testament—as per Christianity.

* Koran-Surath 7:20—As per Islam.

(viii) Satan the son of fire provoked Man and Woman to the forbidden fruit.

* Genesis 2.7 of Hebrew Bible as per Judaism (Jews)

* Genesis 2.7 of Old Testament—as per Christianity.

* Koran Surath-2.30 and 7:23-24—as per Islam—Muslims call Iblish for Satan.

(ix) God expelled both Man and women out of heaven for violating his orders.

* Genesis 3 of Hebrew Bible as per Judaism—(Jews)

* Genesis 3 of Old Testament—as per Christianity.

* Koran-Surath 7:14-18—as per Islam.

(x) On the day of resurrection (Judgment) dead will be raised and judged.

* Genesis 3-2 of Hebrew Bible as per Judaism-(Jews).

* Genesis 3-2 of Old Testament—as per Christianity.

* Koran-Surath—7-24-25.

(xi) Moses is a prophet who was issued with commandments.

* Exodus 20, 31, 32 of Hebrew Bible—as per Judaism (Jews)

* Exodus 20,31,32 of Old Testament—as per Christianity.

* Koran Surath-2:60 and 2:71—as per Islam.

(xii) Prophet Abraham and his sons are initiators of these three religions.

* Torah, in Hebrew meaning "Teaching" the most revered part of Hebrew Bible, The first Book of Genesis.

* The Genesis, the first book of Hebrew was also adopted by Christianity.

* Koran says Ibrahim (Abraham) is most revered and righteous prophet regarded in Islam who built the house of God at Mecca and on whose name Idul-Adah is celebrated and Pilgrimage or Hajj is conducted as one of five commandments of Islam.(KORAN 16:121-123, 21:57 AND 21.70 SURATHS)

(xiii) Abraham's Sons Ismail and Isaac considered as their ancestors:

    * Abraham and Sarah's (first wife) son became first ancestor of Jews(G.21).

    * Abraham and Hagar's (second wife) son Ismail the ancestor of IslamS.21.70)

    * similarly Christians also considered Abraham and his both sons as ancestors.

(xiv) Prophets like Isaac, Jacob, Ismail, Moses, Solomon CONSIDERED AS MOST REVERED PERSONALITIES AMONG all these religions. For Islam Christ in the name of Arabic name of Isa is included as a Prophet and his birth to Mari am (Mary)and David as Dawood in Islam are few examples of prophets common to these three religions. The Ten Commandments revealed to Moses at Mount Sinai as per Judaism is also equally regarded as sacred to Christianity and Islam. Similarly Hebrew Bible (Old Testament) preserves the stories of Judaism became an authoritative scripture for Christianity. Torah, the first five books of Bible are included in Koran. The 613 Mitzvoth or commandments are included in the Sharia of Islamic as Laws of life.

When there are so many aspects are common features of these three Abrahimic Religions why the clash and conflict and bloodshed among themselves is PUZZLING humanity at large. Moreover, the religion is not relevant to modern days of Science and technology. However all religions are born to give ethical approach to human life so that human mind behaves irrationally on so many occasions since man is abode of passions and greed, envy and crazy for the artificial life which is not a permanent feature of life. HENCE RELIGIONS

PROPOSES EITHICAL WAY OF LIFE WITH THREAT OF THE EXISTENCE OF GOD WHO PUNISHES THEM BY SPARING THEM TO HELL AFTER DEATH

This is an human appeal to all these religions to wipe out their differences and join the main stream of civilization and ensure peace and security to human life. Violence breeds violence, war breeds war, hatred breeds hatred but LOVE AND PEACE BREEDS LOVE AND PEACE ONLY WHICH PROVIDES SUSTAINABILITY OF HUMAN LIFE ALTOGETHER. Hence the so called religious leaders let assemble together in same plat form and negotiate to eliminate difference among them and open the doors of democratic, peaceful and secured life to all humans on the earth. Most of the humans around 40% of Global population (which is inclusive of believers of these religions for which God is coming forward to elevate them) are suffering from starvation, malnutrition, poverty and leading dreadful and insecure life. The Clashes, conflicts and wars are nothing but preparation for dooms day for all including you and ourselves. It is requested to prepare an agenda which can depreciate differences and appreciate friendship and love and create an atmosphere of brotherhood/sisterhood among ourselves and I think it is the major agenda of all the religions also. Round table conferences will help to solve the problems since every problem has got certainly a solution. War wrecks both wealth and welfare. An International delegation under the guidance of UN may brought forth for dealing the problems of CLASH OF CIVILIZATION IN GENERAL, solutions can be sorted out and periodical review conducted as many times as possible by THE PROPOSED U.N. GOVERNANCE, so as to ERASE THE WORD OF HUMAN MISERY FROM THE DICTIONARY OF MAN KIND.

Problem IV—Illicit Global Arms Trade

Each year hundreds of thousands of civilians are slaughtered by conventional weapons that are manufactured and sold, transferred by governments or diverted to unscrupulous regimes criminals, illegal Militants and Terrorist Groups.

But the Government and arms brokers that contribute to crimes against humanity by pouring guns and arms into conflict zones are not violating any international law and are often out side the jurisdiction of national laws. This hole in fabric of international security can be patchup by imposing strict vigilance by international security council under affiliation to United Nation Peace Council.

Many countries have weak or ineffective regulations governing the trade of weapons. The result is that there are more international laws governing the trade of bananas than conventional weapons, like AK-47. In the absence of international standards and effective national controls, irresponsible arms suppliers exploit the gaps for profit. For years, for instance Russian firms have supplied helicopters to Syria which have reportedly been used by Bashar Al Assad regime to attack civilian population centers in recent weak.

It is therefore, there shall be a treaty that prevents illicit arms transfers and it should have the potentiality to the behavior of by requiring states to put in place basic regulations and administrate to follow common sense criteria that reduce irresponsible international arms transfer and hold arms suppliers more accountable for their actions. Negotiations must also ensure that the the treaty covers all types of transfers and the full range of conventional weapons and must also cover the import and export of ammunition.

For the treaty to have teeth, it should require States to report regularly and publicly on their sales and purchases.

Finally the treaty under the supervision of U.N. Security Council should require States to regulate the activities of international arms brokers as their desire profit has fuelled gruesome violence against innocent humans in recent conflicts in Sierra Leone, Liberia, Syria and else where. **<u>Today only 52 of the worlds 192 Governments have law</u>** regulating arms brokers and less than half of those States have criminal or monetary penalties associated with illegal broking.

World leaders must act on emergency basis, overtime, this will help prevent HUMAN RIGHTS ABUSES and make the world safer place.

Chapter XVIII
HUMAN TRAGEDY—
PERFORMANCE AUDIT

The 20th century far from uniquely representing advances in post Renaissance 'Civilization' witnessed a great number of systematic slaughter of human beings within any century in history. Indeed 20th century may become historically in famous for introducing a sinister type of aggression, genocide and homicide the terms that did not exist in the lexicon homicide until post World War II. It was coined by RAFEL LIMKIN, a Polish Jew who escaped holocaust and lobbied tirelessly for recognition of form of human killing of groups of people defined in United Nation convention on the prevention and punishment of Genocide in 1948, as acts committed with the intent to destroy in whole or in part a national, ethnical or religious group. Such acts include killing members of the group causing serious bodily harm or mentally harm to members of the group deliberately inflicting on the group, conditions to life to bring about its destruction in whole or part, imposing measures to prevent birth within the groups and forcibly transferring children of the group of another group.

It is apparent that the explanation of specific forms of violence, rape, mutilation, torture etc. is not forthcoming from current psychological knowledge. All are forms of extreme sadism and how sadism is developed in specific was still not clear. We do not know the perpetrators are stressed desentized and view their victims as threat or as subhuman, yet utilize the forms of sadism that require human mores and reactions in order to have effect. Forensic Psychology views such actions as the consequence of pathological developmental issues. Social Psychological explanations have suggested "State" aggression can be produced by pathological situations. ZIMBARDO in 1969, suggests that power imbalances, lack of oversight and competing purposes AMONG GROUP WERE TOXIC MIX AND PRODUE ABUSIVE BEHAVIOUR FROM NORMAL COLLEGE AGE MEN UNDER SUCH CIRCUMSTANCES.

Corroborated information could be sought regarding violent tendencies in civilization settings. Some of the techniques are used in Psycho historical approaches. However in forensic analysis, more weight is put on what information and state of mind would have required for specific actions to occur. DARELY, a great Psychologist has suggested "probes into conceptual world of individuals who are enlisted in to real world-harm doing socialization process. Only such methods may answer the ultimate question of whether normal man who shows no prior propensity for violent crime can act like sexual sadist during the program"

Then what would be sustainability of human development? United Nations Human Development program report 1996, define 'human development as expanding choice for all people in Society, the men and women particularly poor and vulnerable are the center of the development process. It means protection of life opportunities of future generation . . . . and natural system on which all life depends'

However, as seen here under the PROBLEMS OF HUMANS STILL REMAINED UNSOLVED:

NO HUMILIATION MORE ABUSIVE THAN HUNGER: Following statistics shows how humans have been deprived of their basic need HUNGER which is the primary meaning of life-Energy.

15.10 Abuse of Humanity—Poverty Line

List containing the countries where majority of the people living BELOW POVERTY LINE and Poverty line is Internationally standardized as the earning by an Individual to the extent of 1 to 1.25 Dollar per day which can be considered to be the worst state of affair on the part of Humans of the AFFLUENT EARTH.(Major countries where above 30% (population is below poverty line)

Position as on 2010 as per the UNITED NATIONS HUMAN DEVELOPMENT REPORT)

Name of the country percentage of the country's total population

Afghanistan	36 percent
Angola	40 percent
Armenia	32 percent
Belize	43 percent
Benin	37 percent
Bolivia	52 percent
Botsavana	30 percent
Bolivia	52 percent
Burkina Faso	48 percent
Burma (Myanmar)	33 percent
Burundi	68 percent*
Cambodia	31 percent
Central African republic	62 percent
Chad	80 percent***
Columbia	37 percent
Comoros	60 percent
Congo Democratic Republic	71 percent*
Congo Republic	50 percent

Coati devoir	43 percent
Djibouti	42 percent
Ecuador	33 percent
El-Salvador	38 percent
Equatoria Guinea	77 percent*
Eritrea	50 percent
Ethiopia	40 percent
Gabon	33 percent
Fiji	31 percent
Gambia	48 percent
Ghana	30 percent
Grenada	38 percent
Guatemala	54 percent
Guinea Bissau	65 percent
Guinea	53 percent
Honduras	65 percent
Kenya	46 percent
Kyrgyzstan	34 percent
Lesotho	57 percent
Liberia	64 percent
Macedonia, Republic of	31 percent
Madagascar	69 percent
Malawi	53 percent
Mali	47 percent
Mauritania	42 percent
Mexico	51 percent
Mongolia	39 percent
Mozambique	55 percent
Namibia	56 percent
Nepal	31 percent
Nicaragua	46 percent
Niger	60 percent
Nigeria	70 percent

Paraguay	35 percent
Peru	31 percent
Rwanda	50 percent
Sierra Leone	66 percent
Senegal	51 percent
South Sudan	51 percent
Sudan	47 percent
Suriname	70 percent*
Tajikistan	53 percent
Tanzania	33 percent
Togo	62 percent
Turkinistan	30 percent
Ukraine	35 percent
Yemen	35 percent
Zambia	64 percent
Zimbabwe	68 percent

* In Asian, African and Latin-American countries, well over 500 million people are living in what the World Bank has called 'absolute poverty'.

*Every year 15 million children die of hunger.

*For the one Missile a full hungry children of a School could eat every day five years.

*Through 1990' more than 100 million children died of illness and starvation and this could have been averted for the price of ten Stealth Bombers what world spends on its military in two days.

* World Health Organization estimates that 1/3rd of world is well fed, 1/3rd of world is under fed and another 1/3rd of is under starving. Over 4 Million are dying with starvation each

year. At least 200 people would die of starvation for every two minutes.

*One in twelve worldwide is malnourished including 160 million children under the age of 5 as per the United Nation Food and Agriculture Report.

* The Indian Sub-continent has nearly half the world's hungry people. Africa and the rest of Asia together have approximately 40% and remaining hungry people found in Latin America and other parts of the world as per the Report on Hunger in Global Economy of United Nation.

*Nearly one in four people, 1.3 million a majority humanity live less than one dollar (American) per day while world's 358 billionaires have asset exceeding combined annual income of countries with 45% of world income—UNICEF Report.`

*3 billion people in world today struggle to survive on US dollar 2 per day.

* In 2994 the Urban Institute in Washington DC estimated that one out of 6 elderly people in U.S. has an inadequate diet.

* In the U.S. hunger and race are related report 46% of Africa-American children, 40% of Latin America are chronically hungry when compared to 16% of White children.

* Infant mortality rate is closely linked to inadequate nutrition among pregnant women. The U.S. ranks 23 rd among industrial nations in infant mortality. Africa-American infants die at twice the rate of white infants.

* Half of all children under five year of age in South Asia and one third of those in Sub-Saharan Africa are malnutritioned.

* In 1997 alone the lives at least 300,000 young children were saved by Vitamin A supplementation program in developing countries.

* Malnutrition implicated in more than half of all child death world wide—proportion unmatched by any infectious disease since Black Death.

* To satisfy worlds sanitation and food requirements would cost U.S. 13 billion dollar—what people of U.S. and European Union spend on perfumes each day.

* The world's three richest men are more than combined G.N.P. of all the least developed countries.

* Every 3.6. second someone dies of hunger.

* It is estimated that 800 million people in the world suffer from hunger and malnutrition about 100 times as many as those who actually die from it each year.

REGION	TABLE OF POVERTY(%)			1.25US Dollar per day	
	1990	2002	2004	1981	2008
Pacific Region	15.40	12.33	9.70	17.2	14.3
Europe & C Asia	3.60	1.28	0.95	1.9	0.5
Latin America	9.62	9.08	8.64	11.9	6.5
Middle East & NA	35.04	33.64	30.84	61.1	2.7
Sub-SaharaAfrica	46.07	42.63	41.63	51.5	47.5

DISPARITY IN WEALTH POSSESSION BY HUMANS.

*6% of World population own 52% of global assets.

*The richest of world population own more than 51% of global assets the richest 10% own 85% of global assets.

*50% of world population own less than 1% of global assets.

*The whole global assets volumes about 125 trillion US dollar.

*Over 80% of world population lives ON LESS than 10 UD dollars per day.

*Over 50% of world population lives ON LESS than 2 US dollar per day.

*Over 1.5% of world populations are billionaire who own 4.4 trillion US dollars and 4 times more than 505 of poor of the world.

*In 2005 43% of world Population (3.14 billion) people have an income less than 2.5 USD a day

*21.5% of world population (1.4 billion people) has an income less than 1.25. USD a day.

*In 2008 17% of people in developing countries are on the verge of starvation.

*The proportion of poor people with less than 34.70 USD per year is 78%. The proportion of Rich people with more than 8000USD a year is 11%.

*World Health Organization estimates that $1/3^{rd}$ of population is well fed, $1/3^{rd}$ is under fed and $1/3^{rd}$ is under starving.

*over 200 people have died of starvation each minute.

*At least 400 million people have died of starvation each year.

*One in 10 is malnutritioned including 160 million children under the age of 5 as per United Nation Food and Agriculture report.

*Consumers across the Globe now spend an estimated 35 billion (USD) on bottled water and half of the water is thrown into garbage.

*In 2000 one in 5 world populations did not have reasonable access to safe drinking water.

*Providing adequate food and basic education for world\s poorest could be achieved for less than people spend annually on makeup, ice cream (in cold countries) and pet food in European countries.

*300 Million number fire arms valuing 40 billion USD owned by people in the US. It has 88.8% fire arms per 100 people, the highest gun ownership rate in the worldwide (Courtesy CIA the World Face Book).

UNACCOUNTED WEALTH LYING IDLE IN BANKS, TEMPLES AND OTHER ENDOWMENT SHRINES:

As of November 2010 report from Washington based on Global financial Society:

* India lost USD 13 billion dollars illicit financial flow since 1948.

*Underground economy USD 640 billion as of 2008 that marks 50% GDP of nation.

* Black Money (unaccounted money) in Swiss Bank worth 462 million USD as reported by Sri.L.K. Advani Opposition Leader, Government of India during 2010.

*Treasure trove of gold coins, silver jewelry coins precious stones to worth 10.50 billion USD has been found in Hindu Temples in South India as reported by chief Secretary of Kerala Government, Sri. K. Jayakumar on July 2, 2011.

* The Comptroller and Auditor General of India calculated the loss of Government revenue on account of under priced 3G spectrum to be 576.66million which includes SUN TV Scam of 176.6 million, CWG Scam 1.35 million, Delhi Governments DDA, NDMC, MCD and PWD Scam 7.6million, Krishna Godavari Basin Scam with RIL 4.5 million and Reddy Brothers Iron ore Scam 15.6 million)

* The Global financial Integrity (GFI), Washington published illicit amount to the tune of 213 billion.

Poona based Hassan Ali and Kasinath Tripura's illicit accumulated wealth is around 5 billion USD.

* World's countries Black money including Pakistan around 340 billion USD.

Total Cost of War spent by US since 2001—USD 1,347,376,189,136

MILITARY EXPENDITURE BY WORLD COUNTRIES:

Country	percentage of annual budget
USA	41.0
China	8.2
Russia	4.1
U.K	3.6
France	3.6
Next 10 countries combined	21.3
Rest of world	18.2

Thus Total military spending in world is around 780 billion USD as of 2000 and there has been shot up to 1730 billion USD by 2011 almost 140 percent increase within a decade which is an alarming threat to human survival.

LUXURY BECAME BASIC NECESSITY FOR CERTAIN SECTION OF PEOPLE AND THE FOLLOWING TABLE INCLUDE:

Global priority	US Dollars in billions
Cosmetics in U.S.	8
Ice creams in Europe	11
Perfume in Europe and US	15
Pet foods in Europe and U.S.	17
Business entertainment in Japan	35
Cigarettes in Europe	50
Alcoholic drinks in Europe	105
Narcotic drugs	400

641 billion dollars?

BASIC SOCIAL EXPENDITURE REQUIRED TO ERADICATE POVERTY

*Basic education for all	6 billion dollars
*Water and Sanitation for all	9 billion dollars
*Reproductive for all women	12 billion dollars
*BASIC HEALTH AND NUTRITION	13 billion dollars
*Basic need for food for 25 million poor people	25 billion dollars
Total need based expenditure	65 billion dollars

ANOTHER ASTONISHING REPORT OF THE EXPENDITURE ON SUPERFLUOUS HEALTH CARE:

America spending on health care during 2011	2.6 trillion US dollars
Excess administrative cost	190 million US dollars
Prices that are too high and expenditure on aristocracy . . .	105 mission US dollars
Inefficient delivered services and remained unfruitful	130 million US dollars
Unnecessary services	210 million US dollars
Missed prevention	55 million US dollars
Fraud and evasive	75 million US dollars

(Institute of Medical report for 2011-10 M analysis
September 7,2012.)

Ahmed Sayeed

MAJOR INTERNATIONAL ISSUES OF TERRORISM AND INTERNAL CONFLICTS

(POST WORLD WAR II—21st CENTURY DATA)

PERIOD	NAME OF CONFLICT/ATTACKS	NUMBER DEATHS
6 October 1976	Columbia Flight 455 hijack	73
20 November 1979	Grand Mosque Seize	127
2 August 1979	Bologna bombing	85
8 Apr 1983	1983-US bombing	63
23 October 1983	Beirut barracks bombing	299
8 March 1985	Beirut Car bombing	80
14 May 1985	Anuradhapura Massacre	146
23 June 1985	Air India Flight 182 Bombing (Atlantic Ocean)	329
21 Dec 1988	Pan Am Flight 103 bombing over Scotland	270
12 March 1993	Bombay Bombing	257
19 April 1995	Oklahoma City bombing in Kenya & Tanzania	224
11 September 2001	September Attacks in US	3217
12 October 2002	Bali bombing in Indonesia	202
2 March 2004	Ashura Massacre in Iraq	170
11March 2004	Madrid Train bombing in Spain	191
4 September 2004	Beslan School hostage crisis in Russia	344
28 February 2005	Al Hilal Bombing in Iraq	127
7 July 2005	London Bombing in UK	52
11 July 2006	Mumbai Train bombing in India	207
27 March 2007	Tal Afar bombing and massacre in Iraq	152
14 August 2007	Yazd communities bombing in Iraq	796
26-28 November 2008	Mumbai attacks in India	185
22 July 2011	Norway attacks	77
6 December 2011	Ashura Bombing in Afghanistan	80
20 January 2012	Nigeria Attacks	185

21 May 2012	Sana'a bombing in Yemen	101
13 June 2012	Iraq attacks	93
23 July 2012	Iraq Attacks	116
14 August 2012	Human bomb attack in Mosque in Pakistan	89
19 September 2012	Human Bomb attack in Mosque in Pakistan	76
26 October 2012	Myanmar Ethnic violence	56

(In addition many civilian attacks by Military in Syria, Libya, Yemen, Egypt and other middle east countries amounting 1000 of killings and several thousands of people migrated to other countries)

ATTEMPT TO ANALYSE THE SOCIAL CAUSES FOR THE OF CAUSE POVERTY, ACQUISITION OF MASS WEALTH BY INDIVIDUALS THROUGH UNNATURAL METHODS AND REASONS OF CONFLICTS AND MASS ACCRE—A GENERAL ANALYSIS:

UNITED NATION was established after World War II with a motto to maintain world peace. This is well known fact. But the question is was this really successful in doing so? Following list include success and failure of U.N. since establishment in 1945.

SUCCESSES:

*First and foremost is it has prevented occurancy of any further World War. It became instrumental in peace in many parts of the world to some extent.

* It played a significant role in disarming the world and making it nuclear free. Various treaties, negotiations like

partial Nuclear Test Ban treaty and Nuclear-nonprolifition treaty have been signed under the supervision of UN.

*Demise of colonialism and imperialism on one hand and apartheid on the other had UN sanction behind them.

*UN acted as Vanguard for the protection of human rights on the people of the world by Universal declaration of Human rights in 1948.

*Despite crippled by Britton Woods Institution, UN has played limited but effective role in economic matters. Supported North-South dialogue and aspired for emergence of new Economic International order.

*Agencies of UN like WHO, UNICEF, UNESCO have keenly participated in the transformation of International social sector.

*Peace Keeping operations, peaceful resolutions of disputes and refugee concerns and had always been on the LIST OF CORE ISSUES.

* Since 1945 the UN has been credited with negotiations 172 peaceful settlements that have ended regional conflicts.

*The World Body was also instrumental in institutionalization of International Laws and world legal frame work.

* Passage of various conventions and declarations on Child, Women Climate etc. highlights the extra-political affairs of otherwise political World Body.

*It has successfully controlled the situation in Serbia, Yugoslavia and Balkan areas.

*A number peace missions in Africa has done reasonably to control the situation.

FAILURES:

* U.N. opinion on Hungary and Czechoslovakia were ignored erstwhile soviet Union in 1950.

* Israel had been taking unilateral action through decades in its geographical victory and nothing substantial come out even as on date.

*No emphatic role in crisis of worst kinds like Cuban missile crisis, Vietnam crisis.

* UN was nowhere in the picture in the NATO rained bombs over former Yugoslavia.

*Uni-Polarity and Unilateralism has shaken the relevance of the world body. Unilateral action in Iraq was bereft of UN action.

*Failed to generate universal consensus to protect the deteriating world climate even at Copenhagen in 2007.

* Number of nuclear powers in the world has kept increasing. UN could not control the horizontal expansion and proliferation of weapons and arms.

* Financial dependence on the industrialized nations has at times deviated UN from neutrality and impartiality.

* AIDS is crossing regions and boundaries both in spread and intensity.

* Domestic situation of near anarchy in Iraq and many regions of Afghanistan despite on active UN. The US president scheme of withdrawal has not able to bring back specific solutions in the region even after Osama Bin Laden was put to death. In fact the situation has been further aggregated. Human bomb attacks are still going on even at the so called sacred places like Mosques and tombs in Pakistan, resulting into thousands of deaths of innocent prayers.

* The UN totally exposed in the case of invasion on Iraq in the name for the search weapon of mass destruction. US withdrawn its combat forces but the law and order and mutual distrust worsened at this juncture and the UN seems to be clue less.

* North East Asian Islamic countries like Egypt, Libya, Jordan, Syria Yemen have become turbulent due to ethnic and power crisis and UN secretary Kofi Annan's attempts gone waste and UN became a watch dog.

* UN has not intervened in humanitarian crisis in Syria encouraging Al Assad to kill people with an armed aid by Russia. Turkish Premier says "The UN security council has not intervened in the human tragedy that has been going on in Syria for 20 months". On account of crisis in Syria dissident people to the tune of 336,000 have migrated to neighboring countries like Turkey, Lebanon, Jordan and Iraq during the past 20 months. This is one of the recent inaction by apex body.

* Veto powers with five Permanent members of the council are still rests with them and this shows the inability of the World body in taking action against the aggressions that hamper world peace.

Thus I can say humanity's problems remained problems only without any suitable solutions since centuries. The main problems of humanity's include: (i) non provision of Energy (ii) Inadequate food (iii) Unbearable Poverty with 40% of human population (iv) Terrorism and War (v) non-eradication of deadly diseases (vi) non-establishment of Democratical governing in all the countries (vii) Non imparting Education to all humans (viii) Non controlling over population (ix) Inadequate provision of drinking water and (x) non adopting measures to eradicate polluted environment which causes global warming. In this context we need to study the basic causes or say PROBLEMS creating above quoted problems. It can be well determined that the following are main CONCERNS OF ABOVE ISSUES which include:

PSYCHOOLOGICAL PROBLEM:

Micro level that is individual level:

* Disrupted relationship with care givers;

*Unexpected death in the family;

*Abuse (sexual, physical, emotional and psychological);

* Chronic family instability;

*Family dysfunction and break down;

* Conflict and rejection in significant relationship and

* Improper education.

*Addiction to unwarranted habits like drugs and alcohol;

*Preparing for crime and violence for irrational provocations by religious and political fundamentalists;

*Greed and inclination towards artificial pleasures of mass prompts, like communal enjoyment, entertainment and encroachment

SOCIAL AND ECONOMIC PROBLEMS:.

*Forced transactions from living off the land to wage earning and welfare economy;

* high rate of poverty—lack of need based facilities like food, water, shelter, clothing, power, sanitation etc.

* Limited employment opportunities;

*Inadequate housing and health services;

*Deficiency in water and sanitary qualities.

* Cultural and traditions stress;

* Irrational beliefs and ritual expenses.

* Racial and ethnical discrimination;

* Honor and Status incurrence on ceremonies like births, deaths and marriages.

* Classification of humans in multi-class systems which is not a right perspective of humans.

CHAPTER XIX

Russell determined man to the "product of causes, his origin, his growth, his hopes and fears, his love and his belief are but the outcome of accidental collections of atoms that no fire, no heroism, no intensity of thought and feeling can preserve an individual life beyond the grave" that all the labors of the ages, all inspiration, all the noonday brightness of human genius are destined to extinction of vast death of solar system, that the whole temple of MANS ACHIEVEMENT MUST INEVITABLY BE BURIED BENEATH THE DEBRIS OF A UNIVERSE IN RUINS—all these things, if not beyond dispute are so nearly certain that no Philosophy which rejects them can hope to stand.

CULTIVATION OF MIND SHOULD BE THE ULTIMATE AIM OF HUMAN EXISTENCE

The struggles, wars, conflicts of ideological, ethnical, religious and national are mainly due to current generation has forgotten where they and their ancestors came from. Face to face, with untold sorrow, world leaders should determine not to let the HUMANAITY ENGLUFED IN WAR and ensure that it should happen again and again. Affirming their faith in dignity and as an INDIVIDUAL, they should set their minds on the advancement of all peoples. Centuries have passed since civilization and humanity had seen, has seen and seeing still much violence, suffering due to poverty, and injustice in exercising human rights. There remain dangers that could threaten the very civilization and indeed the future of humanity. Due to advancement of Science and technology as discussed in earlier chapters, we came to know that where are we from and what caused us to take birth. We have got more power to shape our future and forthcoming generation shall acknowledge the emancipation and empowerment of their lives.

The time has come to right to foster the wishes of nation and states and people to control their destinies and find what they can do so only by working together with each other. They must secure their future through commitment to common responsibility and shared effort. The need to work together also guided the visionary starts and shift of focus from states to THE PEOPLE. An aspect of this change is growth of INTERNATIONAL SOCIETY.

Let us recall once again how humans who are called INTELLIGENT ANIMAL or SOCIAL ANIMAL and POLITICAL ANIMAL came to existence. Our mind began its development about 500 million years ago in small specie in the "small pond or water based Tank" that barely had enough neurons to orient itself to light. Eventually fish evolved showing further growth in the brain stem. The brain stem is responsible for our bodies' involuntary functions such as breathing, sleeping, heart beating reproduction etc. It is also responsible for much of behavior when were young.

Sea creatures evolved to land animals and the brain grew further quite similar human brain stem today. The mammal cerebrum showed up and with emotions and the capacity to learn emerged. This mammal brain also known as the LIMBIC system, from limbos or cap (around the brain) evolved until it was covered by the THINKING CAP, the cerebral cortex With this, evolution of cerebral cortex in human, human started learning rapidly. Our first brain weighed only about 1pound. As we evolved, the cerebral cortex folded in on itself in order to maximize the surface area, thus enabling greater blood supply. Since its humble beginning, the human brain now weighs in at 3 pounds and consumes 40% of the oxygen in our blood. The brain has grown approximately 3and half pounds in the last hundred years which indicate that human brain is growing at a faster than we have experienced possibly due to increase in availability of printed and digital information (knowledge). And this knowledge causes the brain to grow.

Thus it can suitably be said without any counter that HUMAN (say MAN or ADAM) has not consumed any fruit of "The Tree of Knowledge" grown in the EDEN GARDEN and was ordered by GOD or ALLAH not to eat the fruit otherwise he will die and disobedience of the ORDER caused him to fall on earth" as theorized by all the Three Abrahamic Religions, to whom 2/3 of human population were allowed to be believed and on account of which innumerable wars and massacres took place resulting millions of humans were put to dust. And, surprisingly, clashes are still on footage and put human society to dysfunctions.

The thinking brain can be viewed as an electro chemical organ that run stimulus (external and internal) and process the input in a systematic and reverberating manner. The cycle goes something like this:

INPUT THROUGH SENSES>EMOTIONS>MUSLCE CONTROL>MEMORY>LEARNING.

Under MRI scan the cycle can be seen through different areas of the brain responsible for emotions, muscles, learning etc. The thinking process several distinct brain areas and if one or more of these areas is out of whack out entire thought process and safety could be in jeopardy.

KNOW THY SELF:

(The 100th monkey effect)—The hundredth monkey effect is based upon the principle that after one monkey on an island discovers how to wash a coconut in the water to remove the sand and dirt, the rest follow suit until the last or say hundredth monkey, finally learns this improved methods. At this point monkeys on the other island become aware of this knowledge with direct communication. This same effect has happened repeatedly in human history where inventors simultaneously discovered inventions that around the world were contemplating at the same time. The thoughts become energy and this energy that is available to others that tune into this energy field or UNIVERSAL CONSCIOUSNESS. This brain process of information works in a cyclical fashion that relies heavily on memory, for storing and retrieving data so that we may realize it on and of. If we fail to store information properly it creates problems for us when we try to remember and apply the information. Such is the power and preciousness of our brain.

Scientists are breaking their head in trying to create such brains' simulation artificially. A "HUMAN BRAIN PROJECT" (HBP) funded by European Union, seemed to create world's first SIMULATION OF WHOLE HUMAN BRAIN artificially. The complexity of the Brain with it s billions of interconnected neurons makes it hard for Neuro-Scientists to understand how it works. The human brain is far larger with about one million cortical columns a computer that can simulate would have to carry out of billions of calculations over every second and that would consume the output of an entire Nuclear power station using present technology. It seems by 2014 they hope to have a working copy of entire brain of a mouse with its 1000 cortical columns and which will take 300,000 processors consuming 700,000 pounds (5.6 billion Indian rupees). They also report that our brain consume only TINY amount of energy and it last for 90 years or more. It is also reported that in the coming decades CONNECTOMES (mapping showing how brain cells link up) will dominate our thinking on what it means to be HUMAN.

WISDOM:

Such humans having such invaluable brain have been mercilessly butchered and thrown in to garbage. Here the parody is the Killer and Killed are HUMANS only. Intellect is the functioning of head (mammal brain), instinct is the functioning of the body (the reptilian brain) and intuition or wisdom is the functioning of heart (inspirational brain). And behind these there is a MASTER-ME or YOU or OUR. A wise person creates hormone between the head, heart and body. In this hormone comes the revelation of the source of one's LIFE, the very center of HUMANITY. We all have the past, present and future. Instinct is what belongs to past, Intellect is human which is our present. The intellect is fallible because it is new recent arrival. Intellect lives through prejudice, it is never fair. Intellect is your mind, instinct is your body and the linkage of intellect and instinct is HUMANITY and to enlighten this humanity one must understand our position in the universe, since intellect is a tool and is a servant and not a MASTER.

For getting master one should obtain knowledge through stages of our growth of body from child hood to adulthood and adulthood to old age and finally to the stage of end that is DEATH TO DUST. Nevertheless, it is clear that there will neither temporary nor permanent LIFE after death. Going to hell or heaven after death are nothing but fairy accomplishments. At the most we may become neuron to support to other form of life, and nothing more than that. Thus the life now we are in 'being' is only life and hence we need to live a peaceful and pleasant life as best as possible, rather struggling each other for unknown BETTER LIFE after death. This is wisdom of life by all means.

Knowing things is knowledge and knowing yourself is wisdom since right knowledge is a lifelong companion. Thus knowledge is unity and ignorance is diversity. WISDOM begins with the dawn of reason. When you know better you would do better as knowledge empowers you to change how world works. So the price of wisdom is above diamond. Wisdom and virtue are like two wheels of life's cart.

Man once born and grow until death need to depend on others, for many reasons, like learning earning, flourishing, nurturing and diminishing unto death. We came into the world as a result of other's actions. We survive here on earth in dependence on each other. Whether we like it or not there is hardly a moment of lives when we do not benefit from others activities. And for this reason only our pleasure and pain arises in the context of our relationship with others. Sex with your mate, success in our dealings with others, are the factors of pleasure, where as sickness, disappointments, old age, miseries and mishaps are the causes of pain. Procreation is the purpose of life. These processes are socially related and hence right from our beingness to becomingness should go, eventually, ethical and thus sustenance of society nurtures. This is a universal principle whether he is an Asian or African, Southerner or Northerner and theist or atheist. This is why because, firstly, our every action has a universal dimension, a potential impact on others, happiness and ethics are necessary means to ensure that we restrain ourselves from being violent on others because they too are like ours. Thus right knowledge enlightens right faculty and right faculty provides right individual. Right human assumes right qualities of love, passion, patience, tolerance, forgiveness and son and so forth. This is the foundation of human peace which provides both for individual and universal sustainability.

If the individual is happy, group will be happy, if group is happy society will be happy and society is happy nation is happy and nation is happy UNIVERSALITY will be happy. It is however, this is an Utopian idea still has its own limitations. Aristotle, the great Greek Philosopher and teacher of the Alexander the Great had rightly argued around 2700 years back that "human ability to strive toward higher level of morality, justice and brotherhood is what set them apart from lesser animals" and so we are not lesser animals hence we can achieve that utopian idealism. He further argues that "we must not follow those who advice us to have sub-human thoughts, since we are only man and have mortal thoughts and as mortals should on contrary we try to be as immortal as far as that is possible and to do our utmost in accordance with what is highest in us" (Aristotle—34) Plato, teacher of Aristotle and student of Socrates, also criticized for the "traditional societal structuring, which certainly projects an initial impulse" In his great Book "The Republic" he not only presents the first thorough model of a utopian Society but also represents to some of the first materials in social education. This encouraged peoples to do better for each other. He also states" HUMANITY SHOULD ASPIRE TO THE IDEAS OF JUSTICE, FRIENDSHIP AND MORALITY THAT IT DISCOVERS IN THIS UNSEEN REALM (unseen realm Plato's view was "where ideas born" that is 'THE BRAIN' FOR WHICH HUMANS ONLY HAVE ACCESS).

John Locke, 17th century British Philosopher who wanted individuals to use reason to seek truth rather than relying on authorities and pronouncements as to what truth is. He refutes Ren'e'Descartes(Philosopher) contention that HUMAN BEINGS KNOW CERTAIN CONCEPTS 'INNATELY', and in this contest he profound that human mind was what he called is 'TAABULA RASA' which is Latin word for "clean sheet of paper". He believed infants know nothing when they are born and all the ideas come from EXPERIENCE and acquired by knowledge only. An Experience is of two types: external and internal. External experience is "sensation" referring human being's interaction with objects of real world, including color, motion and number of such objects. He referred "internal experience" as reflection referring to acts of the mind such as knowing, believing, remembering and doubting" He also proposed that all sensation and reflection fell into the categories of being either simple or complex. A simple idea is one which centers on one element such as say 'whiteness'. A complex idea is one which combines several simple elements as an 'an apple contain simple concept of whiteness, redness and roundness'

KNOWLWDGE BREEDS WISDOM

Knowledge comes from learning and application of thought in right way is called wisdom. Real success comes from applying wisdom in our day to day life. In sum, knowledge comes from the left/logical side of brain and knowing comes from right/intuitive side of our brain and the two halves of our brain constitute our mind. Our mind has tendency to talk to us incessantly our mind also has an ego that stops our higher self our true being from gaining control over our mind our higher self has the chance to guide us towards enlightenment (which equates the living in moment, the present, the here and now)

We need left brain to help us to educate ourselves so that we make decent living of ourselves and our family, but perhaps more important is the EDUCATION /use of right brain in order life to be rewarding. Only by utilizing two halves together we become 'WHOLE'. After learning how to utilize both sides of our mind is the next step is to learn to quiet the mind so that we can attain wisdom and enlightenment. We must rise above the ego of the mind and find of our higher self 'TRUE-BEING'. Thus the journey of enlightenment begins.

To conclude "watch your thought, they become words, watch your words they become actions, watch your actions they become habits, watch your habits they become character and watch your character it becomes your destiny". You are the better judge to decide "mental intelligence VS emotional intelligence—which is a better indicator of success. Mental intelligence may have higher correlation to school or college and financial success but emotional relation is more important when seeking the ultimate prizes in life—happiness, peace, love and joy. Thus the point is to be smart enough to know that you need both type of intelligence in order to truly succeed in life. Left brain thinking without right brains support is a little like playing cricket or soccer with only half of your team on the field.

Further no deep resentments are justified! Why means that by harboring resentment against others you are really stopping from obtaining peace. So let us get rid of resentment.

To get wisdom is better than Gold and understanding is more valuable than silver. The more anger you have inside, the more likely you lose ties with your success. Anger usually a sign that tells that you have problems. The real problem is partly or mainly inside you. Admit it and you are half way in solving your problem. To get wisdom is to get right knowledge at a right time.

HUMAN BEING—A GOOD CITIZEN

A good human must be good citizen also in the context of his fellow beings since he is not only a intelligent animal but also a SOCIAL AND POLITICAL ANIMAL. Having acquired a true knowledge and wisdom about himself and his life, he should think of about his mate, children, family, and also about the society and realize his responsibility towards it. As Socrates the father of Philosophy, pronounced that "He is neither a citizen of Greece nor a citizen of Athens but a citizen of world'. This was proclaimed around 2700 years ago. For a good citizen good education is required to be imparted and the education should have curriculum that imparts ethical foundation.

"Modern education is competitive, nationalistic and seperative. It has trained to regard material values as of major importance, to believe that nation is also of major importance and superior to respect other nations and peoples. The general level of world information is high but usually biased, influenced by national prejudice, serving to make us citizen of our nation but not of the world" Albert Einstein, the great Scientist quotes. Such education should not be encouraged otherwise result would be going back to middle ages or say even historic age. Without an integrated understanding life, our individual and collective problems will deepen and extend. The purpose of education is not to produce mere scholars, technicians and job hunters, but integrated men and women who are free of fear. For only between such human beings there can be enduring peace.

Citizenship is sacred honor, a plaque we carry on our back, chests and a burden pressing hard on our back. A citizen is a member of a society, country and global. He has the right to ask for its protection and duty to protect it and obey its laws and rules. In other words citizenship is relationship between individual and state which the individual belong and owes allegiance to country (instead to a particular region or religion). Fortunately being a good citizen does not stop at the exchange of rights and duties, it requires a lot of civilized behavior—respect others, respect others property, respect elders respect the ruler, treat your family and children with love and affection, elect suitable leader for governance, discourage corruption loyal and dutiful to service, discourage pilferage and suitably guard your ecological environment.

SOCIETY IS COLLECTIVITY OF INDIVIDUALS

Individual and Society are inter related and I do not think one exists without the other. Say one person is the most individualistic on earth has reference to as to how that person relates to the rest of society. Similarly Society is collective of individuals who make up the whole. The individual has not obligation except to his or her own rational self interest. The only right that exist are individual right. What exactly are rights? They are ways subordinating society to moral law. The only right exists is mans right to his life—and all rights that exists can be derived from this. They do not come from government or God, but they do depend upon the nature of individual existence only. Rights guarantee man's ability to lead a life as rational being. Natures demand is no less, unlike other animals, man's existence depend upon not upon instincts, but on rational thought. Even if man does not live by his rational thought, he depends on the rational thoughts of others. He can use rational thoughts of others to guide his action for example farmer who use farm machinery or as a parasite existing off rational thought of others for example any common burglar.

The conditions for rational existence are free from coercion and the right to that what that which one produces. This is not a right to an object or service, such as education or healthcare but only to the product of one's labor and rational thought. As the only rights that exist are considered negative, like obligation to do something to someone else. Positive rights are an obligation to do something for someone else who does not exist. This means that another man's need does not constitute a claim to another man's wealth. The condition of man's survival depend on actions of the individual (thinking, acting judgment etc.) and society. A Society cannot or think of individuals in society, individuals in a society can act or act or think, but society is an abstract term that does not exist exclusively but exists in the mind of an individual. Man owes nothing to the society and society owes nothing to him. His only obligation is HIMSELF or HIS RATIONAL SELF INTEREST. If the individual is not helped, Society would not be a fun place to be. There would be no joy to transfer.

Overall balance between individual rights and the good of society is the key, to finding a successful happy society. In general rights of the individuals are more important, when and where they do encroach on the rights of the other individuals, but where they interact the society here comes first. This action followed must be that which will most benefit society. Thus when someone acts out against society, such as a thought of theft or murder, directly violating another individual's right is in the interest of society is to stop them. Thus laws are created as a way determining in those interaction who is right and who is wrong and how society should react to those actions. The structure of power penetrate whole society giving advantage to the norm with in media, the educational system, the law, the economy the political system etc. All types of inequality are interconnected, all oppression is based on elitist system based on the idea that some people are better than others and thus deserving better living condition. The various hierarchical systems interact with and reinforce each other.

In Columbia the structure of war connected to the structure of capitalism, racism and patriacity. The social system of mechanism is linked with militarism; they both based on elitist social order that celebrates aggressiveness and violence, feminizing and victimizing peacefulness. According to the international analysis Power is situational, who is more powerful and indigenous male from working class or a white or middle class female? It depends on the situation. Each person encounters different conditions due to its position within different social categories and depending on the situation. Therefore it is crucial to take into consideration all the dimension of power. The structure of power has to be visualized and opposed to eradicate them and constructive alternative have to be created. On a personal or Micro level this action or behavior can be called change. If this change grows to a higher or macro level this can lead to transformation of society as a whole—using non-violent methods one shows the ability to create a peaceful including equal alternative, symbolizing the type of society that one wants to create.

SUSTAINABLE SOCIETY: The ancient who wished to illustrate illustrious virtue throughout the world, first ordered well their own society and state.

Wishing to order well their States, they first regulated their families. Wishing to regulate their families, they first cultivated their persons. Wishing to cultivate their persons, they first rectified their hearts. Wishing to be sincere in their thoughts, they first extended to the utmost their knowledge.
Such extension of knowledge lay in the investigation of things.
This being investigated, knowledge became complete.
Their knowledge being complete, their thoughts were sincere.
Their thoughts being sincere, their hearts were then rectified.
Their hearts being rectified, their persons were cultivated.
Their persons being cultivated, their families were regulated.
Their families being regulated, their States were highly governed.
Their States being rightly governed, the entire world was at peace.

The Great Learning is significant because it expresses many themes of ethical, philosophical and political thinking and has therefore been extremely influential both in classical and modern thought. Self-cultivation, self investigation and self rectification at individual level are interlinked with individual as good citizen and society as sustainable one. Modern days social problems are over population, abnormal poverty index, global warming and terrorism and regional and communal conflicts. Today our society is developing into more global society, due to more advanced transportation, development of technologies like internet, we are able to travel and communicate with people across the world from our home. Global society can be viewed as the intensification of worldwide social relation in such a way that local happenings are shaped by events occurring many kilo meters away/ miles away and vice versa. Advancement over the years to continue to bring people closer and closer together making it impossible to "make sense of our daily lives or understand processes, organizations and relationships that extend far outside the particular country where we live.

Most new discoveries and inventions are not found by Society as whole but individuals and small groups of people. Individuals can have a positive effect on the global society, but they can also a negative effect as well. This can easily seen in Terrorist where an individual or small group of people have a negative effect on the global society but now every air port you go into has increased their security. The 9/11 attacks "introduced an unparallel as symmetry into global relations, namely asymmetry between states and channeled means of protection and society based means of terror.

DYSFUNCTIONAL SOCIETY:

Terrorism is just an example of having the global society can become society dysfunctional. Another problem our society faces is sustainability. We are currently using many of our resources faster than can be created. Our society also is creating pollution faster than the Earth can decompose it and may be causing global warming. Further our population continues to grow at a rate WHEN WE EVENTUALLY RUN OUT OF ROOM. Because it is easier to travel today but it is also easier for diseases to spread across the world faster than the rate. SWINE FLU, WEST NILE VIRUS and SARS are few such examples. There are problems of poverty, unemployment on account of which there is DYSFUNCTION OF SOCIETY. While the global economy grows rapidly, income gap between the world poorest and richest people continues to widen the doubling in the past 50 years.

In relation to the solutions of individual and social problems we have discussed in detail in earlier chapters how a good citizen is required his duties to be discharged while living in group or society. Only RIGHT EDUCATION BREEDS RIGHT KNOWLEDGE, RIGHT KNOWLEDGE BREEDS RIGHT WISDOM AND RIGHT WISDOM BREEDS RIGHT CITIZEN and SOCIETY IS AN ABSTRACT TERM THAT ENCAMPASSES THE INDIVIDUALS BOTH MEN AND WOMEN. NON— GOVERNMENTAL ORGANIZATIONS ARE ACCUTELY REQUIRED TO ERADICATE SOCIAL EVILS SINCE FOR EVERY THING GOVERNMENT CANNOT ATTEND AND SOLVE INDIVIDUAL PROBLEMS.

HOWEVER, GOOD GOVERNANCE AT NATIONAL OR STATE AND INTERNATIONAL LEVEL IS HIGHLY WARRENTED IN THIS MODERN TIME WHERE SCIENCE AND TECHNOLOGY MADE WORLD INTO A GLOBAL VILLAGE and about which next concluding chapter will focus how best our universe or this global village can be governed and establish peace and harmony among HUMANS.

CONCLUSION:

The Global Society is relatively a newer Society considering Societies that were formed thousands of years ago. It is still developing and making the world seem small through advancements in the advancements in technology. We need to find more ways to fix problems we face now and try to minimize the problems through interference of Global alliances between the SOCIETIES/STATES/NATIONS.

Before finding a clear cut solution let me bring the social and national and Global DYSFUNCTIONS in brief once again in the ensuing chapter.

For I dip into the future, as far as human eye could see,

Saw a vision of the world, and all the wonder that would be,

Till the war-drum throbbed no longer and the battle-flag were furled,

In the parliament of man, the Federation of world,

There the common sense of most shall hold a fretful realm in awe

And the kindly earth shall slumber, lap in Universal law.

—Lord Alfred Tennyson

CHAPTER XX
GLOBAL GOVERNANCE—
A PHILOSOPHICAL SKETCH

Immanuel Kant wrote the essay "Perpetual peace: a Philosophical sketch" during 1795. In his essay, Kant describes three basic requirements for organizing human affairs to permanently abolish the threat of present and future war, and thereby help establishment a new era of lasting peace throughout the world. In 1811, a German Philosopher Karl Krause, suggested in his essay titled" The Archetype of Humanity", the formation of five regional federations: Europe, Asia, Africa and Australia, aggregated under World Republic.

In a simple and broad based definition of world governance, the term is used to designate all regulations intended for organization and centralization of human societies on global scale.

CONTEXT

The political homogenization of the planet that has followed the advent of what is known as liberal democracy in its many forms should make it easier to establish a world governance system that goes beyond market LAISSEZ-FAIRE and the democratic peace originally formulated by Immanuel Kant, which constitutes sort of geopolitical LAISSEZ-FAIRE. Further to secure for all human being in all parts of the world conditions allowing a decent and meaningful life, requires enormous human energies and far reaching problems each related to or even part of the development challenge, each similarly pressing, and each calling for the same urgent attention. No doubt our age is the first generation since the dawn of history in which mankind dares to believe it practical to make the benefits of civilization available to the whole human race.

NEED OF SUCH OCCASION:

Tolerance for inequalities and the growing demand for redistribution, attitude towards risk and over property rights vs human rights, regional conflicts and imbalances mal-distribution of wealth unhealthy classification of humans into so many categories like labor class, middle class, slum dwellers, aristocrats, upper class, business tycoons, drainage-dwellers etc. In such cases, globalization even serve to accentuate differences rather than as force for homogenization. Responsibility must play its part with respect to regional and International Governments, when balancing the needs of its citizenry.

Further we are at the cross roads of most serious economic social crisis in modern history. The process of global impoverishment unleashed at the outset of the 1980's debt has reached major turning point leading to the simultaneous outbreak of famines in all major regions of the developing world, political corruption and unbalanced distribution wealth.

There are many features underlying the global economic crisis pertaining to financial markets, the decline in production, collapse of State Institutions where corruption has opened its dragonic mouth and rapid development of a profit driven war economy. What is rarely mentioned here is this global economy restructuring impringes on four fundamentals of life: FOOD, SHELTER, WATER AND FUEL. The provision of food is a precondition of civilized society; they are necessary factors for the survival of human species. In recent years the prices of these variables have increased dramatically at the global level, with devastating economic and social consequences. These four essential goods or commodities which are in a real sense to determine the reproduction of economic and social life on PLANET EARTH and these are under the control of small number of global corporations and financial institutions. Protest movements directed against the links in the prices food and gasoline has erupted simultaneously in the regions of the world.

To cite very few examples where wealth is abnormally accumulated and lying abused are:

(i)   Reliance Industries Limited Managing Director, Anil Ambani has presented a HELICOPTER AS GIFT TO HIS WIFE ON HER BIRTH DAY

(ii) Mr. Gali Janardhanreddy a business Tycoon of Mines, gifted 45 million dollar worth Gold crown to the Lord Venkateswara, an Idol of God of Hindus, at Tirupathi, South India,

(iii) Gold worth150 million US dollars lying idle in Veerabhadraswamy temple, KERALA, SOUTH INDIA; most abusive incident on INDIAN POLITICISIANS IS AN AMOUNT OF 450 MILLION Us dollar corrupt money is lying in Swiss Bank lockers, where 40% of Indian HUMANS are on the verge of starvation.

(iv) Another astonishing news from America is an old women who had 50 million dollar lying in her Saving account in an American Bank, has nominated to be inherited that amount to her PET DOG after her death and

(v) 1421 Million dollar are being incurred on cosmetics and perfumes, cigarettes and narcotic drugs etc. every year in US when 6.5 % Africa-American citizens are under below poverty line who are living with less than 1.25 USD per day.

Similarly in countries like HAITI NICARAGUA, GOUTEMALA, BANGLADESH the conditions are critical Spiraling food and fuel prices in SOMALIA haprecipated the entire country into a situation of mass starvation, coupled with severe water shortage. A similar and equally serious situation prevailed in Ethiopia. Other countries affected by spiraling food prices include INDONESIA, ZIMBABWE, KENYA, ERITREA a long listed impoverished countries . . . . not to mention those under foreign military occupation including IRAQ, AFGHANISTAN AND PALESTINE. The fate of millions of human being is managed behind by sitting in closed doors in the corporate boardrooms as a part of profit driven agenda. These untold miseries of humanity on one side and an enormous wealth to the tune of trillions of USD lying idle with few rich on the other side (10% of global population) of the planet Earth demands a Universal Governance on Earth. This must be right occasion to have UNIVERSAL WELFARE GOVERNMENT SINCE ALL HUMANS BELONG TO PLANET EARTH. If not now it will never be done. This would be nothing but one of the HUMAN RIGHTS TO BE RIGHTLY RULED BY GLOBAL GOVERNANCE TO PROTECT AND SUSTAIN HUMAN BASIC RIGHTS UNLESS AND UNTIL THAT BASIC NEEDS ARE FULFILLED THERE IS NO RIGHT TO LIVE THE SO CALLED BUSINESS TYCOONS WHO ARE MONITORING THE WORLD ECONOMY.

Challenges of Globalization: the concept of Global Governance is not an academic mental exercise. It is the attempt to find a political answer to the challenges of

Globalization. It is not a myth or a Phantom, but historical reality and for many 'Globalization opponents' a dreadful and threatening scenario. The multilayered development trends in global society, world economy and global politics upon which diffuse and controversial phenomenon is based on consolidat4ed here into the following thesis.

Firstly: globalization is neither something completely new nor the acceleration of the EUROPENIZATION OF THE WORLD that began centuries ago. It is also a not a fateful natural event rather the result of politically desired deregulation strategies. Vilifying it is pointless, since it is however absolutely essential to manage politically its momentum and strengthen the formation of power politics.

Secondly: Globalization holds a risks and opportunities it has winners and losers on the level of the world States and inside the societies of every region in the world. On the other hand it makes the use of the technologically superior ONE WORLD OR WORLD VILLIAGE AND OFFERS COMPETETIVE EMERGING NATIONS NEW OPPORTUNITIES ON THE WORLD MARKET deregulated by the World Trade Organization (WTO). On the other hand, threatens the further marginalize entire regions both economically and politically.

Thirdly: the World market functions as a global court ruling on competitive conditions, Social and Environmental standards are subject to increasingly deregulated free trade increases the temptation to create completive advantages at great cost of humans and nature. If the principles of competition were not tamed through regulation, the social Darwinist principle of "Survival of the fittest "would hold sway".

Fourthly and Finally: the question of controllability of global problems from which no nation can withdraw in our global risky society has become a central issue for Global politics. The Globalization of the economy and Technology, of communication and transport system has also rendered undesirable developments internationally. Problems from regions that seems far removed such impoverishment environmental destruction and migration driven by poverty or wars have global boomerang effects. Three centuries ago in his introduction to the North South Commission headed which came to be known as the BRANDT REPORT— Willy Brandt emphasized that "WHETHER WE LIKE IT OR NOT WE ARE INCREASINGLY FACED WITH PROBLEMS THAT EFFECT THE HUMANITY, SO THAT LOGICALLY THEIR SOLUTIONS NEED TO BE INCREASINGLY INTERNATIONALIZED AS WELL. THE GLOBALIZATION OF DANGERS AND CHALLENGES—WAR, CHAOS, SELF DESTRUCTION, TERRORISM, REQUIRE A TYPE OF GLOBAL DOMESTIC POLITICS THAT GOES WELL BEYOND THE HORIZON OF CHURCH OR MOSQUE STEEPLES BUT ALSO WELL BEYOND NATIONAL BORDERS"

HISTORICAL ATTEMPTS FOR GLOBAL GOVERNANCE:

INTERNATIONAL PEACE CONGRESS: starting in 1843 International Peace Congresses were held in Europe every two years, but lost their momentum after 1853 due to renewed outbreak of wars in Europe (Crimea) and North America (American civil War)

INTERNATIONAL ORGANIZATIONS: International Organizations like Committee of Red Cross in 1863, the Telegraphic Union in 1865 and Universal Postal Union in 1874. In 1883 JAMES LORIMER published "The Institute of the Law of Nations" in which he explored the idea of a world government establishing the global rule of Law. The first embryonic World Parliament, called the Inter-Parliamentary Union was organized in 1886 by Cremer and Passy, composed of legislators from many countries. In 1904 the Union formally proposed an International Congress which should meet periodically to discuss international questions"

LEAGUE OF NATIONS:

The LEAGUE OF NATIONS (LoN) was an intergovernmental organization founded as a result of the Treaty of Versailles in 1919-1920. At its largest size from 28 September 1934 to 23 February 1935, it had 58 members. The LEAGUE's goals included upholding the Rights of Man, such as the non-whites, women, and soldiers; disarmament, preventing war through collective security, settling disputes between countries through negations, preventing war through collective security, settling disputes between countries through negotiation, diplomacy, and improving global quality of life. The diplomatic philosophy behind the league represented a fundamental shift in thought from the preceding hundred years. The League lacked its own armed force and so depended on the Great powers to enforce its resolutions and economic sanctions and provide an army, when needed. Lacking many of the key elements necessary to maintain world peace, the LEAGUE OF NATIONS failed to prevent WORLD WAR II. Having failed its primary goal, the League Nations fell apart eventually and was transformed into the UNITED NATIONS in 1945 after the end of World War II.

NAZI GERMANY:

The ruling NAZI Party of 1933-45 Germany envisaged the ultimate establishment of a world Government under the complete hegemony of the Third Reich. Adolf Hitler in his desire stated political aim of expanding the "Living Space" of the Germany people by destroying or driving out "lesser deserving races" in and from other territories. HE BELIEVED THAT WORLD PEACE COULD ONLY BE ACAUIRED WHEN ONE POWER, THE RACIALLY BEST ONE, AND ATTAINED CONTESTED SUPRAMACY AND WHEN THIS CONTROL WOULD BE ACHIEVED, THIS POWER COULD THEN SET UP FOR ITSELF A WORLD POLICE AND ASSURE ITSELF THE NECESSARY LIVING SPACE.

ATLANTIC CHARTER:

This Atlantic Charter was published statement agreed between Britain and the US. It was intended as the blueprint for the post world war II and turn out to be foundation for many of the International agreement like General agreement on tariffs and trade(GATT), the post war independence of British and French possessions and much more are derived from the Charter. The Atlantic Charted was a stepping stone into the creation of United Nations.

UNITED NATIONS:

World War II, 1939-45 resulted in an unprecedented scale of destruction of lives (over 60 million dead, most of them civilians) and the use of Weapons of Mass Destruction. Some of the acts committed against civilians during the War were on such a massive scale of savagery; they came to be widely considered as crimes against humanity itself. As the war's conclusion drew near, many shocked voices called for the establishment of institutions able to permanently prevent deadly international conflicts. This led to the found of the United Nations in 1945, which adopted the Universal Declaration of Human Rights in 1948. Many, however, felt that the UN essentially a forum for discussion and coordination between sovereign governments was insufficiently empowered for the task. A number of prominent persons, such as Albert Einstein, Winston Churchill, Bertrand Russell and Mohandas Karamchan Gandhi, called on governments to proceed further by taking gradual steps towards forming an effectual federal world government. The United Nations main goal is to work on international law, international security, economic development, human rights, social progress AND EVENTUALLY WORLD PEACE. The United Nations replaced the LEAGUE OF NATIONS in 1945, after World War II. Nearly every country in the UN are member (198 states). The United nations gather regularly in order to solve big problems throughout the world. There are six official languages: Arabic, Spanish, Russian, French, and Chinese. The United Nations is also financed by some of the wealthiest nations. The flag shows the EARTH from a map that shows all the occupied continents.

WORLD FEDRALIST MOVEMENT:

The years between the conclusions of World War II in1950, when the Korean War started and the Cold War mindset became dominant in international politics, were the "golden age" of the World federalist movement. The grassroots world federalist movement in the US, led by people such as Grenville Clark, Norman Cousins, Alan Cranston and Robert Hutchins, organized itself into increasingly large structures, finally forming, in 1947, the United World Federalists (later renamed to World Federalist Association, then Citizens for Global solutions) claiming membership of 47000 in 1949.

Similar movements concurrently formed in many other countries, leading to the formation at a 1947 meeting in MONTREUX, Switzerland, of global coalition, now called World Federalist Movement. By 1950 the movement claimed 56 member groups 22 countries, with some 156,000 members.

GARRY DAVIS:

In France, 1948 Garry Davis began an unauthorized speech calling for world government from the balcony of UN General Assembly, until he was dragged away by the guards. On September 1953, Davis, from City Hall of Ellsworth, Maine announced the formation of the "World Government of World Citizens" based on 3 "WORLD LAWS"—One Absolute Value, One World and One humanity. Its first task was to design and issue a WORLD PASS PORT based on article 13(2) of the UNIVERSAL DECLATION OF HUMANA RIGHTS. To date, over 800,000 of these documents have been issued to individuals worldwide. They have been recognized de facto by over 180 countries.

WORLD PASSPORT:

The world passport is a 45 page document issued by world Service Authority, a non-profit organization citing article 13 (2) of the UDHR. World Passports have reportedly been accepted on a de facto, case-by case basis by over 174 countries and at the one time or another, on an explicit, legal or de jure basis by Burkina Faso, Ecuador, Mauritania, Tanzania, Tog and Zambia.

LEGAL REALISM (1954):

Legal anthropologist E. Adamson Hoebel concluded his treatise on broadening the legal realist tradition to include non-Western Nations. He declared that WHAT EVER THE IDEALIST MAY DESIRE, FORCE AND THE THREAT OF FORCE ARE ULTIMATE POWER IN THE DETERMINATION OF INTERNATIONAL BEHAVIOR, AS IN THE LAW WITHIN THE SOCIAL CONTROL BY WORLD COMMUNITY, BY AND FOR THE WORLD SOCIETY, THEY REMAIN THE INSTRUMENT OF SOCIAL ANARCHY AND NOT THE SANCTIONS OF WORLD LAW . . . . AND THE LAW IS INHERENTLY PURPOSIVE.

EXISTING REGIONAL UNIONS OF NATIONS:

The only Union generally recognized as having achieved the status of a supranational is the EUROPEAN UNION (EU) There number of other regional organizations that have adopted or intend to adopt policies that lead to similar sort of integration in some respects which include:

* African Union (AU)
* Association of Southeast Asian Nations (ASEAN)
* Central American Integration system (SICA)
* Cooperation council for the Arab States if the Gulf (CCASG)
* Commonwealth of Independent States((CIS)
* Eurasian Economic Community (EurAsEC)
* South Asian Association for Regional Cooperation (SAARC)
* Union of South American Nations (UNASUR)
* Union state *Caribbean Community (CARICOM)
* Turkic Council (Turk Kon)

* Arab League into an "Arab Union"
* North American Free Trade Agreement (NAFTA) into the "North American Union"
* Caribbean Community (CARICOM) into Caribbean Federation
* Eurasian Union.
* Shanghai Cooperation Organization (SC0)
* Organization of Islamic Cooperation (OIC)
* The World Constitution and Parliament Association(WCPA)

AMONG THE VOLUNTARY ORGANISATIONS AND INTERNATIONAL ARRANGEMENTS THE FOLLOWING ARE:

* The United Nations is the primarily formal organization coordinating activities between States on a global scale and the only inter-governmental organization with truly universal membership (198 governments). In addition to the main organs and various organs various humanitarian programs and commissions of the UN itself, there are about 20 functional organizations affiliated with the UN's Economic and Social council (ECOSOC), such as the World Health Organization (WHO), the International Labor organization (ILO) and International Telecommunications Union. Of particular are the World Bank, the International Monetary Fund (IMF) and World Trade organization (WTO). Another influential economical international organization is the organization for economic Co-operation and Development (OCED) with membership of 30 democratic members.
* G8, an association of the eight highest GDP nations of the world. The leaders of countries meet annually

in person to coordinate their policies in confronting global issues, such as poverty, terrorism, infectious diseases and climatic change.

*   G20, an association of twenty developing and established nations and entities, including the European Union.

*   Military, the UN deploys peace keeping forces, usually to build and maintain post-conflict peace and stability. When aggressive international military action is undertaken, either ad-hoc coalitions (e.g., multinational force in Iraq) or regional military alliances (e.g., NATO) are used.

*   International Law encompasses international treaties, customs and globally acceptable legal principles. With the exceptions of cases brought before International Criminal Court (ICC) and International Court of Justice (ICJ) is the judiciary organ of the United Nations. It settles disputes submitted to it voluntarily by states (only) and advisory opinions on legal questions submitted by it other organs of the UN, such as the General Assembly or Security Council.

Around 65 years have passed since the CHARTER of UNITED NATIONS was signed in San Francisco. Though there has been no World War since then, but humanity has seen much violence, suffering and injustice. At the same time, nation-states find themselves less able to deal with the array of issues—some old and some new—that face them. States and their people, wishing to control their destinies', find they can do so only by working together with others. They must secure their future through commitment to common responsibility and shared effort.

The need to work together also guided the visionary men and women who drew up the Charter of the United Nations. So many regional organizations and Institutions were framed.

What is new to day is that the interdependence of nations is wider and deeper. What is also new is the role of people and the shift of focus from states to people. An aspect of this change is the growth of international civil Society. The purpose of Article 24 of UN charter to maintain International Peace and Security remained unsolved even after 65 years. These changes and unsolved preambles of UN's Charter call for reforms in the modes of international co-operation-the Institution and process of global governance. The UN charter put in place need to be renewed. The flaws and inadequacies of existing institutions have to overcome. There is a need to weave a tighter fabric of international norms, expanding the rule of law world-wide and enabling citizens to exert their democratic influence of global process.

It is everybody' dream that the World' arrangements for the conduct of its affair must be underpinned by certain philosophical values. Ultimately, no organization will work and no law upheld unless they rest on a foundation made strong by shared values and these values must be informed by sense of common responsibility for both present and future generations. Nothing is impossible if right approach and dedicated will is placed in pursuit. The development of global governance is part of the evolution of human efforts to organize life on the planet and that process will always be going on. Our work is no more than a transit stop on that journey. Let us not presume to offer a blueprint for all time. But we should be convinced that it is time for the world to move on from the designs evolved over the centuries and given new form in the establishment of the United Nations and this is the time that demands freshness and innovation in GLOBAL GOVERNANCE.

The proposal now made here under does not speak of GLOBAL GOVERNMENT but Global governance. No misunderstanding should arise from the similarity of the terms. This is not a proposal for a World government, movement toward establishing one more power or super power or more hospitable to hegemonic ambition and more reinforcing of the role of states and government rather than the rights of people. The challenge is to strike the balance in such a way that the management of global affairs is responsive by basic human values, and that it makes global organization conform the reality of global diversity.

This is a suggestion or an advice which WORLD GOVERNANCE treatises are expected to be adopted for implementation by the year 2015 at least and the treatises are:

* **UN empowerment over the Global commons, like Space, Sky and Sea**
* **An end to the VETO power of permanent members of the Security Council.**
* **Expanding Powers to Secretary General.**
* **Establishment powerful Standing Army in terms of INTERNATIONAL PEACE KEEPING FORCE.**
* **Establishment of Economic Security Council.**
* **A new parliamentary body of CIVIL SOCIETY representation (NGO)**
* **Verdict of International Court of Justice and Crime (ICJ & ICC) should be binding . . . on all nations.**
* **A new council for looking after grievances and petitions thereof**
* **Global taxation.**
* **Global Space Program.**
* **Curb the illicit Global arms trade on priority basis**
* **Curb insane treatment with female humans**

CHARTER:

THE GLOBALL GOVERNANCE IS THE BELIEF THAT WORLD IS NOW READY TO ACCEPT GLOBAL CIVIL ETHICS which is based on a set of core values that can write people of all cultural, political, ethnical, religious or philosophical background. This belief is reinforced by another belief that governance should be underpinned by democracy at all levels and by such enforceable law

FOUNDATION:

WE BELIEVE THAT ALL HUMANITY COULD UPHOLD THE COVER VALUES OF RESPECT FOR LIFE, LIBERTY, JUSTICE AND EQUALITY and MUTUAL RESPECT and CARING INTEGRITY.

Next to LIFE, liberty is what people value most. The impulse to possess turf is a powerful one for all species yet it is one that people must overcome. Another most important factor of life is energy which can be obtained through eradication of poverty. Although States are Sovereign, they are not free individually to do whatever they want.

* The core value of Justice and equality should be basis for sweeping change in United Nations. A broader commitment to equality and justice is basic to more purposeful action to reduce disparities and about more balanced distribution of opportunities around the world. The principle of Intergenerational equity underlies the strategy of sustainable development.
* Promote growth of the group idea so that group good, group understanding, group interrelation and group good will replace all limited, self-centered objectives leading to group consciousness.

* Providing rights (i) to secure life (mean) right to live on secure planet (ii) right to an opportunity to earn fair living (iii) equal access to the Global commons. (iv) special attention to desist gender discrimination in global society (v) delete capital punishment on human from human chapter

In developed countries which contain 20% of population to use 80% of natural resources. It is not fair for the permanent members of the Security Council to have right to VETO. In general it is not fair for one segment of population to be rich while another segment of population is poor. Unfair themselves, poverty and extreme disparities of income fuel both guilt and envy when made more visible in global Television. The demand in recent decades have the RIGHT TO EARN AND FAIR LIVING implies that there must be some kind of a job available from which people may earn their living and this should be the responsibility SECURITY COUNCIL to provide an opportunity to earn for a fair living.

* Pollution of global atmosphere and depletion of ocean fisheries inadequacies of global governance. The Trusteeship Council or Economic Security council should ensure the matter for environmental treaties.

* Global common are defined to be: the atmosphere, outer space, the oceans and related environmental life-support systems that contribute to the support human life. Here one more aspect shall be made included that all space programs should be propelled by United Nation Aeronautical and Space Program (UNASAP) as each nation doing same such programs would be unwarranted and the national exchequer would grossly be affected. The requirement of the States/Nations shall be purported and a consolidated program be launched under the project called UNASA. The nations can share the knowledge and obtain satellite communication system by subscribing with

minimal payment and thus the saving of capital can be utilized on the welfare schemes like education, mobilization of employment schemes to unemployed youth in their development attempts. Instead of accrediting themselves to be members of ELITE CLUB OF SPACE PROGRAMMES AND NUCLEAR EXPERIMENTS, they can as well divert the capital on sustainable development of humanity as a whole.

STRUCTURE OF GLOBAL GOVERNANCE:

It is known fact that U.S. being the most developed and advanced country, holds Security Council of UN under its dictation. It boasts of itself as the Supreme organ of United Nation. Originally the UN Security Council had 11 members of which 5 were permanent members (CHINA, U.S., U.K. FRANCE AND RUSSIA) WITH Veto power. The other six positions rotated in two year term among the remaining members of UN General Assembly. Now, I would propose for the increase not less than 30 members and should have equal power and not to have veto powers. All the resolutions be passed on consensus only and not by dictation. The permanent members should be increased at least to 10. It is reasonably to say that when the UN system was created nation-state, some of them imperial powers, were dominant. Faith in the ability of government to protect citizens and improve their lives was strong. The world was focused More over the world economy was not as closed integrated as it is today. The vast array of global firms and corporate alliances that has emerged is just beginning. The huge global capital market, which today dwarfs even the largest national capital markets and this was not foreseen. The enormous growth in people' concern for human rights, equity, democracy, meeting basic materials, environmental protection, and determination has to day produced multitude actors who can contribute to governance.

PRESENT OCCASSION DEMANDS:

* **All people, no less than all State, have right to existence.**

* **Global Security policy should prevent conflict and war and to maintain integrity of the Planets life supporting system by eliminating economic social environmental, political and military conditions that generate threats to the security of both humans and Planet.**

* **Military force is not a legitimate political instrument except in self-defense.**

* THE PRODUCTION AND TRADE OF ARMS BE CONTROLLED BY INTERNATIONAL COMMUNITY UNDER INTEGRATED SUPEERVISION.

* THE Security Council would also be empowered to raise a standing army. Article 43 of UN Charter authorize such a force but never has been activated. It can be well said that" it is high time that his idea—a UN volunteers force—was to made a reality. Such force would be under the exclusive authority of UN Security Council under day—to-day command of UN Secretary General. It would maintain its own support and mobilization, capabilities and be available for RAPID DEVELOPMENT anywhere in the world. The small highly trained well equipped force not less than 50000 troops for immediate intervention with conventional title UN PEACE KEEPING FORCE.

PERSISTANT POVERTY:

Economic Security Council described as an Apex Body the Economic Security Council (ESC) is proposed to have the standing in relation to international economic matters that the Security Council has in peace and security matter. The new ESC would be a deliberate, policy body rather than executive agency. It would work by consensus without Veto power by any member.

There is no longer an East to be juxtaposed against the West. With the abandonment of communism, Capitalism has become even more of an omnibus term that hides important distinctions between different ways of organizing market economics. Similarly North-South dichotomy is becoming sharp. "The time is now ripe-indeed overdue—to create a global forum that can provide leadership in economic, social and environmental fields." The ESC would ;

* Continuously assess the overall state of world economy;
* Provide long term strategic policy framework to promote sustainable development;
* Secure constantly between the policy goals of International economic institution (World Bank, IMF, WTO, Global Environment facility etc);
* Study proposals for financing public good by international revenue rising (Public Goods are defined to be "the rules and sense of order that must underpin any stable and prosperous system. It is in the nature not to be provided by markets or by individual government action in isolation).

The Economic Security Council's agenda addressed shall include: long term threats to security in its widest sense, such as shared crises, economic instability, rising unemployment, mass poverty and promotion of sustainable development. The ESC should have no more than 30 or 35 members that it is headed by Deputy Secretary General for Economic co-operation and development and that domestic gross product (GDP) of all member nations be measure by and based upon 'PURCHASE POWER PARITY (PPP). Both World trade Organization, International Labor organization would be brought under the authority of the new Economic Security council.

The ESC would be given authority upon telecommunication /internet/multimedia/world wide web (www). Since the atmosphere and outer space are "global commons" assigned to Trusteeship council, business that use the air waves and satellites would be subject to the policies of ESC.

Further ESC is designed to centralize and consolidate policy making for not only World trade but also for the international monetary system and world development t. Since there is a broad consensus on many elements: (i) understanding of the importance of environmental sustainability financial stability and strong social dimension to policy emphasizing education,(especially women and children health) and family planning.

To deal with third World debt a system can be developed for the establishment of "Akin to corporate bankruptcy, when a state accepts that its affairs will be for a while be placed under the management of representatives of international community and a fresh start is made, wiping much of the slate clean. That is the ESC is expected to facilitate technology transfer which is crucial development in developing countries. The ESC is also expected to immigration policies because there is underlying in consistency—even hypocrisy in the many governments treat migration. They claim a belief in free market (including manpower market) but use draconian and highly bureaucratic regulations to control cross-border manpower migration.

Technological advances have made national frontiers more prosperous. States retain sovereignty, but governments have suffered erosion in their authority. They are less able, for example, to control the transborder movement of money or information. They face the pressure of globalization at one level and of grassroots movements and in some cases, demands for devolution if not secession at another. In the extreme case, public order may disintegrate and civil institutions collapse in the face of rampant violence, as in Liberia and Somalia.

Deprivation is passed onto the next generation. In low income developing countries seventy three out of every 1000 babies do not live until their first birthday. The rate of infant mortality is ten times that in rich countries. Of the children that survive, many do not receive an education just over 40 per cent of eligible children attend secondary school. The destitution of perhaps a fifth humanity has to be set alongside the affluence of the worlds rich. For all such unnatural catastrophes provision should be included in the Economic Security council as POVERTY ERADICATION PROGRAME.

THE MECHINARY OF GLOBAL GOVERNANCE: It can be recommended by two bodies(i) as Assembly of people (2) a Forum of civil society 'What is generally proposed is initial setting up of an assembly of parliamentarians, consisting representatives elected existing National legislatures forum among their members and subsequent establishment of world assembly through direct election by the people. The Forum Civil Society would consist of 300-600 representatives of organization accredited to General Assembly. The Forum shall meet annually prior to the meeting of UN General Assembly. "The considered views of Forum would be a qualitative change in the underpinning of global governance.

Non Governmental Organizations participation in Global Governance is an essential feature, and is in fact the dimension of governance that is totally new. It is no longer just an idea. It is demonstrated fact of life for which it should institutionalize through Legal status. The idea of NGO participation in Global governance is as old as UN. According to certain reliable report around 30000 International NGOs are known to exist and are directly involved in advancing agenda of Global Governance NGO community have strong national constituencies and enormous staff and money capabilities. Most often the term "public/private sector partnership "is issued to describe and define 'Civil Society' participation. At the lowest that is ground level, NGO's are present and prepared to lobby on issues relating to particular programs like watershed, local boards under guardianship can also be established to look after ground level requirements.

Strong NGO participation has marked the UN conferences held after Rio: on human rights in Vienna in 1993 on small island states in Barbados in 1994, and population and development in Cairo, also in 1994. Official bodies need, of course to relate to the independent sector on regular basis not simply at or in preparation for a major conference. They must reach out to civil society in positive spirit and seek its contributions at all stages including the shaping of policy.

ENFORCING GLOBAL GOVERNANCE: From the outset the World Court ruling is being marginalized. States were free to take it or leave it whole or in part. The rule of law was asserted and at the same time undermined.

REMEDY: The treaties and agreement s between Nations shall be written to include binding adjudication by World Court and that all Nations should "accept compulsory jurisdiction of the World Court, like wise World trade organization is step in this direction. Members agree in advance to accept WTO decision and not seek bilateral resolutions and disputes.

The very essence of Global Governance is the capacity of International community to ensure compliance with the rules of society. It should be obeyed and adopt as is done with their local Supreme court. The International Criminal court which has been recently formed should deal criminal acts like terrorism, riots, clashes in societies and the verdict imposed and its verdict be binding on the societies or States concern.

FINANCING GLOBAL GOVERNANCE: Previous reports recommending globally redistribute tax principles have short shrift. The time could be right, however, for a fresh look and breakthrough those relating to the physical environment—is now widely accepted. This cannot happen with drip freed approach to financing. And the notion of expanding the role of UN is now accepted to military security.

Currently total UN expenditure is slightly more that of 11 billion USD, although not all the cost of peace keeping activities are reflected through the UN system. The cost of implementing Agenda 21 was estimated in1992 600 billion USD. Currently the costs are paid by member nations in the form of assessment and voluntary contribution. It is also a known fact the USA is due by 17 billion dollars as its contribution to UN. Because, UN has no power to enforce payment of either assessments or voluntary contribution from the Nations. It is suggested that the industrialized countries have severely constrained the exercise of the Assembly's collective authority. A START SHOULD BE MADE in establishing practical, if initially small scale, schemes of Global financing to specific UN operations. As said earlier, the US has often withheld payment as means of influencing UN policy. Let it be an obligatory with all Nations who have a membership (198 nations) to subscribe their contribution to UN on basis of recommendations drawn hereunder so that the UN can be strengthened its Global Governance to ensure to establish its core principals of Peace and Security to entire humankind of the Planet.

It would be appropriate to charge for the use of some common global resources which belong to all humankind of the Globe. Another idea would be for corporate taxation of Multinational Companies. Another proposed scheme is all nations shall share 50% their Defence expenditure and subscribe UNS to get Strengthen it in discharging the preamble of ESTABLISHMENT OF PEACE AND SECURITY GLOBALLY. One more favored scheme as proposed by Nobel Prize winner JAMES TOBIN, is to tax on International Monetary Exchange which would yield an estimated 1.5 trillion USD per year. A carbon tax introduced across a large number of countries or a system of traded permits for carbon emission would yield very large revenue in lead. Besides these proposals following channels are identified to procure more revenue which include

*   A surcharge on air tickets of the Global Commons, on Aviation and space utilization
*   A charge on ocean Maritime transport;
*   User fees for ocean fishing;
*   Special user fees for activation in Antarctica;
*   Parking fees for geo-stationary satellites (if the nations do not agree to endorse space programs to UNASA as proposed earlier.
*   Charges under right of electromagnetic spectrum.
*   An amount of 900 million dollars can be collected from the Wealthiest Tycoons at 20% of their net assets towards Poverty eradication Tax and use the same to wipe out poverty line from the HUMAN CHAPTER.

ENLIGHTENED LEADERSHIP:

Leadership is urgently needed that represents all the world's countries and people, not simply, most powerful. The Global conference in San Francisco was aptly summed up in the phrase NEVER AGAIN. Never again should the word's leaders fail to prevent a global depression. Never again should they fail to stand up to aggression. Never again should they tolerate governments that assaulted the most basic dignities of their citizens. Never again should they squander the chance to create institutions that would make a lasting peace possible. It was these aims that led the delegates in San Francisco—and the July 1944 UN Monetary and financial Conference held in Bretton Woods, New Hampshire—to establish the key International institutions that became the part of the post-war arrangements for Global governance. But the challenges facing the world today are vastly more complicated than those that confronted the delegates in San Francisco. They demand co-operative efforts to put in place a system of global governance better suited to present circumstances—a system informed by an understanding of the important transformation of the past more than half century by an enlightened leadership. The leadership should draw its strength from society as much as the state, from solidarity and philosophical perspective more than from authority. It should operate by persuasion, co-operation, and consensus more than by imposition and fiat. It may be less HEROIC and POWERFUL, but it is the only form leadership likes to prove effective and it prevails too.

LET ME CONCLUDE THIS THESIS WITH TRUST AND HOPE ON ESTABLISHING PEACE AND SECURITY TO ALL THE NATIVES OF THE PLANET.

EPILOGUE

THE ATTEMPT IN WRITING THIS SCRIPT, THOUGH IT IS LENGHTHY, IS TO ENLIGHTEN ALLTHE DOGMATICS WHO ARE STILL IN THE CAGE OF BELIEF AND FAITH IN SUPERNATURAL ELEMENT WITHOUT DISCHARGING THEIR DUTIES ASSIGNED TO THEM BY NATURE, THE MOTHER, OR OUR PLANET EARTH. THE DAYS HAVE GONE WHEN 'BELIEF IS RELIEF' BUT THE DAYS OF UNFORSEEN AND UNIMAGINABLE TECHNOLOGY HAS REVRSED THE PROVERB INTO 'BELIEF IS GRIEF'

I MUST SAY THAT ALL RELIGIOUS FANATICS, FUNDAMENTALISTS, POPULARISTS AND EXTREMISTS MUST DEAL NOT ONLY WITH HUMANITY BUT ALSO WITH THE ENVIRONMENT IN WHICH WE DWELL. THEY MUST, IN OTHER WORDS, HAVE TO SAY SOME THING ABOUT THE PLANTS AND ANIMALS AND MOUNTAINS AND FORESTS THE SOIL AND SKY AND STARS THAT ARE VISIBLE AND TANGIBLE.

NATURE CAN BE EXPERIENCED IN MANY WAYS SOMETIMES IT SEEMS LUSH AND BEAUTIFUL AND FRIENDLY BEYOND ANYTHING ELSE IMAGINABLE AND WE BELIEVE NATURE MUST BE THE VERY FOOT STOOL OF GOD OR MANIFESTATION OF DIVINE REALITY. YET OTHER TIME, IN THE WAKE OF FLOODS OR DRAUGHT OR EARTH QUAKES, NATURE APPEARS CRUEL AND RUTHLESS, THE ENEMY OF ALL HUMAN HOPES AND DREAMS. YET AGAIN THERE ARE TIMES WHEN WE ARE STRUCK

BY HEARTLESSNESS OF NATURE, THE SUFFERING OF SOMANY CREATURES AND HARNESS OF THE NATURAL ENVIRONMENT AGAINST WHICH WE OFTEN STRUGGLE. HERE THE GOD TURNS IN TO THE EVIL SPIRIT. A FEAR AND HELPLESSNESS CAUSES HIM TO BELIEVE IN, THAT GOD IS CURSING FOR OUR MISBEHAVIOUR, MISDEEDS, A KIND OF GUILT AS SEGMUND FREUD TERMED, STARTS IN THOUGHTS OF HUMAN BEING AND THIS THE SEED IS SOWED AS THE PLANT OF BELIEF, BELIEF IN GOOD AND EVIL, GOOD BECOMES GOD AND EVIL, A DEVIL. THUS THE POSITIVE AND NEGATIVE ASPECT OF NATURE'S PLAY MAKE HUMANS TO RESORT TO RELIGION. A BELIEF IN BRAIN GENERATES. A GUILT OF "SIN AND FALLEN" DIFFERENTIATE PSYCHOLOGICALLY. THE INTOLERANCE OF CRUELTY OF NATURE DISTURB THE HUMANS PSYCHOLOGICALLY AND HE FINALLY RESORTS TO EITHER FORGET OR DISCARD PERMANANTLY, HE ADOPTS RELIGION AS RESORT TO OPIUM TO GET SOLACED.

THEREFORE, HUMBLY REQUEST ALL THE RELIGIOUS LEADERS TO REALISE THAT RELIGION IS NOTHING BUT INEVITABLE FEELING THAT SOME SUPERNATURAL BEING EXISTS WHO IS PLAYING WITH HUMANS. IF THAT IS THE CASE, WHAT ABOUT ANIMALS WHO CANNOT THINK BUT FEEL AND THAT FEELING THEY CANNOT PUT INTO WORDS AND ACTION. HAD THEY ALSO BLESSED WITH THE THINKING POWER AS HUMANS POSSESS THEY WOULD HAVE A FEELING OF THEIR OWN RELIGION AND THEIR OWN GOD IN THEIR IMAGE.

EVEN STILL IF YOU ARE ADAMENT IN YOUR BELIEFS OF SOME RELIGION OR OTHER THEN KEEP IT WITH IN YOUR "PREMISES" ONLY WITHOUT BECOMING AN OBSTACLE TO OTHERS, I MEAN, YOUR FELLOW BEINGS SINCE THEY TOO WILL HAVE THEIR OWN BELIEF AND CUSTOMS OF DIFFERENT KIND. IF YOU START IMPOSING YOUR BELIEVES ON OTHERS AND THE RESULT WOULD BE CLASH AND CONFLICT OF IDEOLOGY WHICH FINALLY CULMINATES INTO WAR. THAT IS WE HAVE LEARNED FROM HISTORY WHICH IS FULL OF STRUGGLES AND WARS. LET US NOT REPEAT HISTORY AGAIN SINCE WE ARE LIVING IN THE DAYS OF SCIENCE AND TECHNOLOGY WHICH HAS PUT FORTH DETAILED FACTS AND FIGURES OF HUMAN LIFE IN FULL LENGTH DETAILS.

IF YOU GO THROUGH THIS BOOK ONCE IN YOUR LIFE TIME I THINK THE FACTS OF LIFE WOULD BE KNOWN AND CLOUDS OF DOGMAS WILL BE CLEARED AND YOU START MAINTAINING A BROTHERHOOD WITH YOUR FELLOW BEING. SINCE WE LIVE LIFE ONLY ONCE AND THERE IS NEITHER A PERMANENT LIFE NOR ANNIHILITION IN TO THE SO CALLED GOD AFTER DEATH. HEAVEN AND HELL ARE BOTH HERE ON THE EARTH ONLY. IF YOU LIVE PLEASANTLY THAT IS HEAVEN AND IF YOU LIVE IN PAIN THAT IS HELL. THIS IS THE ONLY SIMPLE FORMULA OF HUMAN EXISTENCE. THIS IS THE WISDOM HENCE IF YOU THINK OF OTHERS IN YOUR PLACE THAT WILL SOLVE ALL THE PROBLEMS. YOU NEED NOT SUPPRESS OR KILL YOUR DESIRES FOR THE SAKE OF UNKNOWN GOD. STRIVE HARD TO REALISE THE TRUTH OF EARTHLY PLEASURES AND TRY TO AVOID PAINS DURING YOUR TENURE OF LIFE

ITSELF. KNOWLEDGE OF THIS SIMPLE RULE WILL CERTAINLY MAKES YOUR MIND FREE FROM THE CAGE OF CONSERVATIVE BELIEVES AND PREVENT UNNATURAL CALAMITIES ON EARTH, SINCE EVERY HUMAN POSSESS HUMANITY IN HIMSELF.

THANK YOU.

ABBREVIATIONS

A.U.	African union or Arab Union
A.L.	Arab Language
A.S.E.A.N	Association of South east Asian Nations.
A.I.D.S.	Acquired Immune Deficiency Syndrome.
C.E.R.N.	European Organization for Nuclear Research.
CH4	Methane.
C.I.S.	Common Wealth of Independent States.
CARI.COM	Caribbean Community.
C.P.P.C.G.	Convention on Prevention and Punishment of Crime Genocide.
C.C.A.S.G.	Cooperation Council of Arab States in Gulf.
D.N.A.	Deoxyribonucleic acid
Eur. As Ec.	European Asian Economic Community.
E.U.	European Union.
ECOSOC.	Economic and Social Council
F.S.H.	Follicular Stimulating Hormone.
GATT.	General Agreement And Tariff and Trade.
G8	Group of 8 Highest GDP Nations.
G20	Group of 20 Developing countries.
G.N.P.	Gross National Product.
G.A.	Gross Assets.
G.R.B.	Gama Ray Burst.
G.D.P.	Gross Domestic Product.
H.G.P.	Human Genome Project
H.I.V.	Human Immunodeficiency Virus.
H.B.P.	Human Brain Project.
I.L.O.	International Labor Organization.

I.C.J.	International Court of Justice.
I.U.P.A.C	International Union of pure and applied chemistry
I.S.B.T.	International Society of Blood Transfusion
ICVCN	International Code of Viruses Classification and Nomenclature
ICZN	International Code of Zoological Nomenclature
ICNBA	International Code of Nomenclature of Bacteria and Animals
I.CC.	International Criminal Court.
I.M.F.	International Monetary Fund.
NH3	Ammonia.
N.A.F.T.A.	North American Free Trade Agreement.
N.A.S.A.	National Centre for Super computing Application.
N.G.O.	Non-Governmental Organization.
N.A.T.O.	Non-Aligned Treaty Organization.
N.A.E.	National Academy of Engineering.
O.I.C.	Organization of Islamic Cooperation.
O.P.E.C.	Oil Producing and Exporting Countries.
P.D.	Per Day.
RBC	Red Blood Cells
R.N.A.	Ribonucleic acid.
S.I.C.A.	Central American Investigating System.
S.A.A.R.C.	South Asian Association of Regional Cooperation.
S.C.O.	Shanghai Cooperation Organization.
S.C.	Security Council
S.T.E.M.	Science Technology Engineering and Mathematics.
TUR.CON.	Turk Council
U.D.H.R.	Universal declaration of Human rights.

U.N.	United Nations.
U.N.E.S.C.O.	United Nations Educational and Social Community Organization.
U.S.D.	United States Dollar.
W.C.P.A.	The World Constitution and Parliament Association.
W.B.	World Bank.
W.H.O.	World Health Organization.
W.M.A.P.	Wilkinson Microwave Antistrophe Probe.

ASTRONOMICAL MARINE AND MATHEMATICAL TEREMINOLOGY

SPEED OF LIGHT	:	1,86,000 Miles per second.
LIGHT YEAR	:	9.4605284X10 to the power of 15.
Or		
LIGHT YEAR.	:	Light travels at distance of 9,500,000,000,000. KM
DISTANCE OF SUN.	:	150 Million K.M.(93 million miles) from earth.
MILKY WAY/GALAXY (our)	:	150.000 light year across.
THE CRAB SUPER NOVA RAMNANT	:	4000 LIGHT YEARS AWAY from earth.
PARSEC.	:	1=3.8567758 X 10 to the power of 16. Or 3.25 light year
	:	years
or ONE METER PERSEC.	:	1/299792458 of Speed of light in Vacuum.
EARTH SPEED	:	C i r c u m f e r e n c e latitude/24.
MARTIME (SEA)	:	It is a unit in measuring Sea in terms of distance.

ONE NAUTDICAL MILE	:	1.852 km(6077 FT) OR (2025 Yards)
Ga	:	Billion years.
Ma	:	Million years.

U.S. CURRENCY.

MILLION DOLLARS	:	10 to the power of 6 = 1000.000
BILLION DOLLARS	:	10 to the power of 9 = 1000,000,000.
TRILLION DOLLARS	:	10 to the power of 15=1000,000.000.000.000.

Glossary

A

ABRAHAMIC RELIGIONS	:	Judaism, Christianity and Islam.
ANTHROPOLOGY	:	Science of Study of humans.
APARTHIED	:	Segregation among humans, Separation.
AUROTIC ANEYRYSM	:	abnormal bulging of portion of blood vessel.
AUTISM	:	Treatment to boost child's brain function.
AESTHETIC	:	Art of beauty and taste.
ARTIUM	:	Denoting communicating process.
ALIMENTARY CANAL	:	Mucus membrane—line tube of digestive system.
APPENDAGES	:	An adjunct body, attachment.
ASPIDISTRAS	:	Kind of Plant of genus in the Lilli family.
ARDUOUS	:	Difficult, strenuous.
ACETYLENE	:	Highly inflammable or explosive gas.
AMINOACID	:	Organic compound of amino group, NH2
ARCHE BACTERIA	:	Bacterial cell-derived from Greek.

ABERRATION : The act of departing the right, deviation from truth.

ANTHROPIC : Relating to human or the era of human life.

ADORNED : Enhanced appearance.

ATMOPHILE : A kind of bacteria.

AMPHIBIANS : Smooth skinned vertebrate of class-like frog.

ARBOREAL LIVING : Adaptation for living and moving about in trees.

AURORA BOREALIS : Glimpses of an aurora/ that occurs in northern region of earth.

B

BIG BANG THEORY : A cosmological theory that the Universe originated approximately 20 billion years ago from violent explosion of a very small agglomeration of matter.

BOOM RANG : A flat curved wooden missile when hurdled returns back to thrower.

BEREFT : Past tense and past of bereave-deprived of something.

BOURGEOSIC : Capitalist.

BIPEDIAL : walking on two legs with feet.

BUREAUCRACIES	:	Administration by Office holders.
BONOBO	:	A species of monkey that enjoys sex, penis fencing.
BUCCAL	:	Relating to cheeks or the mouth cavity.
BARTHOLIN GLAND	:	Glands lying to each side of vigina and secreting lubricating mucus.
BOVIOS	:	Full color thermostat.

C

CALIPH	:	Associate or Deputy of Prophet Muhammad.
CEREBRAL ACQUDUCT	:	Narrow channel in mid brain connectivity.
COMBAT	:	Fight against.
CORRABORATED	:	Evidence that tends to support a proposition.
COSMIC	:	Extra terrestrial vastness; relates universe.
CATASTROPHE	:	Disaster.
CAREDIO	:	OF HEART
CAVITY	:	A hollow area within a body.
CERVIX	:	Lower narrow portion of the uterus
COWPERGLAND	:	Two small glands of one lies on each side of male urethra.
CARTESIAN PHILOSOPHY	:	Relating to French Philosophy of Descartes

CHROMOSOME	:	Thread like bodies that carry the genes in an order.
COMPATABILIST THHEORY	:	Theory of free will to perform action.
CENOZOIK ERA	:	Geological term of plant tonic period.
CETACEANS	:	Marine mammals.
CYANIDE	:	Hydrogen salt containing CN. group—Chemical compound C=n.
CREDULITY	:	Readiness to believe.
CRITIQUE	:	Critical view.
CONCOMITTANCE	:	Collecting all facts about the patience.

D

DYNASTY	:	Succession of rulers.
DICHOTOMY	:	Being two fold-split in to two.
DESENTIZE	:	Something very original.
DISCRETE	:	Detach from others.
DEPREDATION	:	Audio pronunciation.
DELUGE	:	Overwhelmed by floor or like.
DOGMAS	:	Doctrine.
DIALECTIC	:	Logical argument.

E

| EMBRYONIC | : | Early stage of development. |
| ERA | : | Period. |

ETHNICAL	:	Racial
EMANCIPATION	:	Free from bondage.
ECOLOGICAL	:	Bionomics, environmental connected with organisms.
ELITIST	:	Persons who believe they are superior to others.
ESCATACY	:	A stage in total suspension or sensibility.
EPISTOMOLOGY	:	Theory of knowledge.
ESOPHGUS	:	Procedure that allows doctor to dilate or stretches.
EPICARDIUM	:	That closely envelops heart.
ENDOCARDIUM	:	Lining membrane connects interior heart.
EQUIDS	:	Hoofed mammal family having muscular bodies.
ECHINODERMS	:	Sea Cucumbers.
EUKARYOTES	:	one or two celled organism containing bound nucleus.
EMPERICISM	:	Theory that depends on the senses for deriving knowledge.
EPIDIDYMIS	:	Convoluted tubes in each testis.
ELICITING	:	To draw, to educate truth.

F

FEUDALISM	:	Governance by land lords.
FEDARAL	:	States Sovereignty.
FIAT	:	Command without effort.

FOSTER	:	Guardian.
FALLIBLE	:	Capable of making an error.
FEMER	:	Bone of leg situated between pelvis.
FUNGI	:	Aerobic organism like mushroom, smut.
FOSSIL ENERGY	:	Petrol
FRAGMENT	:	An isolated portion, a bit.
FORMAL DEHYDE	:	A colorless pungent gas CH_2O.

G

GENOCIDE	:	Systematic extermination or killing of entire racial group.
GRUESOME	:	Causing horror.
GONDWANA	:	Super continent.

H

HEGEMONY	:	Domination by culture, cultural imperialism.
HOMICIDE	:	Massacre by Government.
HOMOERUCTUS	:	Scientific name for primitive man.
HOMOSAPIANS	:	Scientific name for primate human family of hominids.
HEMISPHERE	:	A half of sphere bounded by great circle in to right and left.

HYPOTHALAMUS	:	Part of brain in vertebrate animals that lies below the thalamus.
HOLOCENE CALANDER	:	Period starting with 10000 years-present 11703 years.
HOLOCENE EXTINCTON	:	Extinction of species around 10,000 years BCE
HOMOGENUS	:	Similar generations.
HETERO	:	Pressing two different forms-sexually oriented.
HOMERIC	:	Relating to Greek famous writer of mythology HOMER, his period.
HORMONAL STENT	:	Hormone replacement therapy like estrogen stent etc.
HYPOTHESIS	:	To suppose, to presume.

I

IMPOVERISHED	:	Reduce to poverty.
INFLICTING	:	Causing harm.
INCESSANTLY	:	Continuous without interruption.
INDEGENOUS	:	Originating in and characterizing a particular region.
INNATE	:	Talent from within.
IMPEDE	:	undermine, block.
IMPARTING	:	to bestow, to make know.
IOTA	:	Not the slightest amount.

J

JUXTAPOSED	:	To place side by side.
JEOPARDY	:	Peril, hazard, danger.

L

LOCOMOTION	:	The act of power of moving from.
LACTOSE	:	Intolerance.
LIBIDO	:	Psychic and emotional energy, sexual desire.
LETHAL	:	Causing death, fatal
LYMPHATIC SYSTEM	:	Clear, yellowish fluid derived from body tissue containing blood.
LEPTONS	:	Scientific term-a family of elementary particles.
LAUGHING GAS	:	Nitrogen gas.
LAURASIA	:	Hypothetical land mass that broke into North America.
LAISSEZ-FAAIRE	:	French word meaning state enterprise.

M

MYTH	:	Fiction, not factual.
MUTILATION	:	to disfigure, cutting limbs.
MORES	:	Moral significance.
METALLURGY	:	Science related to metals.

MAMMAL	:	Body covered with hair, nourishing young with milk.
MAMMOTH	:	Great in size, large extinct animals.
MASTADONS	:	Extinct Mammals.
METAPHYSICS	:	Spiritual, non-physical discourse.
MYOCARDIUM	:	Heart wall composed of cardiac muscle.
MICROBE	:	A minute life form.
MAZE	:	Confusion, not real.
MOLTEN	:	A huge red bed of coal blazing.
MAKGANYENE	:	Glaciations, much earlier period, snow ball earth.
MULLUSKS	:	Marine invertebrate of phylum.
MESOZONIC	:	Middle period geological period of early mammals like Jurassic.
MALAYSIANS	:	Country where Malays live.

N

NEO CORTEX	:	New portion of cerebral cortex.
NENDERTHALS	:	Subspecies of HOMOSAPIANS
NEOLITHIC	:	Relating polished stone age, refined implements used after stone age.

NICHE	:	Recess wall for statue, private space.
NIHILISM	:	Extreme form of skepticism that denies all existence.
NEBULA HYPOTHESIS	:	Hypothesis concerning origin of solar system according to which rotating nebula contracted.

O

ORACLE	:	Communications from God, Greek belief.
OPPRESSION	:	To keep down by severe and unjust use of force or authority.
OCCIPITALOBE	:	Visual processing center of the Mammal brain having cortex.
OPTIC CHIASM	:	Structure of fore brain with fibers of optic nerve.
OBESITY/OBSE	:	Fat, plump.
OBSTACLE	:	To hinder, against.
OVUM	:	Egg cell.
ONTOLOGY	:	Branch of Metaphysics propelling the theory of beginning of life.
OMNICIANT	:	Complete unlimited knowledge, total sense.
OMNIPOTENT	:	All powerful.
OZONE	:	Layer from atmospheric oxygen by electric discharge.

P

PARASITE : Sheltered specie while contributing nothing to the survival of host.

PERIETAL LOBE : Front lobe, occipital lobe, uses learning tools.

PESSIMISM : Always being negative about everything, a philosophical term.

PERFRONTED CORTEX : Gray matter of anterior part that is highly developed in humans.

PENETRATE : To enter, pierce.

PERCEPTION : Act of seeing, perceiving, sensing.

PILFERAGE : Petty thievery by employees, theft.

PHYLOSENETIC : Evolutionary development of history.

PHYNOTYPE : Trait that physically explained.

PLEISTOCENE : last ice age, a geological term.

PLAQUE : Flat plate, slab.

POSTERIOR : Rump of body, buttocks.

PHOTONS : Quantum of electromagnetic energy.

PROPENSITY : A tendency, an innate inclination.

PROCREATION : To produce or create, originate.

PRIMATE : Highest form of mammal including humans.

PROTEROZONIC EON : Pre Cambrian explosion or eon.

PROKARYOTE : An organism of kingdom of Monera bacteria.

POLEOGENE : Origin of iron.

PITHECANTHROPUS ERECTUS : Former genus primitive ape like man now homo erectus.

PURSUITE : The act of chasing, striving.

Q

QUARKS : Group of six elementary particles having electric changes of 1/3 or 2/3 electron.

R

RESILIENA : Ability to recover quickly from illness.

RECTUM : Terminal portion of large intestine.

REPLICATING : To reproduce.

REPRESSION : To hold back by an act of violation.

REALM : Community, territory, area, field.

S

SCELODERMA	:	Auto immune disease that affects the blood vessel and tissues.
SJOGREN, S DERMA	:	Disease that causes arthritis, dry eyes and mouth.
SCORUTUM	:	Tumor in veins.
SEMINAL VESILE	:	Disease in prostate gland.
SCUM	:	The extraneous matter or impurities which rise to the surface of liquid boiling of fermentation.
SHOVED	:	To push forward.
SKEPTICISM	:	The theory of doubting authority of accepted belief.
SPIRALLING	:	A curve on plane that winds around a fixed counter point.
SPURRING	:	A short spike wheel that attaches the heel of rider's feet.
SHRIFT	:	Remission of sins pronounced by a priest.
STEALTH BOMB	:	A type of military aircraft bomb used undetectable of sight or radar.
SUSTAINABLE	:	Maintenance of factors of quality.
SEMINAL	:	Containing semen or seed.
SIMULATION	:	Technique of imitating the behavior of some system.
SPAWING	:	To bring forth, to generate.
SWAY	:	To swing, to wield.

SQUANDER   : To spend extravagantly,
                           foolishly,

SYMMETRY   : Arrangement in regular
                           form.

SOLOR COLORATION   : Leaving sun with yellow
                           color.

SHROVED   : Confess and receive
                           absolution.

STROMATOLITES   : A laminated rock formed by
                           growth of blue green algae.

SYNAPSIDS   : An aspidereor vertebrates
                           that possess skulls with no
                           major fenestrate.

T

TANTOLOGY   : Needless repetition of the
                           same sense in different
                           words.

THIRD REICH   : Third Empire in German
                           language, Hitler's rule.

TREATISE   : Systematic, usually
                           extensive discourse.

TOXIC   : Causing injury to death,
                           chemically speaking
                           poisoning.

TROVE   : Collection of valuable
                           items discovered.

TEMPORAL LOBE   : Lower lateral lobe-sensory
                           center of hearing in the
                           brain.

TRAIT   : Particularity, a mark,
                           specific quality.

TENDEM	:	A two wheeled carriage like bicycle.
TRAUMAS	:	Shock or serious injury to the body.
TUSKS	:	Elongated pointed tooth.
TUMBLING	:	Somersault, twist.
TSUNAMI	:	Japanese word for larger thrusting wave.
TRIASSIC	:	System of rocks, sedimentary deposits.
TANTALIZING	:	To teach or torment to keep out of reach.
TRAGECTORY	:	Orbiting, path of planet.
TRNQUIL	:	Peaceful, unaffected by emotions.

U

UNILATERALISM	:	Tendency of nation to conduct affairs individualistically.
UNI POLARITY	:	produced by single magnetic or electric pole.
UTOPIAN	:	High place, high ideals.
URETHRA	:	Canal that discharge urine from bladder.
UNIFORMATARIANISM	:	Holy attribution to man's origin and act accordingly.

V

VILIFYING	:	To make vicious or derogatory statement.

VULNERABLE	:	Susceptible to physical or emotional injury.
VENTRICLES	:	Two chambers of heart that involved in pumping blood.
VASCULAR	:	Related to blood vessels.
VAS DEFERENCE	:	The main duct through which semen is carried from epididymis to the ejaculatory duct.
VERTIBRAL	:	Having spinal column.
VALATILE GAES	:	An organic compound that have high helium etc.

W

| WHACK | : | Slap, strike with sharp blow. |
| WIELD | : | To handle weapon with skill and ease. |

X

| X-LINKED RECESSIVE | : | Genetic adjective referring to mode of inheritance in which gene on the X |

Y

| YELL | : | To cry out loudly. |

References

1. HERSHEL EDEL HEIT , ABRAHAM J. EDELHEIT , History of ZIOSM
2. Haarper Douglas, "religion"
3. KURODA, ROSHIO and JAQUILINE "The Imperial Law and Buddhist Law"
4. Colin Turner" Islam without Allah"
5. Monaghan John, Just Peter (2000) "Social and cultural Anthropology"
6. "Encyclopedia of World Religions" Robert S. Ellwood and Gregory, D. ALLES
7. A. Critique of GEERETZ MODEL BY TALAL ASAD categorized religions "an anthropological category"
8. OLD TETSAMENT AND NEW TESTAMENT in simple English
9. Nicholas de Lange and Mieri Freud Kandel an Oxford Guide, New York.
10. Ahmed Ali Translation Al Quran N.J. Princeton University Press 1988.
11. "Allah and His Prophets" Al-Arabi Abu Hamzah
12. "Adam to Mohammad "—Abdul Rah man shad Islamic Book Service, 2011.
13. James Wilson Coleman (New York, Oxford University)
14. Rick Fields-How Swams Came to the lake.
15. Dr. Mrunalini—A Philosophical Foundation of Education.
16. John E. Cord "Jains in the World"
17. P.S. Jain-The Jaina path of Purification, Berkeley University California press 1979.

18. V. Parthasaraathy—Hindu Heritage, Prgnanabharathi A.P. Hyderabad.

19. Dr. T. Mrunalini Philosophical Education—Neel Kamal Publication, New Delhi.

20. Michael M.J. Fisher—Iran, from religious disputes to Revolution (Madison University of Wisconsin Press 2003)

21. HENIZ HALM-"Shiism "Columbia University, New York.

22. RUSSEL KIRKLAND, TAOISM-An Enduring tradition (New York Rutledge 2004)

23. CATHERINE DESPEUX AND LIVIA KOHN, "Women in Daoism"(Cambridge, Mass three Pine press 2003)

24. JENNIFER OLD STONE—MOORE, TAOISM, origins beliefs, Practices, holy Texts, Sacred Places (New York, Oxford university press 2003.

25. Thomas P. Kasulis, Shinto: The Way of Home (Honolulu University of Hawaii press 2004).

26. GURINDER SINGH MANN, "Sikhism" Upper Saddle River, N.J Prentice Hall 2004.

27. PATWANT SINGH: "The Sikhs" (London john Murray, 199).

28. V. PARTHASARATHY—PRAGNANA BHARATHI Publication Hyderabad A.P Publication.

29. KIM KNOT—"Hinduism: a very short introduction New York Oxford University press 2000.

30. John Ferray: All things made new—a comprehensive outline of BAHAS FAITH (London—BAHAIS Publishing trust 1975)

31. The book of Mormon (Salt lake City, Utah Church of Jesus Christ of latter-day Saints 1982

32. Helen Hard acre, Lay Buddhism in contemporary Japan, Princeton N.J.P. Univeersity 1984.

32. Donna Lee Bowen and Evelyn A. early ed. Every Day life in Muslim Middle East Blooming Indiana University press 2002 & Sunni Path Saddle Broke NJ. HIAZMATH Books 1993. Ii. PHILOSOPHICAL PERSPECTIVE:

33. Martin Cohen—Philosophical Tales (2008) ISBN—1—4057—2.

34. SARAH KOFMAN—Socrates: Fictions of a Philosopher 1998.

35. HADOT P (19950 Philosophy a way life Oxford Black Wells Popper (K.1962) "The Open Society and its enemy Volume I

36. "PLATO" Encyclopedia Britannica 2002.

37. Mc. LEISCH KENNEYTH COLE (1999) "Aristotle The Great Philosopher"

38. Treasure Theological-Politics—Chapter V.

39. BAILEY. C (1928) The Greek Atomist and Epicurus—of Moral Science—Basil Black Well Oxford University.

40. Peter Gay "the enlightenment—An Interpretation "Volume 2 Science of freedom—Wild Wood House London 1973.

41. David son, Ian Voltaire 'a LIFE' Profile books London 2010.

42. Story of Philosophy Will Durant.

43. Broad C.D. (2000) Ethics and History of Philosophy—U.K. Rout ledge.

44. SCHOPENHAUER ARTHUR, Gunter Zoller, Eric F.J. Payne (1999) Cambridge University. press.

45. Walter Kaufmann (1966)—Hegel: A reinterpretation—Anchor Books.

46. Bertrand Russell—Fartlex—Inc retrieved 23 June 1970.

47. Dr. T.M. Mrunalini: Philosophical Foundation of Education—Ne3el Kamal publication Delhi.

SCIENTIFIC PERSPECTIVE-HUMAN ACHIEVEMENT.

48. WEBMASTER—BRIT GRISWORLD—NASA OFFICIAL DR. EDWARD & J. WOLLACK-26 April 2010.

49. ROELAND VANDER MAREL ASTRONOMER—Gulf News 2 June 2012.

50. REUTERS—Gulf News 5 July 2012.

51. Galaxy—Cluster and Large Scale Structure University of Cambridge—Retrieved 15 Jan.2007.

52. NASA Telescope Sees Black Hole Munch on a Star—NASA—5 December 2006.

53. KNAPP G.R. 1999) Star formation i9n Early type Galaxies—Astronomical Society of Pacific Bib code 1998.

54. General Knowledge Category—SCIENCE SPACE AND ASTRONOMY-PTI-DC HYDERABAD A.P. 27 July 201`2. GEOGRAPHICAL CONNETION OF HUMAN LIFE:-ASTRONOMICAL CONNECTION:

55. CATTLERMOLE, peter Moore, Patrice 1985— The Story of Earth Cambridge University press.

56. BLEEKER, B.W. DAVIS (MAY 2004) 'WHAT IS CRATON' American Geo-physical Union.

57. CONDIE KE, KENT (1999) 'Plate tectonics and crustal evolution' (4th edition) Oxford: Butter Forth HEINEMANN.

58. Gale Joseph (2009) 'Astro biology of Earth: the Evolution and Future of life on a Planet in Turmoil 'Oxford; Oxford University press.

59. Kasting James F; M. Tazewell Howard, September 7, 2006 "Atmospheric composition and Climate on the Early Earth"

60. Morbidelli, A; Chambers, J. Lunine J.I., Perit, J.M. Robert, F. Valsecchi, G.B. Cryr K>E.(2000) Source

of regions and time scales for the delivery of water to the Earth" Meteoric tics and Planetary Science 35.

61. A. LAZCANO, J.L. BAD (June 2004) 'The 1953 Stanley L. Miller experiment: fifty years of prebiotic organic chemistry" Origins of Life and Evolution of Biosphere"

62. MOSKOWITZ, CLARA (29 March 2012) "Life Building Blocks may have formed in Dust Around Young Sun"

63. Dawkins 2004. Oxford University Press.

64. FORETY, RICHARD (September 1999) Land Wards Humanity/Life: A Natural History of First Four Billion Years of life on Earth: New York Vintage Books.

65. McClellan (2006) 'Science and Technology in World History; An Introduction' Baltimore Mary land JHU Press.

66. Gibbons, Ann (2003) "Oldest members of Homosapiens Discovered in Africa Science 300.

67. "The Human Evolution" Atlas World History, New York Oxford University Press.

68. Dawkins, Richard (1989) "Memes: The new replicators" The Selfish Gene: Oxford U. Press

69. Tudge Colin (1998) "Neanderthals, Bandits and Farmers: How Agriculture began" London Weidenfield & Nicolson.

70. "Human Spaceflight and Exploration—European Participating States ESA 2006.

71. Expedition: 13 Science, Assembly prep on Tap for Crew NASA January 11, 2006.

72. Gulf News Dt. June 29, 2012 and Deccan chronicle Hyderabad Dt. July 19 & 20, 2012.

73. ENCYCLOPEDIA OF WOLD GEOGRAPHY—R.W McColl, PhD-General editor facts on on Fine Inc. published by 2005

Gilson Book ltd. ANTHOPOLOGY: HISTORICL HUMAN CONNECTION.

74. Broth well; D. Dental Anthropology: Oxford Perammon press 1963.

75. Historical Physical Anthropology, An Encyclopedia: New York Inc. 1989.

76. Selkirk, D. and Burrow, f. "CONFRONTING CREATIONISM: DEFENDING DARWIN", Kingston: New South Wales University Press 1992.

77. Story of Man Kind by HENDRIC WILLIAM VALOON BONI AND LIVE: copy right 1921 Bon and Live right Inc printed in USA.—Wikipedia Free online. SOCIAL SICENCES—HUMAN CONNECTION.

78. TRIGG. R(2001) Understanding social Science.

79. SHINOYA. Y (1997) SCHUMPETER AND THE IDEQA OF SOCIAL SCIENCES Cambridge University Press 1997.

80. E.F. & COLANDER D.C. 2008—Social Science An Introduction to the study of Society: Boston Peason/Allyn and Bacon. NATURAL SCIENCES—HUMAN ACHIEVEMENT.

81. THEODORE L. BROWN, H. EUGENE LEMAY, BRUCE EDWARD, BURSTEN, H. LEMAY: Chemistry the Central Sciene-Prentile Hall 8 Edition (1999). and Wikipedia Sciences. Free online.

82. Vision Learning "Chemical Bonding by Anthony Carpi Retrieved June 12, 2011.

83. http://www.newis.columbia.edu/—Phyphram|intro|intro.html.

84. Paul s. Agutter and Denys N. Whealtly (20080 "Thinking about life: the History and Philosophy of Biology and other Sciences.

85. MagnerW: A History of Life Sciences.

86. Black, J. (June 2002) "Darwin in the world of emotions".

87. Zoology—Wikipedia free online.

88. Dean, Laura "The ABO Blood Group"

89. Miller L.H. Mason S.J., Clyde D.F, Ginny's M.H. (august 1976) The resistance factor to Plasmodium".

90. Kremner Haringa I, Koopmans M, de Heer E, Bruijin, J. Bajema I (2007) Change in Blood group in systematic lupus erythematosus.

91. Rose and Goos DNA-A practical guide, Toronto: Creswell publications.

92. Anne Hart (July 2003) the Beginners' Guide to interpreting Ethnic DNA origins for family History.

93. World Conservation Union 2010 IUCN Red list of Threatened Species by LIZOSBORN.

94. The Times News Paper/ Ltd London 2012—Gulf New 4 May, 2012.

95. Wikipedia free online—Enchanter learning.com

96. Genocide in history from Wikipedia, the free encyclopedia.

97. NATURAL DISASTER; from Wikipedia, the free encyclopedia.

98. Meteorites, Asteroids and comets: Damages, injuries, Deaths and very close calls: Laura Knight—JADCZYK Scot.net 27 March 2009

99. Top Engineering Achievements of the 20th Century at http://www.greatachivements.org.

100. Globalization and Workers Right: http://www./cgg.ch/

101. Socialist International Congress demands Global Governance Wealth Redistribution. Monday 10 September 2012.

102. Blin, Arnaud; Marin, Gustavo "Rethinking Global governance" (http://www.World-governance. Or/ spip.php? article 15

103. Thomas G. Weiss and Ramesh Thakur, The UN Global Governance: An Idea and its Prospectus Indiana University press, forthcoming.

104. CHAARNY 1988 GENOCIDE ARTIFICIAL BIBLIOGRAPHY REVIEW-Stephen|Curtois Black book on communism 1995.

105. Matthews Warfare and Armed Conflict 1992-Clodefelter Warfare and Armed Conflict 1992.

106. Eliot Twentieth Century Book of the Dead 1992—Buthoul: A list of 366 Major Armed Conflict of the period 1740-1974—peace research-1978.

107. R.J. RUNNEL—death by Government-Genocide and Mass murders 1994-Matt white website.

108. BERENBAYM, MICHAEL Editor: witness to the Holocaust New York, Harper Collins.(1997)

109. KRUPA, FREDERQUE PARIS URBAN SANITATION BEFORE 20th century. 1 1 0 . Edward Gibbon-D.M Low 1960-the Decline and fall of Roman Empire New-York HOLOCAUST.

111. LUCIAN GUBBY (1999) Sunlight and Shadow-the Jewish Experience of Islam New York other peers.

112. Daud Ibrahim IBD(2007) retrieved July 9, 2011.

113. HISTORICAAL Record JENSON Volume 7 & 8 GENETICS

114. NASSAUM ROBERT L. ROBERICH, R. MCLINE and HUGTINGTON M.F. WILLIARD—Genetic Medicine 7th Edition Philadelphia.

115. Freeman, Scott and John. Cherron, Evolutionary Analysis 4th Edition Upper Saddle River, Pearson Pentice Hall2007.